Modular Evolution
How Natural Selection Produces Biological Complexity

Natural selection is more than the survival of the fittest: it is a force engendering higher biological complexity. Presenting a new explanation for the tendency of life to become more complex through evolution, this book offers an introduction to the key debates in evolutionary theory, including the role of genes and sex in evolution, the adaptive reasons for senescence and death and the origin of neural information. The author argues that biological complexity increased through the process of 'modularity transfer': modular phenotypes (proteins, somatic cells, learned behaviours) evolved into new modular information carriers (regulatory proteins, neural cells, words), giving rise to new information systems and higher levels of biological organisation.

Modular Evolution makes sense of the unique place of humans in evolution, both as the pinnacle of biological complexity and as inventors of non-biological evolution.

Lucio Vinicius is a Postdoctoral Fellow at the Leverhulme Centre for Human Evolutionary Studies in Cambridge, UK. He has published articles in various fields including life history evolution, *Drosophila* genetics, brain evolution and human growth.

Modular Evolution

How Natural Selection Produces Biological Complexity

LUCIO VINICIUS
Leverhulme Centre for Human
Evolutionary Studies, Cambridge

CAMBRIDGE UNIVERSITY PRESS
Cambridge, New York, Melbourne, Madrid, Cape Town, Singapore,
São Paulo, Delhi, Dubai, Tokyo

Cambridge University Press
The Edinburgh Building, Cambridge CB2 8RU, UK

Published in the United States of America by Cambridge University Press, New York

www.cambridge.org
Information on this title: www.cambridge.org/9780521429641

© L. Vinicius Castilho 2010

First published 2010

Printed in the United Kingdom at the University Press, Cambridge

A catalogue record for this publication is available from the British Library

ISBN 978-0-521-42964-1 Hardback
ISBN 978-0-521-72877-5 Paperback

Thus we cannot say that evolution consists simply in the development of higher from lower forms of life; it consists in raising the upper level of organization reached by living matter, while still permitting the lower types of organization to survive. This general direction to be found in evolution, this gradual rise in the upper level of control and independence to be observed in living things with the passage of time, may be called *evolutionary* or *biological progress*. It is obviously of great importance, and can be seen, on reflection, to be another necessary consequence of the struggle for existence.

Haldane and Huxley (1927: 234), Animal Biology

Contents

himself at the same time a believer in the power

Preface

This book deals with a classic problem in macroevolution: how do we reconcile the Darwinian 'tree of life', which implies that every single branch or living species is historically and adaptively unique, with apparent differences in levels of complexity between organisms such as bacteria and humans? The first author to deal with the issue was Darwin himself, at the same time a believer in the power of natural selection to create biological diversity and in evolutionary 'progress', or the emergence of complex organisms from humbler beginnings. Besides Darwin, I was also inspired by Erwin Schrödinger and his insightful definition of life; by J. B. S. Haldane, Julian Huxley, John Maynard Smith and Eörs Szathmáry and their aggregation model; by Marcello Barbieri, Eva Jablonka and Marion Lamb and the study of biological codes of inheritance. This book is an attempt at melding together those ideas so as to present one possible answer to the problem of evolutionary complexity.

My intention was to offer at the same time an update on classic themes (including the evolution of sex and the role of genes in adaptive evolution) and an introduction to new debates (in particular the controversies surrounding the comparisons between social behaviour in humans and other species). Many important topics could not be addressed: plants are rarely mentioned, as emphasis was given to animals, behaviour and communication; Price's equation and Kimura's neutral theory were not discussed; and the chapter on evolution and development is necessarily tentative due to the constant transformation of the field. However, the biases can be justified: my aim was not to present a thorough review of evolutionary theory but to develop a thesis: namely that the evolution of complexity should be understood as the transformation of Schrödinger 's Principle of Order from Order. This thesis is meant to harmonise Darwinian evolution by natural selection with the concept of a dynamical Chain of Being in which organisms are characterised by different levels of complexity.

This monograph resulted from a few years of study and work at Cambridge and grew out of an undergraduate course that I offer in the Department of Biological Anthropology. I would like to thank St John's College and the Department of Zoology at Cambridge for their support during my PhD, and the Leverhulme Trust for funding my research at postdoctoral level. I am especially grateful to LCHES (the Leverhulme Centre for Human Evolutionary Studies) that has hosted me for the past few years. I am indebted to Professor Robert Foley for discussing some of the ideas in the book and for continuous support. Dr Marta Mirazon Lahr has inspired me as a teacher and convinced me that the book should be written in the first place, and I cannot express my gratitude highly enough. I am also grateful to Andrea Migliano and Rudy Schlaepfer and especially Philip Schlaepfer for useful suggestions. I am indebted to Dominic Lewis at the Cambridge University Press for his patience and assistance. Finally, I could not have finalised this project without the support of Hannah Mumby, and I am counting on her help in future endeavours.

1

From natural selection to the history of nature

For their key role in the revival of heliocentrism, we may certainly excuse Copernicus, Kepler and Galileo for being less successful at explaining *why* planets move. It was only 150 years after Copernicus anonymously circulated his pamphlet *Commentariolus* in 1510 that Isaac Newton's *Principia Mathematica* offered a theory of planetary motion and established the first modern paradigm for celestial mechanics. Darwin's theory of evolution represented a scientific revolution of the same importance and magnitude, but its historical development bears a crucial difference from heliocentrism. Despite a number of forerunners in Britain and France and the work of his contemporary Alfred Wallace, most of us associate both the substantiation of biological evolution as a fact, and the theory of natural selection as evolution's first and only theoretical paradigm, with Charles Darwin and the *Origin of Species* (1859). First, Darwin made species intelligible by setting them in motion as Copernicus had done with the planets. Biological evolution, or the movement of species in time, implied that the ultimate cause of species features is their history. And second, Darwinism found its fundamental law of motion in the principle of natural selection, the consequence of variation and competition within populations. For his contributions to the facts and theory of evolution, Darwin can be seen both as the Copernicus and the Newton of biology (Padian, 2001).

Although the triumph of Darwinism is denied by few, scientific revolutions also demonstrate that even the most successful and influential theories may be wrong or incomplete. The Newtonian paradigm, for example, started to crumble when some of its predictions at the very large (cosmological) and the very small (atomic) physical scales were refuted by experiments and theory; although still an essential component of physics, the Newtonian world picture is no longer accepted as a satisfactory account of the nature of space, time and physical causality (Penrose, 1989). For us, it is important to notice that the major debate involving Darwinism since its origin is also a matter of scale, namely the relationship between microevolution and macroevolution. This is more than coincidence. While natural selection is widely accepted as the microscopic cause of change in populations, when it comes to accounting for the big picture of life in all its forms, living and extinct, it has become commonplace to question the power of selection against a background of virtually infinite and unique events accumulating for billions of years in every line of descent, and then to appeal to contingency and history as the true cause of evolution at larger scales (Gould, 2002). In summary, while Darwinism introduced natural selection as a fundamental law of biological change, it established at the same time that nature had a history; for this reason, the main challenge of evolutionary theory since the *Origin of Species* has been to discover the missing links between the *law* of nature and the *history* of nature.

NATURE AFTER NATURAL LAW

The theory of evolution by natural selection was a late product of the Modern Scientific Revolution and its emphasis on efficient causes and natural law (Cohen, 1987). The rise of natural law meant that science should rely on purely mechanistic explanations, and the study of life should be no exception. The biologist, even when familiar with the appearance of design in living organisms, should 'disregard for a time, as in physical philosophy, the immediate *purposes* of the adaptations which he witnesses; and must consider these adaptations as themselves but the *results* or *ends* of the general laws for which he should search' (Carpenter, 1839: 461). The principle of natural selection provided biologists with a classic example of general law, but its formulation exhibited a distinguishing feature. Newtonian dynamics and the field theories of electromagnetism and general gravitation were originally formulated as sets of deterministic laws (Penrose, 1989). As such, their experimental predictions were meant to be exact (apart from measurement error): given similar conditions, all objects were expected to free-fall predictably, all negatively charged bodies were expected to respond equally to an electric field, and so on.

In contrast, Darwin saw natural selection from the beginning as a statistical or probabilistic principle (Hempel, 1966). The aim of statistical laws is to extract information from systems or populations when the behaviour of their components is either unknown or unpredictable (Menand, 2002). A good example of the logic of statistical laws is the analysis of radiocarbon decay into nitrogen (Bowman, 1990). A radiocarbon (^{14}C) is a carbon atom with six protons and eight neutrons, instead of the six neutrons found in the more common and stable ^{12}C isotope. In the Earth's atmosphere, it is produced when a thermal neutron derived from cosmic rays collides with a ^{14}N atom (the most common nitrogen isotope, with seven protons and seven neutrons) and converts one of its protons into an extra neutron. The resulting ^{14}C atom is unstable and eventually decays back into ^{14}N by emitting a β-particle. In living organisms, a constant ratio of ^{14}C to ^{12}C is maintained on the one hand by the absorption of new radiocarbons into organic matter through photosynthesis (and their subsequent transfer to organisms that feed on photosynthetic plants and algae), and on the other hand by their loss through decay. But after death there is no further absorption of radiocarbons, and the decay of the ^{14}C trapped into the dead organism causes their ratio to ^{12}C to decrease gradually with time.

The work of Willard Libby and collaborators (Arnold and Libby, 1949) showed that such decrease followed an exponential curve and could be used as a method for dating organic samples, provided only that the parameters or calibration of the curve were obtained from fossil or archaeological material of known dates. Among other things, Libby's exponential model showed that 50% of the radiocarbon atoms trapped in a dead organism are expected to decay into nitrogen after 5568 ± 30 years. In other words, if we start with a sample of one million radiocarbon atoms, half a million are expected to disappear after 5568 years, plus or minus an error of 30 years. The error exists because the calibration method itself is based on a finite sample of ^{14}C atoms: larger initial samples of radiocarbon atoms would reduce the error. Thus, provided the amount of organic material in the specimen (i.e. the trapped radiocarbon sample) is large enough, dating of fossils can be very precise.

However, precision completely vanishes at the level of individual atoms (Gell-Mann, 1994). The reason is that radiocarbon decay is spontaneous and unpredictable: whether a particular ^{14}C atom decays instantly after its formation in the atmosphere, decays after a thousand years, or never decays, depends on contingent factors – namely, the outcome of an unrehearsed and never-ceasing dance of particles in the atomic nucleus (Libby, 1955). For this reason, although we know almost with certainty that 50% of radiocarbon atoms in a large sample will decay in about 5568 years, all we can say about an *individual* radiocarbon atom is that the probability that it will decay in less than 5568 years is 50%; we cannot determine when the decay will happen, or whether it will happen at all.

The point is that the principle of natural selection relies on the same distinction between population-level predictability and individual-level uncertainty. Natural selection is, after all, a 'statistical bias in the relative rates of survival of alternatives' (Williams, 1966: 22). Based on the radiocarbon example, natural selection may be described as the decay or rise of allele frequencies across generations, of phenotypic traits towards certain character states, or of organisms towards higher levels of fitness. Provided certain conditions are met, it is even possible to predict fairly accurately the direction and speed of change in measurable traits or gene frequencies in populations (Charlesworth *et al.*, 1982).

However, as far as individual fate is concerned, the struggle for survival is to a large extent a matter of chance. This is because an individual carrying the genes and phenotype corresponding to a fitness peak may (and very often does) simply fail to survive or reproduce for a variety of contingent factors, such as an accident, a disease, or a competent predator. In other words, under the hypothesis of natural selection the link between individual variation and individual fitness was never meant to be deterministic. We can certainly describe or even sometimes predict changes in proportions of alleles or phenotypes in populations; and based on that, we may ascribe individuals a probability of reproductive success. But as in the case of radiocarbon decay, the difference between individual and population scale is all there is between chance and order.

REDUCTIONISM AND EMERGENCE

A possible interpretation of the differences between deterministic and statistical law is that they imply a distinction between exact and historical sciences. If natural selection or the law of evolution itself rests upon statistical ground, how can we avoid the conclusion that evolutionary history is to an even higher degree the domain of contingency and unpredictability? The view that historical sciences deal with subjects too complex to be grasped in terms of exact causality dates back at least to Laplace (1774):

> Chance has no reality in itself; it is only a term fit to designate our
> ignorance concerning the manner in which the different parts of a

> phenomenon are arranged among themselves and in relation to the
> rest of Nature.

According to Laplace, chance is not an objective property of things.
Parts are always well 'arranged among themselves' as described by
deterministic laws; the problem is that our brains are limited devices,
able to calculate the outcomes of a few interactions, but not an exact
event equation whenever the event consists of too many parts or
interactions – that is, whenever the event is too complex. When too
many parts or interactions are involved, Laplace argued that it was
necessary to appeal to a statistical approach and to the use of aver-
ages and error estimates. In summary, chance and uncertainty are not
objective properties of entities, but effects of scale transitions from
simple to complex; in our mind, those transitions are manifested as
the transition from determinism to probability.

Despite its intuitive appeal, reasons for rejecting the Laplacean
view have accumulated for more than a century. The advance of
reductionism, the belief that 'all the complex…things and processes
that we observe in the world can be explained in terms of universal
principles that govern their common ultimate constituents' (Nagel,
1998), has provided compelling evidence that the very foundations of
reality, or its 'simplest' elements, lie on uncertainty and probability
(Feynman, 1965). The most fundamental laws of atomic physics and
quantum mechanics, such as Heisenberg's principle of uncertainty,
Pauli exclusion principle and Schrödinger's wave function, are probabilistic laws; even when applied to a single electron, they imply
respectively that simultaneous measurements of variables such as
speed and position will necessarily exhibit greater-than-zero variance
and confidence intervals, that there is only a probability that it will lie
at a certain region around the atomic nucleus, and that there is a certain probability that it is at a given quantum state (Penrose, 1989).

But if uncertainty is the fundamental rule of reality, why does
the world around us appear so orderly? The current answer, which
completely inverts the logic proposed by Laplace, is complexity itself:
while simple parts or ultimate constituents of matter such as atoms
or atomic particles are intrinsically uncertain, predictability often
emerges at the larger macroscopic scale as a very special kind of statistical effect; this effect we call physical 'order'.

> Only in the co-operation of an enormously large number of atoms do
> statistical laws begin to operate and control the behaviour of these
> assemblées with an accuracy increasing as the number of atoms

involved increases. It is in that way that the events acquire truly orderly features. All the physical and chemical laws that are known to play an important part in the life of organisms are of this statistical kind; any other kind of lawfulness and orderliness that one might think of is being perpetually disturbed and made inoperative by the unceasing heat motion of the atoms (Schrödinger, 1944: 10).

Thus, it is only *because* of the large number of atoms and their complex interactions in ordinary macroscopic objects such as a table that we grasp an appearance of order. Well before the expression became fashionable, Schrödinger was describing our surrounding reality as an 'emergent property' (Bunge, 2003) of a complex system of innumerable microscopic parts. He summarised his views in the classic 'Principle of Order from Disorder', or the origin of macroscopic predictability from microscopic uncertainty. Any other kind of lawfulness claimed by science – in particular the deterministic lawfulness implied by classical physics – was illusory, or just the name we give to our ignorance of the probabilistic roots of reality.

As importantly, for Schrödinger the Principle of Order from Disorder was valid for physical laws too. An electromagnetic field, originally described by Maxwell through deterministic laws, is in a sense just like a table. It is produced when a source (for example an atomic nucleus) emits so many photons that both the probability of a passing electron absorbing them and the number of photons absorbed depend only on the position of the electron in space and time (Feynman, 1985: 122). For this reason, the predictable and seemingly deterministic response of any electron to a magnetic field is in fact the orderly appearance of a system involving countless probabilistic interactions between many photons and the passing electron. If in another example we replaced the photon source with the Sun, and the passing electrons with two glasses of water sitting on a beach, we see that although each interaction between photon and water molecule is unique and probabilistic, the liquid from each of the two glasses would take very similar times to evaporate.

In summary, the dichotomy between chance and determinism proposed by Laplace was radically inverted by contemporary science. Rather than exact expressions of pure and deterministic physical laws, simple interactions and particles of reality are intrinsically uncertain and probabilistic; and rather than the cause of ignorance, complexity or the statistical composition of entities and their interactions is the very reason for predictability and order that we observe around us.

Remarkably, Darwin seems to be closer to Schrödinger than to Laplace; in fact, his definition of natural selection in the *Origin* did not sound too far from the contemporary views on complexity and order:

> Then, considering the infinite complexity of the relations of all organic beings to each other and to their conditions of existence, causing an infinite diversity in structure, constitution, and habits, to be advantageous to them, I think it would be a most extraordinary fact if no variation ever had occurred useful to each being's own welfare...But if variations useful to any organic being do occur, assuredly individuals thus characterised will have the best chance of being preserved in the struggle for life...This principle of preservation, I have called, for the sake of brevity, Natural Selection (Darwin, 1859: 127).

For Darwin natural selection was a pattern or principle of preservation observed in populations and across generations, resulting from virtually infinite interactions among organic beings; but at the level of isolated individuals, the best we can do is to ascribe a better or worse chance of being preserved. Natural selection is another example of natural law, and of order emerging as a scaling effect against a background of individual events inextricably tangled with chance.

HISTORY AND INHERITANCE

If the ultimate components of reality are intrinsically unpredictable, what is the appeal of the 'simple' in the natural sciences? In other words, why is reductionism so influential? The answer is that reductionism was never meant to be a tool against chance; it is a tool against *history*. An enlightening example is given by the work on antiparticles by the physicists John Wheeler and Richard Feynman. According to Dirac's antiparticle theory, every existing electron implied the existence of a positive sister particle (a positron) somewhere in the universe (Wheeler and Ford, 1998: 117). Wheeler then proposed a very original explanation for why electrons and positrons existed in pairs: all observed electrons and positrons would be a single existing particle, travelling back and forth in time and drawing a continuous 'world line' or trajectory of its existence. This single electron could be seen many times simultaneously, as its swaying world line intersects the present multiple times and creates the perception of many existing electrons. When the world line crosses towards the future, an electron is observed, and a travel back to the past would correspond to a positron; hence their similar mass, but inverse charge. Finally, since there is a single continuous line moving back and forth, it follows that between two travels to the future there must necessarily occur a travel to the past; hence the existence of one positron for every electron.

Although Wheeler's idea of world lines was incorporated into quantum mechanics, explaining antiparticle theory as a cosmic *déjà vu* was considered too extreme. Wheeler was aware of flaws in the argument, but what matters for us was his justification for reducing all electrons and positrons to a single particle:

> We realized that such a way of thinking made sense because of the extreme simplicity of the electron. You can tell by looking into a person's face something about what that person has been through. You cannot tell anything about an electron's history by looking at it. Every electron is exactly like every other electron, unscarred by its past, not blessed with a memory – of either human or the computer variety (Wheeler and Ford, 1998: 348).

Since electrons do not have memory and do not bear a record of their past accidents and scars, they lack individuality. Exactly for this reason, they are the ideal starting point for the study of more complex macroscopic entities that do display physical memory and uniqueness. Reductionism thus serves two main purposes. The first is the understanding of things composite or complex, such as tables or electromagnetic fields. The second purpose is the conquest of *history*. While statistical composition generates order from disorder as claimed by Schrödinger, it may also generate history or a record of past events when time is a relevant variable (i.e. when systems are not in equilibrium). This category of problem has come to the fore only recently in the physical sciences as the study of dynamical systems (Nicolis and Nicolis, 2007) and shows that the concept of history can be extended well beyond its original use as a feature of human societies.

Galaxies have persistently eluded cosmologists for their gigantic scale and morphological variability accumulated over billions of years. Spiral galaxies are currently the prevailing form in the universe, but the reasons for their larger number were not obvious (Smolin, 1997). Some sophisticated thermodynamic (*n*-body/gas dynamical) models have been proposed but were not particularly successful; surprisingly, until recently the best simulations of spiral arm dynamics were derived from evolutionary biology, more specifically from simulations of host–parasite interactions, with the forming stars in a spiral arm sweeping through the galaxy playing the role of infecting parasites, and the dark matter that becomes the material source of the forming stars playing the role of hosts.

In a review suggestively named 'The morphological evolution of galaxies', Abraham and van den Bergh (2001) pointed to further similarities between cosmology and organic evolution. They recognise that cosmology also needs to cope with taxonomic problems (the standard 'tuning fork' classification scheme proposed by Hubble in 1926 fails to describe most of the distant galaxies), phylogenetic problems (spiral galaxies seem to be primitive, while elliptical galaxies are probably derived from collision of spirals; however, elliptical galaxies may revert back to spirals due to gas accretion) and especially evolutionary problems:

> At this stage, all that is clear is that the morphology of spiral galaxies is evolving rapidly and systematically, even at quite low redshifts [i.e. at shorter distances from the Earth]. Familiar types of galaxies, such as barred and grand-design spirals, appear to be relatively recent additions to the extragalactic zoo. The nature of the many morphologically peculiar galaxies at high redshift remains a complete mystery. These objects might be mergers, protogalaxies, new classes of evolved systems, or a combination of all three (Abraham and van den Bergh, 2001).

The use of various biological terms and the analogies with organic evolution is possible because galaxies are historical objects whose number, size and configuration depend not only on first principles, but on original conditions and accidental factors occurring over long periods of time. In other words, physical sciences also aim at the eventual conquest of complex historical entities, and this blurs the boundaries between 'exact' and 'historical' sciences. This also means that the reliance of evolutionary biology on the statistical law of natural selection does not tell it apart from the other natural sciences: first because natural laws are statistical, or attempts to grasp patterns against a background of contingency; and second because even the physical sciences aim at accounting for the history of nature.

Undeniably there is a fundamental difference between physics and evolutionary biology, but contrary to the common belief it does not lie in a distinction between exact and historical sciences: the distinction is in the type of *memory* behind physical and organic history. Both galaxies and cells must bear some principle of order that opposes their decay towards randomly moving atoms and molecules; but the principles operating in living and non-living entities are different. As seen above, for Schrödinger the Principle of Order from Disorder operating in non-living matter is the result of statistical averaging, and 'is never the consequence of a well-ordered configuration of atoms'. In contrast, Schrödinger postulated a second Principle (of 'Order from Order'), unrelated to statistical averaging and derived from organisation at the level of atoms and molecules, perhaps in the form of 'aperiodic crystals' within chromosomes.

Less than a decade later, the structure of DNA, the aperiodic crystal behind living organisation, was determined. It is now known that in all living organisms macroscopic order, or phenotype, is symbolically stored in a microscopic sequence of nucleotides or genotype. Since the possible configurations of DNA are virtually unlimited but resources are not, selection arises as the result of competition between alternatives (Eigen, 1971). As discussed below, unlimited inheritance, the material and functional distinction between genotype and phenotype, and competition in the form of natural selection explain why there is more history and complexity to a single cell than to a galaxy.

DARWINIAN PROGRESS: ORDER AT THE MACROEVOLUTIONARY SCALE

Organic history is the record of the scars, accidents and contingent factors crossing the path of evolutionary lineages; but, as seen, contingency must coexist with the operation of the universal law of natural selection. Darwin believed that the logic of inheritable variation and competition would apply not only to individuals within species, but also to the origin, divergence, extinction and succession of species themselves. The title *On the Origin of Species by Means of Natural Selection* is in fact a statement of Darwin's controversial theory (which later became known as 'reinforcement') that speciation between sympatric (physically overlapping) populations can evolve as an adaptation, rather than as a consequence of other adaptations or of accidental factors (Coyne and Orr, 2004). Darwin did not deny that speciation occurs mostly due to allopatry (physical isolation) and therefore by accident, but emphasised that species resulting from allopatry derived their existence from the absence of competition rather than selection of the fittest. Owing their existence to luck, they were destined to play a secondary role in the history of life.

> I conclude that, although small isolated areas probably have been in some respects highly favourable for the production of new species,

yet that the course of modification will generally have been more rapid on large areas; and what is more important, that the new forms produced on large areas, which already have been victorious over many competitors, will be those that will spread most widely, will give rise to most new varieties and species, and will thus play an important part in the changing history of the organic world (Darwin, 1859: 106).

In Darwin's argument, it is clear that some species are 'better' than others due to selection; that those species change or set in motion organic history; and that organic history or macroevolution is a large-scale pattern or order bearing the signal of natural selection. Thus, Darwin postulated not only that natural selection was a pattern emerging within populations over time; he also suggested that organic history is a pattern that emerges from selective interactions among species. The extrapolation from microevolution to macroevolution occurs because Darwin strongly believed that competition took place not only between individuals, but also between populations or species.

It is the most closely-allied forms, – varieties of the same species, and species of the same genus or of related genera, – which, from having nearly the same structure, constitution, and habits, generally come into the severest competition with each other. Consequently, each new variety or species, during the progress of its formation, will generally press hardest on its nearest kindred, and tend to exterminate them (Darwin, 1859: 110).

Darwin's view was that while competition among individuals leads to adaptation, competitive extermination of intermediate varieties may lead to speciation. The extermination of species by natural selection has an obvious effect on the distribution of biodiversity and higher taxa: whereas intraspecific competition implies the supremacy of the fittest individuals, competition between species must lead to the supremacy of 'higher' forms at the macroevolutionary scale.

But in one particular sense the more recent forms must, on my theory, be higher than the more ancient; for each new species is formed by having had some advantage in the struggle for life over other and preceding forms (Darwin, 1859: 336–7).

As in the case of individuals, the fate of a particular species is to a large extent a matter of chance; but with large numbers and long periods of time, competitive interactions between species generate a historical pattern: the appearance of organic 'advance' at the geological scale. When we describe population change driven by selection, we refer to adaptation. When we refer to species succession, Darwin was clear: we should name it progress.

> All the other great leading facts in palaeontology seem to me simply to follow on the theory of descent with modification through natural selection…The extinction of old forms is the almost inevitable consequence of the production of new forms.…The dominant species of the larger dominant groups tend to leave many modified descendants…As these are formed, the species of the less vigorous groups, from their inferiority inherited from a common progenitor, tend to become extinct together…The inhabitants of each successive period in the world's history have beaten their predecessors in the race for life, and are, in so far, higher in the scale of nature; and this may account for the vague yet ill-defined sentiment, felt by many palaeontologists, that organisation has on the whole progressed (Darwin, 1859: 343–5).

For Darwin, both adaptation and progress were consequences of natural selection. Microevolution and macroevolutionary history were instances of order emerging from the interaction of many parts (individuals or species). But in the framework of Darwinism developed by his successors, adaptation remained a central concept whereas 'progress', frequently denounced as a Victorian or anthropocentric prejudice, became an almost forbidden word in evolutionary biology (Ruse, 1996). Ironically, the exclusion of the concept of progress from evolutionary theory was driven both by the enemies of Darwinism and by its most ardent supporters.

MACROEVOLUTION AS HISTORY

Darwin's claim that evolutionary progress is an integral feature of macroevolution has been strongly rejected by most active evolutionary biologists (Ruse, 1996); as a rule, they prefer to assume that macroevolution is just the accumulation of microevolutionary processes at the level of populations, and not a separate level of order. As summarised by Dobzhansky (1937: 12), 'there is no way toward an understanding of the mechanisms of macroevolutionary changes, which require time on a geological scale, other than through a full comprehension of the microevolutionary processes observable within the span of a human lifetime'. Later, Simpson's (1944) account of modern horse evolution became a classic example of how ecological specialisation, speciation and extinction occurring over a period of 25 million years were reduced to a narrative of the workings of natural selection within populations – without any reference to higher forms or progress of any kind. For Simpson, the Equidae (the family that now includes horses, donkeys and zebras) underwent a transition from browsing (leaf eating) to grazing (grass eating) during the Miocene period as a response to selection for larger body size, which led to larger organs and structures such as teeth as a correlated outcome. Although only an indirect product of selection for increased body size, the larger and higher tooth crowns in ancestral browsing taxa (*Mesohippus*, *Miohipus*) 'incidentally evolved in the direction of grazing adaptation', and were then captured by natural selection:

> A segment of the population broke away, structurally, under this selection pressure [for grazing adaptations], climbed the grazing peak with relative rapidity during the Miocene, and by the end of the Miocene occupied its summit … the competition on both sides from the well-adapted groups caused the intermediate, relatively inadaptive animals on the saddle to become extinct. The browsing types … became extinct, while the grazing types persist today (Simpson, 1944: 92).

It is now known that intermediate types between browsing and grazing should not be described as inadaptive animals. Those extinct species are currently seen as a third niche of mixed browsers that evolved in parallel with the grazing types, displayed equivalent levels of diversity during the Eocene, and disappeared at the same time as the browsing taxa (McFadden, 2005). Despite some problems with the interpretation of fossils, Simpson's account perfectly exemplifies the belief that the fossil record is a window into the selective forces that guided changes in populations and species in the past.

But can the logic be inverted? In other words, can the knowledge of selection patterns or microevolution taking place in a population be used to predict history or macroevolution? Simpson made it clear that the answer is no; the reason is the set of material conditions under which selection operates.

> The cause of evolution thus includes all the genetic, structural, physiological, and behavioural states of populations right back to the origin of life. Even slight changes in earlier parts of the history would have profound cumulative effects on all descendant organisms through the succeeding millions of generations (Simpson, 1964: 773).

Even when the state of a population is well known, 'it is impossible for population genetics to predict any pattern at all in the fossil record' (Charlesworth *et al.*, 1982), since after a few generations the present state will be altered by a number of chance events. For this reason, macroevolution is nothing more than historical reconstruction or recapitulation: although lineages are impossible to predict, they are at least accountable on hindsight when fossils are available to tell us the story. The human evolutionary lineage, for example, is a product of probabilities that make the evolution of a second 'humanoid' or human-like species extremely improbable, either on Earth or anywhere else in the universe.

> There are four successive probabilities to be judged: the probability that suitable planets do exist; the probability that life has arisen on them; the probability that such life has evolved in a predictable way; and the probability that such evolution would lead eventually to hominoids…the first probability is fair, the second far lower but appreciable, the third exceedingly small, and the fourth almost negligible. Each of these probabilities depends on that preceding it, so that they must be multiplied together to obtain the over-all probability of the final event, the emergence of hominoids. The product of these probabilities, each a fraction, is probably not significantly greater than zero (Simpson, 1964: 771).

Simpson's conclusion will sound familiar to most readers: 'evolution is not repeatable. No species or any larger group has ever evolved, or can ever evolve, twice' (Simpson, 1964: 773). That would be, according to current mainstream Darwinism, the ultimate limit of macroevolution as a science. Watched from the Simpsonian perspective, the fate of any evolutionary lineage is similar to the decay of a single radiocarbon atom: dependent on contingent factors, unpredictable, and only accountable on hindsight. It should be clear that Simpson does not refer to a humanoid as a species *exactly* like ours (the evolution of which would in fact be unrepeatable): it simply denotes a 'living organism with intelligence comparable to man's in quantity and quality, hence with the possibility of rational communication with us. Its anatomy and indeed its means of communication are not defined as identical with ours' (Simpson, 1964: 771). In other words, it is not just the evolution of *Homo sapiens* but also of human intelligence and language that are considered unique, unrepeatable, and mostly the product of chance.

We must ask how Darwinians came to differ so much from Darwin in the subject of macroevolution. For Darwin, large numbers of individuals and their interactions generate natural selection as a statistical pattern, whereas large numbers of interacting species over long periods may generate evolutionary progress as a higher-order statistical pattern or a sort of Order from Disorder in organic evolution. But although Dobzhansky, Simpson and others accepted that macro-evolution is an extrapolation of natural selection, they rejected the idea of additional forms of order beyond the species level. In other words, the appearance of biological progress cannot be derived from the fundamental law of natural selection: progress can at best be accepted as a contingent feature of evolution (Simpson, 1949), or a mystery beyond science (Dobzhansky, 1967).

CONTINGENCY AS THE STARTLING CONSENSUS

Simpson's argument defined evolutionary history or macroevolution as the scale at which natural selection becomes an insufficient power, so that the 'states of populations' themselves become the causes of evolution. This idea was reshaped by critics of Darwinism as the con-cept of evolutionary constraint.

> Organisms must be analyzed as integrated wholes, with baupläne
> so constrained by phyletic heritage, pathways of development, and
> general architecture that the constraints themselves become more
> interesting and more important in delimiting pathways of change than
> the selective force that may mediate change when it occurs (Gould and
> Lewontin, 1979: 147).

To use an analogy, natural selection is as irrelevant for under-standing species diversity as gravitation is for explaining why river courses differ. The flow of water from high to low potential energy levels does require gravitation, but gravitation is virtually the same for all rivers: what makes the Thames different from the Nile is the unique topography of their surroundings. Now, if a given topography is turned upside down, we may interpret rivers as evolving lineages; and selection can be seen as the force constantly and universally driv-ing populations, whether of green algae or arboreal primates, towards points of maximum fitness. The reason why algae and primate lineages end up at different points, despite moving in the same upward direc-tion from a common ancestor and being driven by the same force, is that their lineages ran through different hills and valleys.

Evolutionary constraints are the hills and valleys that guide or direct evolutionary lineages. A negative constraint (a hill in the evo-lutionary topography) is defined as a limitation to possible evolu-tionary outcomes, or the absence of inheritable variation in certain directions (Maynard Smith *et al.*, 1985). Development is seen by many authors as a major source of negative constraints, as exemplified by the mechanism of body segmentation in British geophilomorph centipedes (Arthur and Kettle, 2001). Geophilomorph centipedes are among the few known organisms to exhibit both within- and between-species variation in leg-bearing segment numbers. Populations of centipedes show an approximately binomial distribution of segment number, suggesting stabilising selection. What is intriguing is that the number of leg-bearing segments in centipedes is always odd. It is not easy to understand how and why this pattern would result from natural selection; why would 49, 51 and 53 similar body segments be an advantage to an individual, but 48 or 50 segments a disadvantage?

A possible explanation is that even-numbered mutants simply do not occur (or are much less frequent) in nature, as suggested by recent studies in the mechanisms of segmentation in *Strigamia maritima* (Chipman *et al.*, 2004). In this centipede, segments are formed in a two-step process: first, segments are produced as a result of the growth of the anterior–posterior axis, and then subdivided into two due to intercalation of an additional boundary within the segment. If for some reason viable mutants exclusively occur at the first step but not at the second, then they will necessarily either gain or lose segments in pairs, and segments will necessarily jump numbers.

Segment number variation in *Strigamia maritima* provides a convincing example of discontinuous phenotypic variation determined by developmental constraints rather than natural selection. It is true that the mechanism of double periodicity and segment subdivision must have evolved by natural selection; but it evolved as a mechanism of segmentation rather than segment number determination. For this reason, segment number jumps in centipedes would be a by-product of inherited 'pathways of development'. Thus, although developmental constraints may result from the operation of selection in the past, their presence directs the evolution of a lineage in the future:

> Adaptations may then 'congeal' to limit directions of potential alteration in descendant taxa (the negative meanings), or to channel future change in preferred directions that often accelerate or grant easier access to adaptive solutions (the positive meanings) (Gould, 2002: 1173).

As much as topographies can be the source of rivers and waterfalls, constraints can also be positive (acting as valleys in the evolutionary topography); in other words, constraints might channel, direct or even accelerate evolutionary trajectories. For example, shared developmental mechanisms might predispose evolutionary lineages towards similar directions or evolutionary outcomes. Accordingly, traditional examples of adaptive convergence, such as the allegedly independent evolution of eyes in six separate animal phyla (Salvini-Plawen and Mayr, 1977), have been radically reinterpreted by some as 'a case of homoplasy in final results based upon significant homology in underlying developmental architecture' (Gould, 2002: 1128).

Morphologically, the compound eyes of arthropods and the camera eyes of vertebrates are blatant examples of homoplasy or analogy (superficial similarity derived from convergence) rather than homology (similarity due to inheritance from a common ancestor). Even the more similar camera eyes of vertebrates and cephalopods develop in different ways (the former as a projection from the brain, the latter as a differentiated region of the epidermis). However, it was found that vertebrates and cephalopods share a homologous 'master control gene' known as *Pax-6*, whose expression in the embryo triggers the differentiation of cells into a fully formed adult eye (Gehring, 1998). This was soon interpreted as evidence that 'absent an "internal" direction supplied by the pre-existing *Pax-6* developmental channel, natural selection could not have crafted such exquisitely similar, and beautifully adapted, final products from scratch, and purely "from the outside"' (Gould, 2002: 1129). The evolution of animal eyes would be just one example of the failure of natural selection to account for many aspects of organic diversity above the species level.

> Macroevolution cannot simply be scaled-up from microevolutionary mechanics if the phenomenology of this larger scale depends as much upon the potentials of evolvability as upon the impositions of selection (Gould, 2002: 1294).

In summary, while microevolution is the study of biases in the distribution of genotypes and phenotypes within populations, macroevolution is a science of a different kind: it is the historical study of how evolutionary constraints and random historical events have guided and commanded selection through unlikely and irreproducible walks. Evolutionary history should be seen as a sequence of hierarchical 'tiers of time': the first and lower tier is selection operating at the level of populations; the second is species competition; and the third and most important, represented by episodes of catastrophic mass extinction caused by extraneous factors such as asteroid collisions or radical climate change, results in random sampling of species and the actual pattern of biodiversity that we observe. Macroevolution has to be for this reason the science of 'narrative explanations' and the domain of contingency, 'or the tendency of complex systems with substantial stochastic components, and intricate nonlinear interactions among components, to be unpredictable in principle from full knowledge of antecedent conditions, but fully explainable after time's actual unfoldings' (Gould, 2002: 46).

Startlingly, the essentially anti-Darwinian concept of constrained macroevolution is remarkably similar to the views expressed earlier by Simpson. As surprisingly, Gould's narrative view of macroevolution, based on the old-fashioned, Laplacean view of complexity as a source of unpredictability, is favoured by many Darwinians over the processual view proposed by Darwin and based on a more contemporary view of complexity as a source of order through composition. In summary, macroevolutionary theorising has been characterised by an unexpected consensus between ardent supporters of Darwinism and some of its most vociferous critics: all seem to agree that the history of life can only be described *a posteriori* as a procession of unique and unrepeatable lineages.

CONVERGENCE

Despite its wide acceptance, the apparent consensus over historical contingency may be unjustified. The reason is that it seems to depend on the assumption that the focus of analysis in macroevolution is the lineage itself; under this assumption, macroevolution is nothing more than the exhaustive or encyclopaedic study of evolutionary trajectories.

> Wind the tape of life back to Burgess times [over 500 million years ago], and let it play again. If *Pikaia* [a primitive chordate] does not survive in the replay, we are wiped out of future history … And so, if you wish to ask the question of the ages – why do humans exist? – a major part of the answer, touching those aspects of the issue that science can treat at all, must be: because *Pikaia* survived the Burgess decimation. This response does not cite a single law of nature; it embodies no statement about predictable evolutionary pathways, no calculation of probabilities based on general rules of anatomy or ecology. The survival of *Pikaia* was a contingency of 'just history' (Gould, 1989: 323).

Each evolving lineage is by definition unique, but does this prove that macroevolution must be the historical narrative of case studies? As seen above, nuclear physics is not limited to particle history narratives despite the fact that each β-decay event of ^{14}C into ^{14}N is unique and unpredictable. For the same reason, natural selection can be seen as an emerging statistical pattern or bias in populations. But can statistical composition be applied to evolutionary lineages too? In other words, if we strip species and lineages of their unique features and analyse them as data points from a large sample, do we observe any patterns or regularities at the larger scale of evolutionary history?

A hint at the answer is offered by the phenomenon of evolutionary convergence, or independent evolution of functionally or morphologically similar traits (Haldane and Huxley, 1927; Simpson, 1953; Rensch, 1960). A much debated phenomenon, convergence, was recently reinstated by Conway Morris (2001, 2003) as an answer to Gould's challenge. He convincingly argued that the tape of life has indeed been rerun not once, but multiple times: it was rerun when Cretacean mammals adapted to marine environments previously occupied by extinct Jurassic reptiles; it was rerun when ancestral mammals, isolated from each other in North America, South America and Australia by continental drift, were exposed to similar selection pressures; and it is rerun when different parasites adapt to different hosts (or to the same host multiple times). Those reruns frequently generate surprisingly similar outcomes: the incredibly similar placental wolf in North America and the marsupial Tasmanian wolf; the fusiform dolphins and ichthyosaurs; or the eyes, legs and wings that independently evolved in the most diverse taxa.

Convergence conveys the idea that selection has repeatedly driven distinct species to the same evolutionary ends, irrespective of the particularities or historical scars of each lineage; it is therefore a cogent response to the positive constraint argument. When Gould (2002: 1129) pointed to the discovery of *Pax-6* genes in a wide range of organisms, including even planarians whose eyes do not include lenses (Pineda *et al.*, 2000), his conclusion was that 'the basic genetic cascade had already been originated, and already regulated visual systems, indicating the pre-existence of the developmental pathway as a positive constraint of parallelism'. The fundamental problem with this argument is that conservation of genetic pathways does not mean predisposition towards parallel evolution: it is as often associated with evolutionary divergence. The *pdm/apterous* cascade, for example, is another conserved developmental cascade across arthropods, which instead of positively constraining taxa towards similar parallel evolution, evolved to specify limbs in crustaceans and wings in insects (Averof and Cohen, 1997). Since in insects wings are evolutionarily derived from ancestral dorsal limbs, the conservation of a developmental cascade was in this case a condition for divergence and innovation driven by selection.

If parallelism, convergence and divergence are all possible outcomes of conserved developmental mechanisms, we may conclude that evolving lineages are not primarily channelled by constraints but guided by natural selection. But if all those results are possible, why does natural selection often lead to convergent results? The Earth is a finite environment offering a finite set of adaptive niches, and this may ask for a finite and repeatedly deployed set of adaptive solutions. From this perspective, it is not surprising that evolutionary history must sometimes repeat itself. Vermeij (2006) showed that in a set of 78 major evolutionary innovations (ranging from the genetic code to venom injection), 70% are convergences that evolved more than once. The remaining traits, or unique events in evolutionary history, had a significantly older origin than the convergent traits, suggesting that their uniqueness may result in some cases not from singular and contingent creation, but from loss or non-preservation of lineages that once exhibited convergent traits.

In summary, it may be true that our existence depended on the unlikely survival of *Pikaia*. Nevertheless, had it not survived and chordates did not evolve, the Earth would not have been deprived of organisms exhibiting mineralised skeletons, muscularised appendages, image-forming eyes, teeth, bipedalism, endothermy, placentas and social behaviour; all those traits evolved in many other lineages.

THE DENIAL OF 'PROGRESS': DARWINISM'S PREJUDICE AGAINST DARWIN

The frequent occurrence of evolutionary convergence frontally challenges the prevailing scepticism regarding selection-driven macroevolutionary patterns. Other arguments suggest that evolutionary history is more than a random walk of living forms. A hypothetical visit to the Earth four billion years ago would reveal the presence of self-replicating molecules in oceans or atmospheric water droplets (Hazen, 2005); three billion years ago, we would find unicellular organisms and the genetic code; half a billion years ago, macroscopic multicellular organisms resembling extant life were already present. Thirty million years ago, complex social networks had already evolved in insects, mammals and other animal groups; now, members of one species use words and written symbols to communicate. The evolution from molecules to human societies seems to suggest that evolution has some sort of direction; but does it move 'forward' in any objective (and non-anthropocentric) sense? As seen above, Darwin was clearly sympathetic to the idea of evolutionary progression and believed that extant forms are better adapted than extinct ones; a few Darwinians such as Mayr (1982: 532) were also fully convinced that 'on almost any measure one can think of a squid, a social bee, or primate, as more progressive than a prokaryote'.

A main problem in the debate over evolutionary progress is the lack of agreement on how to define and measure it objectively. To be fair, even those who reject evolutionary progress are not clear about a definition. The denial of progress in evolution is commonly based on three different features: linearity, inevitability, and increase in complexity. Maynard Smith and Szathmáry (1995: 4), for example, denounced the 'fallacy of progress' as the view of evolution as 'a simple image of progress on a linear scale'; against that mistaken view, they argued that 'life is better visualised as a branching tree than as a single ascending line'. Gould (2002: 1321), describing progress as the product of 'anthropocentric hope and social tradition', stated that evolution does not necessarily and linearly 'ascend': 'after all, two of the three great boughs on life's phyletic tree remain prokaryotic [Eubacteria and Archaea], while all three multicellular kingdoms extend as twigs from the terminus of the third bough'.

However, arguments against linearity and inevitability in evolution are based on a straw man fallacy. The most vociferous and outspoken progressionists, starting with Darwin himself, recognise that evolution is a branching process: even Haeckel (1896), a symbol of anthropocentric progressionism (Ruse, 1996), placed humans not on top of a ladder but of a living tree alive from its unicellular roots to the human high canopy. Haldane and Huxley (1927: 234), also strong believers in evolutionary progress, never argued that evolution implies the replacement of lower forms; instead, evolution 'consists in raising the upper level of organization reached by living matter, while still permitting the lower types of organization to survive'. Mayr (1988) expressed similar views:

> Who can deny that overall there is an advance from the prokaryotes that dominated the living world more than three billion years ago to the eukaryotes with their well organized nucleus and chromosomes as well as cytoplasmic organelles; from the single-celled eukaryotes to metaphytes and metazoans with a strict division of labour among their highly specialised organ systems; within the metazoans from

ectotherms that are at the mercy of the climate to the warm-blooded endotherms.

Mayr was aware that metaphytes and metazoans represented two divergent branches descending from unicellular ancestors; and by referring to extant ectotherms and endotherms (and in general only to extant groups), Mayr acknowledges that the most 'advanced' form does not necessarily replace its ancestor.

Moreover, when Ruse (1996: 419) interprets Mayr's belief in biological progress as a product of 'cultural convictions, especially those about scientific and technological progress', he is right for the wrong reasons. Ruse's remark that 'there is no reason to think that nature – or biological theory – makes this progress mandatory' is based on a misunderstanding: the belief that cultural progress itself is linear and inevitable. In fact, it appears that the history of technology and science can only suggest a useful parallel with biological evolution because they are *not* linear and inevitable. *Homo sapiens* evolved in Africa in the Middle Pleistocene (at present the earliest fossil evidence dates back to 200 000 years) and had dispersed as far as Australia at around 60 000 years ago (Lahr, 1996; Lewin and Foley, 2004). In Europe, modern humans made their first appearance over 40 000 years ago, bringing with them the Aurignacian stone tools that define what is known as the Upper Palaeolithic Revolution, characterised by a 'Mode 4' lithic technology for obtaining blades from prepared cores and use of alternative raw materials such as bone, ivory and antler. While in Europe this was only the first of a long series of revolutions, various human populations currently living in Australia, Asia, Africa and the Amazon remain in the Stone Age (Lee and Daly, 1999) – proving that technological change is not inevitable. A similar rationale applies to scientific theories. Heliocentrism (Thurston, 1994), atomism (Gregory, 1931) and relativity (Einstein and Infeld, 1938) were originally proposed in Antiquity, discarded or forgotten, and then reinstated, indicating that linearity is not a necessary rule of scientific progress. Rejecting evolutionary progress on the basis of inevitability and linearity does nothing but solve a pseudo-problem; linearity and inevitability are not the reason why Darwin, Mayr and others believe that biological organisation has on the whole progressed.

BIOLOGICAL COMPLEXITY AND INFORMATION

Finally, progress is also frequently defined as an increase in biological complexity. Even those who denounce the fallacy of progress admit that 'there is surely some sense in which elephants and oak trees are more complex than bacteria, and bacteria than the first replicating molecules' (Maynard Smith and Szathmáry, 1995: 3), and 'appreciate the appeal of an argument based on "ratcheting" for an accretion of levels of complexity through time' (Gould, 2002: 1321). Contrary to linearity and inevitability, arguments for evolutionary increases in biological complexity are as a rule more sophisticated and resistant to criticism, and therefore more difficult to disqualify. Whereas Ruse's (1996: 416) somewhat puzzling assertion that 'ancient forms (like trilobites) were more complex even possibly than humans' should not be taken too seriously (for a convincing demonstration, see Simpson, 1949: 254), more serious objections to evolutionary increases in complexity were made by Williams (1966) and McShea (1996). Both listed a series of possible definitions of complexity (including number of body parts, number of cell types, and phenotypic specialisation), analysed their distribution during evolutionary history, and then concluded that none provided any substantial support for the belief in a trend towards evolutionary increases in complexity.

On closer inspection, the negative conclusions of Williams and McShea seem to derive from a fundamental deficiency in their own criteria of complexity. What the measures of complexity proposed by Williams and McShea have in common is their strictly phenotypic (or organisational) character, and a deliberate attempt to avoid possible genotypic (or informational) criteria which measure or define complexity based on the 'information content' in the DNA sequences (Wicken, 1987). For example, Williams (1966: 35–6) hastily discarded Kimura's (1961) suggestion that increases in complexity could be measured as the accumulation of genetic information during the evolution of a lineage, criticising his proposals as naïve preconceptions, and then concluded without further justification that genetic information has 'changed enormously since Cambrian time, and natural selection has guided these changes, but it need not have increased the total information content'.

McShea (1996) also rejects genotypic measures of complexity, but bases his view on the unclear statement that 'much of the information in development is cytoplasmic and not present in DNA'. He also appeals to what we might call the 'Mayonnaise over DNA argument' to demonstrate that the complexity of an organism cannot be measured by its information content or genetic recipe. McShea's point is that the complexity of mayonnaise, 'a simple, homogeneous substance (at ordinary scales of observation)', will be highly overestimated when judged from the very complex recipe required to produce it. It is easy to see the fundamental problem in the argument: it assumes a priori that phenotypic or organisational criteria have priority over genotypic or informational ones, and then tries to prove the same point. In the example of mayonnaise, McShea implicitly and incorrectly assumed that homogeneous substances *must* be simple (an organisational criterion); therefore, organisational heterogeneity must be a standard for complexity.

Given the importance of inheritance to both life and evolution, it would be surprising if genetic information played no role in a possibly objective definition of biological complexity. Addressing the problem of defining life, and inspired by Schrödinger, Crick (1981) proposed a distinction between the Earth's geological history (the outcomes of physical and chemical processes, or all that depends on statistical averaging and Schrödinger's Principle of Order from Disorder) and its biological history (life itself, or anything that requires genetic material or DNA; or all entities and processes that depend on Schrödinger's Principle of Order from Order). That definition neatly grasped the inseparability of life from genetic inheritance, evolution and common descent. The distinction also offers the bonus of setting a lower boundary or root to the scale of biological complexity: viruses. Viruses are organisms that rely on phenotypes encoded by genes, store and transmit their 'recipe' across generations via DNA (or RNA), and share a nearly universal genetic code with other living beings (or more specifically with their specific hosts; Shackleton and Holmes, 2008).

From this perspective, it is hard to imagine how one could ever think of viruses, despite their extreme phenotypic simplicity, as not being living organisms. However, those who prefer phenotypic definitions of life based on key metabolic or morphological features, such as cellular organisation or self-maintenance (autopoiesis), tend to exclude viruses from the domain of life. For Margulis and Sagan (2000: 18), viruses are 'too small to self-maintain, they do not metabolize. Viruses do nothing until they enter an autopoietic entity; a bacterial cell, the cell of an animal, or of another live organism'. This argument has some clear weaknesses too. Margulis and Sagan explain in their own words why viruses do not metabolise: this is a consequence of their parasitic lifestyle. Parasites tend to rely on the phenotypic features of their hosts, thereby 'stripping themselves down to bare essentials' (Keeling, 2001). For example, intestinal parasites of vertebrates such as tapeworms live on food digested by the host, and therefore lost their guts completely; the same explains the loss of sensory and locomotory organs in other endoparasites (Ruppert and Barnes, 1994). To sum up, phenotypic redundancy with hosts is what often leads to simplification of parasites.

It so happens that some organisms, including viruses, are endoparasites of cells; in this case, one predicts the absence of some structures present in the cellular host. Whether viruses lost such structures or never possessed them is still debatable (Burnet, 1945; Forterre, 2006). In some cases, loss of structures in cellular parasites was demonstrated. For example, the microsporidian *Encephalitozoon cuniculi*, a unicellular parasitic eukaryote that only lives inside animal cells, lacks key organelles such as mitochondria and peroxisomes (Katinka *et al.*, 2001; Keeling, 2001). Structural simplification of microsporidians also occurred in the genome, with the loss of core eukaryotic genes and whole metabolic pathways. Genome size, gene number, protein size and cell size have been equally reduced and are comparable to what is found in some bacteria. Although highly atypical, *E. cuniculi* is undeniably a eukaryote, as shown by the presence of a nucleus and various eukaryotic genes and phylogenetic analysis indicating that microsporidians are in fact derived fungi (Hirt *et al.*, 1997). But for being too small, unable to self-maintain, and unable to survive and replicate outside an animal cell, microsporidia (as well as viruses) probably do not qualify as living organisms in Margulis and Sagan's scheme. In summary, it seems that definitions of life that exclusively rely on phenotypic criteria tend to be flawed. Genetic information must be taken into account in definitions of life, and as seen below, also of biological complexity.

ORGANISMS AS DNA PROGRAMS

Biological information must be included in definitions of biological complexity, but analysing genetic information carries its own difficulties. It is possible to interpret a living organism as a DNA program (Mayr, 1974) and use information theory (Shannon, 1948; Avery, 2003) to estimate its information content from objective variables such as genome length, information entropy (a measure of the probability of a DNA sequence in a universe of possible ones), or algorithm complexity (the size of the algorithm necessary to generate an observed DNA sequence from a randomly generated one; Li and Vitanyi, 1997). However, comparisons using variables such as amount or size of DNA in species tend to yield counterintuitive estimates of complexity: lungfish carry over 50 times more DNA than other fish species or humans, while grasshoppers carry 80 times more DNA than fruit flies (Maynard

Smith and Szathmáry, 1995). This is no surprise, since most DNA is 'junk' and does not code for protein (Orgel and Crick, 1980). Gene number is an alternative and in principle more appropriate measure of complexity, but existing evidence is equally frustrating: humans and chimpanzees differ little in both genome size and gene number (Mikkelsen *et al.*, 2005).

The main problem with strictly genetic comparisons is that the information content of a genome (however defined) cannot be an intrinsic property of the sequences themselves; it depends on its effect on a target or receiver (Wicken, 1987). In other words, the same DNA sequence may code for a product with different functional or structural effects when expressed in bacteria, a plant or a mammal; much as the same letter sequence 'as' conveys different meanings in English from German (meaning 'ace') or Dutch ('axis'). Trying to incorporate the functional or adaptive effects of genetic information into the definition of biological information, Adami (2002) proposed the concept of 'physical complexity' as the 'amount of information that an organism stores, in its genome, about the environment in which it evolves'. This definition has certain advantages, especially the link it establishes between increasing adaptation to a niche and increasing complexity. But such a link is also the reason for its intrinsic limitations. Physical complexity is a genetic mapping of niche complexity, and is therefore a niche-specific measure: one may be able to compare the complexity of two fish species living in the same lake, but not the complexity of a fish and a terrestrial mammal. As reckoned by Adami itself, physical complexity does not allow comparisons across adaptively divergent taxa, and such comparisons (between bacteria, chimpanzees and humans, or between unicellular and multicellular organisms) are exactly what evolutionary biologists expect from an objective measure of complexity.

The same comment applies to the study of developmental complexity by Azevedo *et al.* (2005). Based on the Kolmogorov criterion (Li and Vitany, 1997), they proposed the length of the shortest algorithm required to specify a cell lineage in a developing multicellular organism as the measure of developmental complexity in metazoans; that algorithm specifies various commands such as the number of cell divisions in the cell lineage, the number and distribution of resulting cell fates, and the pattern of cell division. According to the authors, metazoan development was shown to be extremely simple: that is, near the shortest possible generative algorithm. However, their interpretation of complexity and simplicity is questionable.

The finding that selection seems to have favoured the evolution of the most parsimonious or simplest developmental pathways is hardly surprising, given the advantages cited by the authors themselves: it allows for faster development, and 'might require less genetic information, and thus be more efficient'. The point is that efficiency is not what is meant by complexity in macroevolutionary debates. Rather than efficiency in the development of a cell lineage, it is the existence of genetic algorithms specifying cell lineages, or multicellularity itself, that suggests higher complexity in multicellular organisms. Azevedo *et al.*'s argument for selection as a process producing simplicity does not address a more fundamental question; as seen later, this question is the role that natural selection played in the evolution of 'complex' multicellular organisms from 'simpler' unicellular ancestors.

MAJOR TRANSITIONS: THE AGGREGATIONAL MODE OF EVOLUTION

It seems that a sound definition of biological complexity cannot be based solely on either information criteria (genotype) or organisation criteria (phenotype). By offering a definition that integrates information and organisation, the most fruitful account of biological complexity is the theory of 'major transitions' presented in its most popular formulation by Maynard Smith and Szathmáry (1995, 1999). It is rarely acknowledged that the basic principles of the theory are found almost fully developed in Haldane and Huxley's (1927) *Animal Biology*. Surprisingly, Maynard Smith and Szathmáry fail to cite or mention the book (although Maynard Smith was Haldane's student and colleague at University College London).

A possible reason for the neglect is the explicitly progressionist perspective of *Animal Biology*. Haldane and Huxley were firm believers in evolutionary progress, which would result from two processes. The first was individuation, or 'improvement of the separate unit' or organism, measured in terms of control over the environment; some examples are the origin of a central nervous system, sense organs, terrestrial life, instinct and intelligence, and reason and language, which place humans at the summit of evolutionary progress (Haldane and Huxley, 1927; see their Figure 77).

The second process, evolution by 'aggregation', was a groundbreaking idea. Aggregation was the 'joining together of a number of separate units to form a super-unit, as when coral polyps unite to form a colony' (Haldane and Huxley, 1927: 235). Since individuation can turn the 'mere aggregate into an individual', the two processes act together in progressive evolution: aggregates may evolve new adaptations by individuation, and the improved units may merge into new aggregates. Unfortunately Haldane and Huxley's book focuses almost exclusively on examples of individuation, but decades after its publication a series of works rescued the idea of aggregation as the key to the understanding of biological complexity. Buss (1987: 171) reinstated Haldane and Huxley's case by proposing that 'the history of life is the history of transitions between different units of selection', represented by the sequence of self-replicating molecules, self-replicating complexes, cells, multigenomic cells, multicellular individuals, and kin groups. But it was the joint effort of Maynard Smith and Szathmáry that contributed the most to reviving aggregation by taking the concept to its logical and most general consequence. In redefining evolutionary aggregation, Maynard Smith and Szathmáry (1995: 6) proposed what is named here the biological unit concept (BUC):

> Entities that were capable of independent replication before the transition can replicate only as part of a larger whole after it.

The super-unit evolved by aggregation bears an implicit analogy with Mayr's (1942) classic biological species concept (BSC). According to the BSC, a new species is formed when potentially or actually interbreeding natural populations become reproductively isolated from each other. Similarly, a major transition in evolution occurs when entities become reproductively isolated within a larger whole – that is, a new super-unit or level of biological organisation. The BUC is important for allowing the distinction between a mere aggregate or group (for example, a colony of unicellular organisms) and a true super-unit (for example, multicellular organisms that evolved from unicellular ancestors). Their list of eight major transitions starts with the origin of protocells (the transition from self-replicating molecules to compartmentalised populations of molecules) and ends with the relatively recent origin of human societies that communicate through language (Table 1.1).

However, super-unit formation is not the only aspect of a major transition. For Maynard Smith and Szathmáry the function of gametes in sexually reproducing species, or queens in eusocial species, is the replication of the previously independent, turned-sterile components of an evolved super-unit; examples of sterile components are somatic cells in multicellular organisms and non-reproductive castes in eusocial insects. Thus, evolutionary transitions also 'depended on a small number of major changes in the way in which information is stored, transmitted, and translated' (Maynard Smith and Szathmáry,

Table 1.1 *The eight 'major transitions in evolution'*

(1) Replicating molecules	→	Protocells
(2) Independent replicators	→	Chromosomes
(3) RNA World	→	DNA World
(4) Prokaryotes	→	Eukaryotes
(5) Asex	→	Sex
(6) Protists	→	Multicellular animals, plants and fungi
(7) Solitary individuals	→	Colonies with non-reproductive castes
(8) Primate societies	→	Human societies

Adapted from Maynard Smith and Szathmáry (1995).

1999: 16). Examples of new ways of transmitting information include the origin of template replication, the genetic code, developmental and epigenetic regulation, and human language.

The theory of major transitions has the merit of defining evolutionary increases in complexity both at the phenotypic-organisational (the newly evolved super-units) and genotypic-informational (the new methods of transmitting biological information) levels. A second advantage is that it avoids anthropocentric criteria of complexity. For example, the genes required for the maintenance of individual cells are only a subset of the information transmitted by a eusocial queen to her descendants (other levels of information include multicellular organisation, and organisation of eusocial behaviour); the eusocial queen is more complex than a single-celled organism not because it is more similar to a human, but because its phenotype requires more types of biological information: a multicellular organism is more than a group of cells, and therefore cannot be less complex than separate cells. By implicitly appealing to the classic Aristotelian motto that 'the whole is more than the sum of its parts', major transitions imply that biological wholes (or super-units) must be more complex that the biological parts that preceded them in evolution. For this reason, social wholes must be more complex than their individual parts, and multicellular wholes must be more complex than single-celled organisms. Finally, since asocial organisms coexist with social ones, and unicellular organisms coexist with multicellular ones, major transitions imply neither linearity nor inevitability in evolution. Major transitions and the rationale they present for evolutionary increases in complexity suggest that Darwin's belief in evolutionary progress was not completely unjustified.

The theory of major transitions is an appealing account of patterns in macroevolution, but it shows a conceptual flaw. According to Maynard Smith and Szathmáry, major transitions represent new super-units formed by aggregation of formerly independent units, maintained and replicated by new systems of biological information. However, it is clear that not all the proposed transitions exemplify *both* sides of this definition.

1   Not all transitions involved aggregation. The transition from primate to human societies has certainly required language as a new system of biological information, but human societies are not aggregates of primate societies. Although human societies may be qualitatively different from other primate societies, they do not bear a part-to-whole relationship exemplified by the unicellular–multicellular transition.

2   Not all transitions involved a new system of transmitting information – unless a 'new system' is vaguely defined. The definition of a 'new system of transmission of biological information' offered by Maynard Smith and Szathmáry is not precise enough. There is an obvious appeal to the idea that the information stored in genes and transmitted from ancestors to descendants is of a different nature from the information stored in animal brains and transmitted between organisms through learning, or from information stored in words and transmitted between humans via speech. In contrast, characterising German and Latin as 'different systems of information' would describe differences at a less fundamental level: they are just two variants of the 'same' human language. For the same reason, a visual display and a bird song can be seen as two forms of animal communication transmitting the same type of 'behavioural' information stored in animal brains (Jablonka and Lamb, 2006).

From this perspective, some of the eight major transitions did *not* engender the origin of a truly new type of biological information. The symbiotic origin of the eukaryotic cell involved the aggregation of previously independent bacteria (Margulis, 1970); but both bacteria and the first unicellular eukaryotes were transmitting the 'same' *genetic* (or protein-coding) information for maintenance and reproduction of their descendants. A similar argument applies to the comparison between asexual and sexual reproduction: both a sexually reproducing roundworm and an asexual bdelloid rotifer (Fontaneto *et al.*, 2007) transmit to offspring the 'same' genetic (protein-coding) and developmental information (required for organising the multicellular body plan) and thus represent the same level of biological complexity.

3   Some transitions describe a new level of selection, but not a new level of biological organisation. The origin of social groups from solitary individuals can at best describe a case of *incomplete* evolutionary transition. Many colonies of single-celled organisms are better interpreted as nearly multicellular: slime moulds, social amoebae and volvocine algae, for example, display some features of multicellular organisation (division of labour and reproductive specialisation), but their members are still independent individuals competing for reproductive success against each other (Buss, 1987; Bonner, 2006), contrary to somatic cells in a multicellular organism. The same is true for animal societies: there are various degrees of sociality between the hypothetical extremes of solitary living and full eusociality. In summary, groups of co-operative or even interdependent organisms (from lichens and slime moulds to social mammals and humans) can certainly be a product of selection as social life often increases the fitness of social individuals (Lewontin, 1970; Maynard Smith, 1988; Keller, 1999), but social groups (including eusocial ones as discussed later) are not a new level of organisation equivalent to a multicellular 'super-unit'. In fact, the transition from unicellular to multicellular organisation is a rare example satisfying both aspects of a major transition (being a super-unit and requiring a new type of biological information).

4   Aggregation is convergent rather than unique. Multicellular super-units have evolved independently in fungi, algae and plants, and animals (Gerhart and Kirschner, 1997; Bonner, 1998). Convergence also characterises eusociality, since sterile castes and division of labour occur not only in insects, but also in other groups such as crustaceans (Duffy, 1996) and vertebrates (O'Riain *et al.*, 2000). This suggests that super-unit formation may be only one of the recurrent *consequences* of evolutionary increases in biological complexity, which may rest on much rarer and important macroevolutionary episodes.

All the points above will be discussed in more depth in the following chapters. What can be concluded now is that the theory of major transitions proposed by Maynard Smith and Szathmáry has the merit of defining objective parameters for the study of biological complexity. However, it seems to imply a mismatch between the informational and organisational sides of transitions: while new types of biological information are rare and unique (with the genetic code and language, for example, evolving only once), aggregation processes (either complete or incomplete) are an exuberant example of evolutionary convergence. As argued below, an alternative equation between information and organisation can be derived from the very definition of life proposed by Schrödinger.

THE EVOLUTION OF BIOLOGICAL ORDER

Schrödinger's Principle of Order from Order was a significant step in our understanding of life by pointing to nucleic acids as the source of order in living organisms. It has not been realised that the principle has another far-reaching consequence: it may also be an answer to the problem of biological complexity and its evolution. Schrödinger's Principle of Order from Order defines life through a simple formula: it is the microscopic order of DNA that carries and transmits information about phenotypic order. However, the principle fails to capture another defining feature of life: evolutionary change. Can the static link between information and organisation found in living beings be dynamically established in macroevolution? The hypothesis presented here (and developed in more detail in the final chapter) is that *evolutionary increases in complexity represent macroevolutionary transformations in Schrödinger's Principle of Order from Order*. The hypothesis consists of some elements. First, it states that the evolution of new 'biological codes' underlies changes in levels of biological complexity, in agreement with the views pioneered by Buss (1987) and Maynard Smith and Szathmáry (1995), and more recently given an explicit formulation by Barbieri (2003) and especially Jablonka and Lamb (2005, 2006).

Second, new levels of complexity evolve with a new biological code or type of biological information, and then with a corresponding new type of phenotypic entity. For example, the genetic code consists of a system of DNA, RNA and amino acids, thus generating disposable proteins as the first and most fundamental phenotypic tools used by all living organisms. Later, multicellularity brought about the origin of somatic cells as a new form of disposable phenotypic units, as a consequence of a new 'developmental code' based on transcription factors (modified proteins) and gene regulatory regions. A third category of

Table 1.2 *The four codes representing the transformation of Schrödinger's Principle of Order from Order*

Information carrier	Disposable phenotype
Genetic code:	
genes	Proteins
(modified RNA)	
Developmental code:	
regulatory proteins	Somatic cells
(modified proteins)	
Behavioural code:	
neural cells	Learned behaviours
(modified somatic cells)	
Linguistic code:	
words	Human cultural traits
(modified behaviours)	

Source: Based on Maynard Smith and Szathmáry (1995) and Jablonka and Lamb (2006).

phenotypic unit present only in animals is behaviour, which requires neural cells (modified somatic cells) and brains as sources of information and organisation. Finally, *Homo sapiens* has relied on words (modified vocalisations or behaviours) and language, a new mechanism for storing and transmitting human culture, our species-specific system of learned extended phenotypes and social norms. In other words, levels of organisation can be primarily defined by categories of phenotypes and their corresponding codes, rather than stages in aggregation of phenotypes. The list of four fundamental levels of organisation described above (genetic, developmental, behavioural and cultural), although implicit in previous works, was explicitly proposed by Jablonka and Lamb (2005, 2006) as the 'four dimensions' of evolution (Table 1.2).

Third, new biological codes gradually evolve from previously existing ones, in contrast to the thesis of 'sudden appearance' (Barbieri, 2003: 235). It also seems that Jablonka and Lamb's main interest was to argue that the existence of three systems of inheritance other than the genetic one was evidence for 'Lamarckian' or non-Darwinian aspects of evolution. This is probably why they were unable to present a model for the *evolution* of those new systems, a process that was essentially Darwinian. Thus, the evolutionary version of Schrödinger's Principle proposes that *a new biological code evolves when entities that originally performed phenotypic functions gradually evolve into informational carriers themselves.* For being the ancestor to all codes, the genetic code poses a special problem (similar to accounting for the origin of life or the 'first species') and is given a special solution (the RNA World hypothesis; Gilbert, 1986). The genetic code, assumed as a starting point, converts information stored in DNA sequences into protein sequences. However, proteins gradually evolved new functions including a particular one: the function of information carriers in molecules such as transcription factors. The modulation of gene activity by transcription factors was the condition behind the multiple origins of multicellularity (Kirschner and Gerhart, 2005). The same applies to the gradual origin of the behavioural code from the developmental code: multicellularity implies differentiated somatic cells originally evolved as disposable units; but in some organisms, neural cells and their networks evolved with the function of storing and transmitting the information underlying animal behaviour. Finally, behaviour is a category of phenotype engendering forms of interaction with the environment and organisms from other species, as well as intraspecific interactions such as competition, co-operation, signalling and communication. In *Homo sapiens*, words evolved from modified vocalisations or behaviours and are the units of language, our unique system of information.

Fourth, the gradual origin of new information carriers and their corresponding phenotypes is possible due to the process of *modularity transfer*. DNA is an efficient carrier of information due to its modular organisation consisting of nucleotide units, whose combination gives rise to potentially infinite combinations or sequences (or unlimited inheritance; Maynard Smith and Szathmáry, 1999). On the basis of the RNA World model, we may assume that DNA inherited its modular organisation from RNA. The genetic code implies not only that DNA is able to specify protein sequences; it implies at the same time that modular organisation is transferred to proteins (which are organised as amino acid sequences). This process has a crucial evolutionary consequence: if proteins are modularly organised like their DNA 'hard copy', they could at least in principle evolve into information carriers themselves. Thus, transcription factors, neural cells and brains, behaviour and cognition, and human language all derived their modular organisation from previously existing disposable, modularly organised phenotypic entities. Not by accident, the modularity of DNA and proteins (Maynard Smith and Szathmáry, 1999), developmental processes (Wagner *et al.*, 2007), brains and cognition (Fodor, 1983) and language (Nowak *et al.*, 2000) are central concepts in evolutionary studies, but tend to be treated separately. The evolutionary formulation of Schrödinger's Principle of Order from Order and the concept of modularity transfer unify those debates to a certain extent.

All the biological codes are different manifestations of Schrödinger's Principle of Order from Order: they are ways in which different types of microscopic order or information is converted into different forms of macroscopic or phenotypic order. The idea that the principle has evolved has another important consequence: it establishes a hierarchy of levels of organisation.

THE EVOLUTION OF ORDER:
MACROEVOLUTIONARY CONSEQUENCES

The hypothesis that new biological codes evolve when phenotypic entities become carriers of information is based on Maynard Smith and Szathmáry's concept of new systems for transmitting biological information, but aims at being more precise in its definition of the new information carriers. For example, although the joint replication of genes in chromosomes was listed as one of their eight transitions in evolution, chromosome formation did not correspond to the origin of a new biological code but was simply a new form of replication of genetic information. The definition also excludes various codes proposed by Barbieri (2003), such as a 'histone code' or the 'sugar code', which are different ways of transmitting the 'same' type of information.

A further consequence is that since the evolution of a new biological code relies on a previously existing one, a functional and evolutionary hierarchy is established between them. Barbieri (2003) pointed out that new organic codes do not replace previous ones, but the hypothesis that a new code derives from transformation of a previously existing *phenotypic entity* implies more than that: it implies that the previous code *cannot* disappear. The developmental code based on specialised proteins (transcription factors and others), for example, was built upon proteins that require the existence of the genetic code. Learned behavioural phenotypes depend on information processed by neural cells and brains, and for this reason cannot exist without somatic cells and the developmental code. The same is true for human language that requires the existence of learned behavioural phenotypes.

Ultimately, the hierarchy of codes and dependence of levels of organisation on previously existing ones explain why human culture, despite being a phenotype inextricably linked to human language, rests simultaneously upon linguistic, behavioural, developmental and genetic foundation. Thus, the hierarchical structure of biological codes points to the continuity and complementarity of information systems. The hierarchy of codes proposed above may also provide a more powerful criterion of biological complexity than super-unit formation: more complex organisms may be defined as those whose phenotypes require more biological codes; four levels of biological complexity can be defined as genetic, genetic-developmental, genetic-developmental-behavioural, and genetic-developmental-behavioural-linguistic. Thus, biological complexity (or the evolution of Order from Order) is classified as a different phenomenon from physical complexity, which as seen previously results from statistical averaging (or Order from Disorder). The hierarchical view does not imply linearity or inevitability either: the genetic code, for example, does not necessarily lead to the developmental code, since transcription factors and other proteins still perform various functions unrelated to the transmission of information in unicellular organisms.

Since the evolutionary version of Schrödinger's Principle implies that new categories of phenotypic entities have been evolving since the origin of life, natural selection has also changed and adopted new forms with the emergence of new levels of biological organisation. Not accidentally, the most general principles of Darwinian evolutionary theory are statements about the operation of natural selection at a given level of organisation; they are equally crucial to an understanding of how phenotypic entities may have evolved into new information carriers. Thus, to each of the four levels of genes and proteins, development and multicellularity, animal brains and learned behaviour, and human language and culture, there corresponds a fundamental axiom of natural selection. The first is Fisher's (1930) 'fundamental principle of natural selection', which would hold true even in a world exclusively consisting of genes as units of inheritance and proteins as units of phenotype. The second can be named as Weismann's principle, and states that the power of natural selection decreases with age in multicellular organisms and rules the transformations of somatic bodies (Weismann, 1889). The third, more recent generalisation of the theories of kin selection (Hamilton, 1964) and reciprocal altruism (Trivers, 1971) is Dawkin's memetic principle, according to which the animal brain became the host of 'memes' or units of information communicated between brains (Dawkins, 1976). Finally, the importance of cultural transmission via human language is expressed by the concept of 'cultural group selection' (Gintis *et al.*, 2001) unique to our species.

The next chapters will develop the thesis that the perception of evolutionary increases in complexity is neither an anthropocentric illusion nor a macroevolutionary accident: it is a historical product of the hierarchical operation of selection. Evolutionary changes in levels of biological complexity are fundamental changes in the character of life – in the nature and carriers of information, in the phenotypic entities that they code for, and in the way biological codes convert information into organisation. The challenge is to understand how the operation of selection has transformed Schrödinger's Principle of Order from Order by setting it in motion.

2

From the units of inheritance to the origin of species

By the time of Darwin and Wallace's death the belief in evolution and descent with modification of species was well established, but enthusiasm for natural selection as the mechanism or law of evolution remained meagre until the 1930s (Bennettt, 1999). The most likely reason for scepticism was that the genetic theories considered by Darwin and other naturalists, including pangenesis (the origin of the hereditary material from the fusion of body organ samples or 'gemules'; Darwin, 1868), Nägeli's blending theory (the averaging of parents' traits in sexually produced offspring; see Ospovat, 1980 and Berry, 2000) and inheritance of acquired characters (see Mayr and Provine, 1980) failed to account adequately for inheritable variation in natural populations and were at odds with experimental work done by geneticists (Osborn, 1926). Crampton (1928) believed that 'little if any understanding of the origin of organic types can be gained through the study of genera, species or even varieties, *after* they have arisen...the geneticists and they alone are working on the fundamental dynamics of organic differentiation'. For this reason, natural selection was still struggling to gain respect among biologists 70 years after its birth: as summed up by Watson (1929), 'the only two "theories of evolution" which have gained any general currency, those of Lamarck and of Darwin, rest on a most insecure basis'.

Less than a decade after Watson's remarks were published, natural selection had become the one and only theory of evolution for most biologists. In 1934, the previously sceptical American Society of Naturalists dedicated its annual dinner to the centenary of the birth of Weismann and Haeckel, respectively 'the arch selectionist and the arch genealogist'; the meeting was described as an opportunity for selectionists to 'pause to congratulate ourselves upon our accomplishments'. The reason for the enthusiasm was that 'at the hands of Wright, Fisher and Haldane, we are gradually being shown what the course of evolution must be in the light of the Mendelian mechanism' (Shull, 1935).

Mendel's genetic theory published in 1866 was a breakthrough that postulated the existence of 'constant characters' or units of inheritance (which we now associate with genes), while his laws of dominance, segregation and independent assortment of constant characters successfully predicted distributions of phenotypic characters. However, although Mendel's laws provided the safe foundation that genetics needed, they were derived from experiments based on small populations and a few generations of domesticated garden pea varieties. Thus, it was necessary to extrapolate the consequences of Mendel's laws to larger, natural populations and to many generations before they could play any role in evolutionary debates. The theoretical extrapolation from Mendel's garden to the course of evolution was mostly the product of Fisher's *The Genetical Theory of Natural Selection* (1930), Haldane's *The Causes of Evolution* (1932) and Wright's classic essays (1931, 1932), which jointly redefined Darwinism as the study of how natural selection and other demographic processes affect the survival and transmission of inheritance units in natural populations.

Despite all the progress that followed the synthesis of natural selection with Mendelism, some controversy still surrounds Darwinism both at the microevolutionary and macroevolutionary scale. At the level of microevolution, debates are still ongoing as to how gradual or punctuated is the process of adaptive evolution (Orr, 2005). At the macroevolutionary level, the relative roles of selection versus physical isolation in the origin of new species also remain highly controversial (Coyne and Orr, 2004; Gavrilets, 2005).

Underlying those controversies there is an even more important question: what is the most fundamental consequence of Mendelian or particulate inheritance for the evolutionary process? A popular answer is the 'selfish gene' hypothesis: since the gene is the unit or particle of inheritance, it must also be the unit of selection (Williams, 1966; Dawkins, 1976). A second and radically opposite answer is that the gene is a molecule playing a reduced role in evolution and only relevant for the chemistry of life (Goodwin, 1994). Both views seem to be incorrect: Mendelism and the discovery of genes are relevant for macroevolution because they revealed the existence of a *modular* system of biological information underlying inheritance and evolution. The principles behind the operation of genetic modularity and their far-reaching consequences for the evolution of biological complexity are discussed below.

THE GENE AS THE MODULE OF INHERITANCE

Contrary to old and recent prejudice (Henig, 2000), the late fusion of Darwinian and Mendelian principles was probably not accidental (Mangelsdorf, 1967; Berry, 2000). Mendel's classic study of garden peas was published in a journal circulated to about 120 libraries in the United States and Europe including England, and was cited in the influential botanical treatises of Hoffmann and Föcke that were held in Darwin's library. Mendel travelled to London in 1862 (when his experiments with garden peas had already been finalised) and later read a German translation of the *Origin*. Since Darwin and his fellow naturalists were interested in evolution and continuous variation whereas Mendel was a creationist by faith and profession, it is more likely that mutual lack of interest and understanding prevented an early synthesis of evolution and Mendelian genetics.

The first attempt at incorporating Mendelism into evolution is known as mutationism, and is associated with a rediscovery of Mendel in the early 1900s and a hostile attitude towards natural selection. The logic of mutationism was simple: mutation is the origin of new gene alleles (de Vries, 1906); different alleles produce different phenotypes; species and higher taxa are characterised by different phenotypes; therefore, mutations, rather than natural selection, must be the origin of new species. In summary, 'the discontinuity of species follows from the discontinuity of variation' (Bateson, 1894), and both derive from gene mutation.

More than any other work, Fisher's *Genetical Theory of Natural Selection* (1930) was responsible for the demonstration that natural selection is fully compatible with Mendelian laws. The book can be understood as a long argument against mutationism; for a secondary role of mutation in evolution; and for natural selection as the true creative power in evolution. The starting point of Fisher's argument was the statement that the most important contribution of Mendelian genetics was the atomisation of inheritance into independent factors and an unambiguous rejection of all previous theories of soft inheritance (Mayr, 1980).

Fisher showed that the 'blending theory' proposed by Nägeli and accepted by Darwin was not only wrong but also incompatible with natural selection. The reason is intuitively simple: in sexual organisms, blending theory proposed that inheritable factors were averaged in descendants, explaining for example why a tall and a short parent tend to generate offspring of average size. But blending creates a problem: it implies that the offspring of a mutant will be 'less mutant' and deviate less from the population average than the mutant parent. For this reason, after a few generations of averaging, descendants of the original mutant will be virtually indistinguishable from non-mutants (Box 2.1). More specifically, Fisher showed that the genetic variance in phenotypic traits, the essential condition for the operation of natural selection, is reduced by half every generation under blending inheritance purely as a result of sexual reproduction. This was the reason why Darwin was forced to postulate high rates and multiple sources of mutations (use and disuse, environmental effects, nutrition habits) constantly replenishing populations with a minimum level of genetic variation required by selection.

Fisher argued that the problem of vanishing genetic variation magically disappears under Mendelian genetics, which assumes that inheritance factors are transmitted as particles that do not blend in

---

Box 2.1 The effect of mutations under blending inheritance

Suppose a large, randomly mating population under the operation of blending inheritance. A body size mutant occurs and is larger than the population average size x by an amount e (the 'average excess'), so that its size is $x + e$. If the mutant mates with a random member of the population of body size x, the expected size of their descendants will be the average of $x + e$ and x, or $x + (e/2)$. Therefore, descendants deviate from the population average by an amount $e/2$, half the original deviation e in the mutant parent.

Now, if this descendant with body size $x + (e/2)$ mates with another random member of the population, the expected size of their offspring is the average of $x + (e/2)$ and x, or $x + (e/4)$; the deviation between the mutant's grandchild and the population average is $e/4$. Thus, the effect of the rare mutation under blending inheritance is quickly diluted across generations due to mating with non-mutant individuals. The deviation from the population average in the mutant lineage decreases by $e/2^n$ (where n is the number of generations) and the phenotypic effect of the original mutation rapidly tends to zero.

It should also be noticed that the mutation e increases the average body size in the population. However, the effect on the average is e/N, where N is population size; thus, the effect approximates zero unless the population is unrealistically small. Under the assumption of blending inheritance, the effect of a mutation on the population where it occurs is as irrelevant as a drop of black ink in an ocean.

descendants. As we now know, sexually reproducing species are typically diploid organisms carrying two separate alleles or copies of each gene (one paternal and one maternal). As demonstrated by the Hardy–Weinberg theorem (Fisher, 1930), frequencies of Mendelian factors and genotypic distributions remain in equilibrium in a randomly mating population, meaning that sexual reproduction by itself cannot destroy genetic variation. For this reason, much lower mutation rates are required to maintain variation in populations under the Mendelian scheme.

By accepting Mendelism and the integrity of alleles and their phenotypic effects across generations, Fisher's evolutionary genetics can be defined as the study of the effects of allelic variation on individual adaptation and population change. Fisher defined the average excess of an allele on a trait (for example, the effect of a given allele on body size) as the difference between the trait in individuals carrying the allele and those not carrying it (for example, the difference in average body size between carriers and non-carriers). Since alleles and their effect on traits are not diluted across generations under Mendelian inheritance, Fisher defined a second and related quantity, the 'average phenotypic effect produced … by the substitution of one type of gene [an allele] for the other' (Fisher, 1930: 31). This quantity is better understood as the effect that a mutant gene introduced into a population has on a trait average, and was named 'genetic variance' by Fisher; it is currently known as 'additive genetic variance' (additive means that only effects caused by the presence of the individual allele are considered, but not the effect of its interactions with other alleles such as dominance and epistasis).

Additive genetic variance, or the power of alleles to affect phenotypes as a consequence of their mere presence, is in Fisher's theory the most fundamental evolutionary consequence of genetic mechanisms. For this reason, the rejection of blending theory and the concept of additive genetic variance represented the true birth of the gene as a Darwinian concept. In the Fisherian scheme, the average effect manifests the essence of an allele in the same way that mass, charge or spin manifest the nature of an electron. This is why Mendelism was so crucial to the development of the theory of natural selection: it postulated the existence of inheritance factors which were constant, followed clear dynamical rules (the Mendelian laws), and manifested an essential or intrinsic power in the form of an observable phenotypic quantity (their additive effect). From this Mendelian or particulate foundation, Fisher was able to propose a complete reformulation of Darwin's troubled hypothesis of natural selection.

Particulate inheritance solved the problem faced by Darwin by showing that genetic variation is neither lost due to sexual reproduction nor created by environmental factors such as climate, nutrition or use and disuse of organs. Fisher no longer needed to postulate high mutation rates, and the first experimental studies in the fruit fly *Drosophila melanogaster* confirmed that mutation rates were very low in that species (Morgan *et al.*, 1925). But if genetic variation is created by mutations but not destroyed by blending, what prevents it from indefinitely accumulating in populations? The answer is natural selection itself; this is one of the meanings of Fisher's (1930: 35) 'fundamental principle of natural selection'.

> The rate of increase in fitness of any organism [i.e. population or species] at any time is equal to its [additive] genetic variance in fitness at that time.

The principle, one of the most important in evolutionary biology, makes intuitive sense: it states that the more variation in fitness is found in a population, the higher the gap between the fittest and the less fit individuals. Therefore, the faster the bias of selection towards the fittest operates, the faster the unfit are selectively outcompeted and wiped out. For this reason, Fisher's fundamental principle implies that natural selection is a self-inhibiting process. As selection eliminates the unfit, only the fittest survive; among the survivors, selection proceeds in the following generations to keep only the fittest among the fittest; eventually, one expects a single allele at each locus to survive, corresponding to the survival of a single 'fittest' combination of alleles in an originally variable population. In other words, additive genetic variance in fitness is now predicted to vanish not as a result of sexual reproduction (as in the case of blending inheritance), but as a consequence of natural selection itself. For this reason, Fisher had to redefine the role of mutation in adaptive evolution: mutation provides the raw material upon which selection can act (Fisher, 1930: 48), or the fuel that continuously propels adaptation and prevents evolution from coming to a halt.

If mutation fuels inheritable variation, one might conclude that an increase in mutation rates could increase genetic variation and therefore accelerate the rate of adaptive evolution. However, this interpretation is incorrect for various reasons. The first is that mutations introduce random deviations into organisms moulded by selection, and for this reason are mostly deleterious; this is why selection favours mechanisms that correct errors in DNA replication and reduce mutation rates (Cromie *et al.*, 2001).

But the main reason why mutation does not determine the rate of adaptation in populations is that the fundamental principle refers to genetic variance in *fitness* rather than genetic variance per se (or pure allele polymorphism). The difference between the two concepts is of key importance. For Fisher, additive genetic variance is a factor in adaptive evolution only when it produces effects on fitness. For example, a laboratory study might find genetic variation for resistance to subzero temperatures in a species of present-day Amazonian monkeys; this might be done by relocating a sample of monkeys from the Amazon to the Antarctica, by measuring individual survivorship, fertility and reproductive output in the new environment, and finally by identifying genes and alleles responsible for variation in fitness. However, even if genetic variation in response to low temperature existed in the species, it can never be actually expressed as variance in fitness in the native Amazonian habitat where temperatures never reach values under 0 °C.

In other words, it is only the competitive context faced by individuals in their actual environment that converts some aspects of additive genetic variation into components of additive variance in fitness; it is selection itself, and the effect of different alleles in the struggle for survival, that determines the rate of adaptive change by relying on a 'useful' fraction of the stock of genetic variation and mutations found in all populations. Fisher's fundamental principle therefore inverted the mutationist view according to which populations were interpreted as virtually waiting for the 'right' (adaptive) mutations for evolution to occur (for the classic formulation of 'mutation pressure', see Morgan, 1932; for contemporary and perhaps naïve examples, see Klein, 2000 and Stedman *et al.*, 2004). In contrast, the view inspired by Fisher's fundamental principle is that populations are constantly carrying a reserve of hidden inheritable variation with no immediate adaptive relevance, until a change in demography, environment or other factors creates an opportunity for alternative alleles to reveal some fitness effects. Barrett and Schluter (2008) have concluded that adaptation based on already present (or 'standing' genetic variation) is even expected to be faster than adaptation based on new mutations (although the two processes are complementary).

In addition to the fundamental principle, Fisher offered other arguments against a major role for mutation in evolution; one of them refers to the role of the mutation event itself, or the moment of its first appearance. Fisher pointed out that the odds of survival of any mutant allele, however advantageous, are necessarily low due to genetic drift (or random loss due to change factors). Because a given mutation is represented by a single copy in the individual where it first occurs, the likelihood that it will be eliminated by change after a few generations is high (Box 2.2).

Box 2.2 How important is the occurrence of a new advantageous mutation?

Suppose that a new mutant allele occurs in a sexually reproducing, diploid species; that the mutation is neutral (i.e. has no effect of fitness); and that population size is large and constant. The individual carrying the mutation is expected to leave two descendants (the replacement rate in a constant sexual population). Mendel's first law implies that the likelihood of the mutant allele being lost due to chance is ¼ or 25% after one generation, or the likelihood that it is absent both in the first and the second descendant (i.e. ½ times ½). This probability increases to ¼ + (¾ · ½) = ⅝ or 62.5% after two generations; this is the probability of allele loss in the first generation (¼), plus the probability of allele survival in the first generation (¾) multiplied by the probability of allele loss in the second generation (½).

Now suppose that the mutation is not neutral and confers an unrealistic fitness advantage of 50% to its carrier over the population average. This means that the mutation carrier is expected to leave three descendants (50% over the population average of two). Even in this case, the likelihood of loss due to drift (of one ninth or 11% in one generation) is still high. Fisher calculated the probabilities of loss of an advantageous mutation based on the more realistic value of a 1% fitness advantage, and showed that after only 15 generations the likelihood of its extinction is 88%, and about 97% after 100 generations. Therefore, even favourable mutations are mostly lost due to pure chance factors.

But the prospect changes in the case of a recurrent mutation. For example, although the chance of loss faced by the mutation above is 97% after 100 generations, if it occurs 100 different times this likelihood is reduced to less than 5%; it does not survive only if it is lost in all 100 individuals, a probability of only $0.97^{100} = 0.048$ or 4.8%).

Does that mean that the alleles we carry, and by extension adaptive evolution itself, result from a few lucky mutations that escaped genetic drift? The answer is no; the reason is that an allele may be produced multiple times by new mutation events, until it eventually overcomes the statistical likelihood of its extinction (Fisher, 1930: 77). For example, the same mutant allele with a chance of extinction of 97% after 100 generations has a chance greater than 50% of avoiding loss by drift if it occurs 23 times in different individuals. It is true that multiple occurrences of the same mutation are unlikely, especially if we take into account that mutation rates are typically low. However, large populations can theoretically solve the problem, and are in fact a frequent assumption in Fisher's model. Thus, whereas each single mutation event is random, individual and unique, the fixation of a new allele in a population should be seen not as an event, but as a demographic process under the control of selection.

Fisher also made it clear that the random loss of new mutations does not establish genetic drift as a relevant factor in evolution. Random elimination of alleles only occurs at the stage of initial introduction due to the small numbers involved (Fisher, 1930: 87). When applied to alleles at frequencies greater than 0.25%, Fisher demonstrated that genetic drift would take $1.4N$ generations to halve the additive genetic variance in a population of N individuals. If N is not unrealistically small, the power of genetic drift will be irrelevant in comparison to selection.

Thus, mutations are required at low rates, are mostly deleterious, and only make adaptive sense in the light of a given selective context. In addition, mutation events and genetic drift play a limited role in adaptation. In summary, Fisher's fundamental principle implies that evolution is under the strict control of natural selection.

GRADUALISM: THE COST OF BIOLOGICAL COMPLEXITY

Darwin was no natural born gradualist (Desmond and Moore, 1991: 225). In the *Red Notebook* written during his trip to South America, Darwin expressed an early enthusiasm for the saltationist views of evolutionists such as Geoffroy Saint Hilaire (who argued that birds could be generated at once from ancestral reptiles) and later revived by Bateson (1894), Osborn (1926), Goldschmidt (1940) and others in the form of mutationism. Speculating on the origins of sympatric (geographically overlapping) species of South American rheas, Darwin concluded that 'change [was] not progress if produced at one blow', and recognised that the extraordinary and rare birth of a successful monster might 'present an analogy to the production of species'. Such enthusiasm was short lived; by the time of the publication of the *Origin*, Darwin was already fully converted to a gradualist view of evolution.

> Natural selection can act only by the preservation and accumulation of infinitesimally small inherited modifications, each profitable to the preserved being; ... so will natural selection, if it be a true principle, banish the belief of ... any great and sudden modification in their structure (Darwin, 1859: 95).

With this argument Darwin was addressing the still controversial issue of 'missing links' in evolution and the impression of jumps between characters or closely related species. Against the temptations of saltationism, Darwin proposed the alternative gradualist explanation for the evolution of traits and species, including highly divergent ones. His rationale was that if a trait shows continuous distribution in populations, individuals may differ in those traits by infinitesimal amounts; for this reason 'inherited modifications' or mutations might also be of reduced magnitude; those small mutations and nothing else should be seen as the raw material of selection, and once and for all 'banish the belief' in evolutionary saltations. Fisher's contribution was to offer a first mathematical demonstration of the gradualist argument, by showing that small mutations (micromutations) are the most likely to increase the fitness of their carriers.

To understand Fisher's argument, let us imagine a population of birds migrating to an island and still poorly adapted to their new habitat. For the sake of simplicity, let us neglect standing genetic variation and only consider the contribution of new mutations occurring after the arrival of founders to the island. Let us also focus on adaptive change in only one or two phenotypic traits affecting fitness. The question asked by Fisher was: how does the 'size' of a new mutation (i.e. its phenotypic effect) relate to its contribution to the adaptive evolution of the population (i.e. its fitness effect)?

Let us begin with the one-dimensional case of a single phenotypic character such as body size (Figure 2.1). A representation of the level of maladaptation of the immigrant population to the new environment is the distance d separating the current character average (S_0) (the average size of the migrant birds) and the value at the fitness or adaptive peak (S_p) (the optimal body size favoured by selection on the island). It should be noticed that the fitness peak is empty until populations evolve and occupy it; Fisher was therefore defining it as the

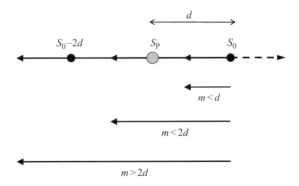

Figure 2.1   The effect of mutation size on single-trait evolution. The horizontal axis represents the magnitude of a trait such as body size; S_0 is average body size in an adapting population; S_P is optimal body size. Mutations increasing body size (dashed arrow) are necessarily deleterious; mutations reducing body size by the amount d are favoured by selection.

theoretical destination of the adapting population. Let us assume that the average body size of the newly introduced birds may be too large for the island by d grams.

Suppose that a new mutation occurs and changes the body size of an average carrier (a bird with body size S_0) by an amount m. It is clear that if $m > 2d$, the mutation is necessarily deleterious. If m is positive (i.e. if the mutation increases size by m), mutant body size is even larger than average and more distant from the fitness peak. If m is negative, the mutation decreases body size towards the adaptive peak, but its magnitude is so large that it overshoots the fitness peak: the parent is too large, but the mutant descendant is too small. Thus, according to Fisher's argument, exceedingly large mutations are necessarily maladaptive.

Now consider mutations with a smaller magnitude $m < 2d$. In this case, mutations increase fitness when m is negative (by reducing the size of the mutant bird and moving it towards the adaptive peak); but they reduce fitness when m is positive (increasing size and moving it away from the adaptive peak). Since the direction of mutations is random, the likelihood of mutations of magnitude $m < 2d$ being negative, and therefore advantageous, is 50%. Thus, in the world of one-dimensional adaptive evolution, natural selection would favour 'hopeful monsters' (Goldschmidt, 1940) produced by relatively large mutations of magnitude d: that is, macromutations able to hit the adaptive target in one single blow. If mutations of the exact magnitude d

did not happen in the population, selection would be expected to favour the mutation with the magnitude closest to d. If this second-best mutant allele is fixed, a new (and smaller) distance d_1 to the adaptive peak would be defined. Although smaller jumps are favoured as adaptation proceeds, at any stage of adaptive evolution the optimal mutation size m favoured by selection would be the distance between current trait value and the adaptive peak. In other words, when a single trait is concerned, natural selection does not favour gradual evolution but saltationism.

The scenario completely changes if we just add a *second* phenotypic trait (Figure 2.2). Let us now assume that both average body size and average bill size in the founding bird population are larger than the optimal value favoured by selection on the island, and that mutations in the two traits occur. Fisher's model is compatible with mutant phenotypes being caused by a single pleiotropic gene (i.e. able to affect multiple traits) or by mutations in two different genes. With two phenotypic dimensions under consideration, Fisher represented the distance between the current state of the population and the adaptive peak as the radius d of a circle around the adaptive peak. Any mutant inside that circle is closer to the adaptive peak and exhibits higher-than-average fitness. Mutations of magnitude m must also be represented by a circle, in this case of radius m, around the non-mutant average; in other words, instead of only two directions (decrease or increase in body size) in the one-dimensional case, there are many possible combinations of changes in the two traits corresponding to

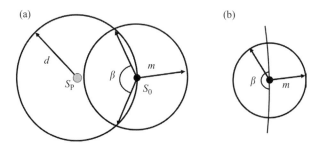

Figure 2.2   The effect of mutation size on two-dimensional evolution. The likelihood that a random mutation of size m increases fitness (i.e. the likelihood that the mutant is inside the circle of radius d) is $p = \beta/2\pi$. (a) When the mutation of size m is similar to the distance d from current average (S_0) to the adaptive peak (S_P), the likelihood that it increases fitness is $p \approx 0.3$. (b) When the mutation of size m is much smaller than d, the likelihood that it increases fitness is $p \approx 0.5$.

the same mutation size m. The question is: what now is the effect of the magnitude m on the adaptive evolution of a two-dimensional mutant?

First, as in the one-dimensional case, if $m > 2d$, the mutation is necessarily deleterious: even if it points in the right direction (reducing both body and bill size), it overshoots the adaptive peak; geometrically, that means that the circles of radii d and m do not intersect. Second, if mutations are of smaller magnitude ($m < 2d$), a fraction (or arc) of the circle m will be inside the circle d, representing mutants closer to the adaptive peak. This arc can be calculated as the quotient between the central angle β (derived from the intersection of the circles d and m) and the full extension 2π of the circle m, thus, the fraction p of mutations that improve adaptation, or the probability that they increase fitness, is $p = \beta/2\pi$.

Since β can be written as a function of d and m, Fisher could also estimate the relationship between mutation size m and the likelihood p that it will increase fitness. While the analytical solution is not simple (and will not be discussed), its meaning is straightforward: mutations of infinitesimally small size are the most likely to be favoured by natural selection. A geometrical and intuitive justification is that the arc of the circle d that intersects the circle of mutants m divides the latter into two regions: one inside the circle d, representing mutants closer to the adaptive peak; and an external maladaptive region. It is clear that as m decreases, the curvature of the arc of the circle d becomes less perceptible. This is why the floor underneath us looks virtually flat: we are too small compared with a much larger (although spherical) Earth. Therefore, when m approaches zero, the arc of the circle d becomes a straight line (the diameter of the mutant circle) dividing it into two virtually equal halves. Hence, the likelihood p of a mutation being on the adaptive side tends to a maximum value of 50% when its magnitude m tends to zero. For Fisher, the chance of winning the lottery of adaptation increases to 50% if one plays little money on the random roulette of mutation; for a chance event, those are extremely favourable odds.

We should remember that this result only follows because of the addition of a second phenotypic dimension. When only body size was considered, large hopeful macromutants of magnitude $m = d$ had a chance of 50% of being adaptive, the same as any other non-overshooting mutant. But when bill size is introduced, mutants of the same magnitude $m = d$ see their chance of increasing fitness being reduced to less than 40%. More specifically, Fisher showed that the probability that mutations of size m improve adaptation decreases by a factor $\sqrt{n}$, where n is the number of traits involved. Adding phenotypic dimensions significantly reduces the probability of improving adaptation, and this means that the larger the number of traits involved, the smaller the mutation size has to be in order to approach the maximum value of 50%; and we know that real organisms display a very large number of traits simultaneously affecting fitness.

The result is the 'cost of complexity' (Orr, 2000): the more 'complex' (here meaning 'multi-trait') the organism, the more likely a mutation of a given size is deleterious: there is simply too much that can go wrong. Thus, evolution must rely on micromutations and on relatively smaller steps, even when populations are maladapted and distant from an adaptive peak. This is why adaptive evolution must be gradual rather than punctuated. In Fisher's model, the evolution of complex organisms is gradual and slow because although mutations occur independently in separate genes or atoms of inheritance, from the point of view of selection the phenotypes encoded by genes are a unity: in our example, a given mutation size reflects changes both in body size and bill size. In the following chapter we will see how Fisher's views on phenotypic integration were transformed by developmental genetics.

THE ADAPTIVE WALK IN THE REAL WORLD

Under closer examination, Fisher's gradualist argument exhibits a logical problem. Although it is true that the odds of winning the lottery of adaptation are maximised when the amount gambled (the size of the mutation) is minimal, it is also true that any prizes won (the increase in fitness), if proportional to the bet, will be equally microscopic; in other words, if micromutations have very small phenotypic effects, they will also tend to produce very small positive effects on fitness (m measures phenotypic effect in Fisher's original argument, but it is reasonable to assume that m is proportional to fitness effect; see Orr, 1998). For this reason, they may be barely distinguishable from neutral mutations with no fitness effect. Fisher himself had shown that new mutations, even when significantly advantageous, are at a high risk of random loss; such risk has to be much higher for micromutations. Since mutations of small effect are the most likely to be advantageous, but are also the most likely to be eliminated by genetic drift, Kimura (1983) showed that the mutations contributing to adaptive evolution must be of intermediate size rather than micromutations.

Later, Orr (1998, 2000) confirmed that the size distribution of adaptive mutations shows an intermediate peak, and significantly improved on Kimura's argument by revealing new properties of the adaptive process. For example, we know that as adaptation occurs, the size of mutations improving adaptation decreases in magnitude; the distance d between the population average and the adaptive peak decreases, and the optimal mutation size m is accordingly scaled down. Therefore, d and m should remain proportional to each other. Orr demonstrated that during adaptation the size of the most advantageous mutations relative to the decreasing distance d is constant and surprisingly large. His conclusion is a direct challenge to the gradualism of Darwin and Fisher, and 'flatly contradicts the intuition of most evolutionists (or at least those raised on micromutational dogma): Small random mutations do not yield the fastest adaptation' (Orr, 2000: 18).

Orr's results are robust and significant, but they do not imply a rejection of gradualism. Orr's findings seem to refute Fisher's proof, but they do not say much about the original question that Darwin addressed with his gradualist hypothesis. Darwin postulated that gradualism could explain the evolution of most if not all biological structures; but his argument was clearly interested in those structures seen as highly divergent and unique. After all, it was those cases of extreme phenotypic divergence and of 'complex' traits, classically exemplified by the giraffe neck, the elephant trunk, the human brain and others that inspired the saltationist alternative.

Unfortunately, the emphasis on what really needs to be explained, namely the apparent jumps and missing links in the distribution of adaptations and species, is absent in the theoretical work described above. When presenting his version of gradualism, Fisher chose the microscope to exemplify why sequences of small changes in settings have a much higher chance of improving adjustment than a large derangement, but he gave no biological example; Kimura and Orr preferred not to illustrate their conclusions with any hypothetical or empirical examples. As seen below, consideration of concrete examples can change our interpretation of their mathematical models.

Let us examine one case study: the highly enlarged and derived brain of *Homo sapiens*. Fossil evidence suggests that brain size in the earliest hominin ancestors living more than 5–6 million years ago was around 400 g, similar to values observed in chimpanzees, gorillas and orang-utans (in those species, average brain size is in the 300–500 g range; Kappeler and Pereira, 2003). Modern humans show average brain size of about 1400 g, or 1000 g larger (Cabana *et al.*, 1993). Due to its significant enlargement, human brain size is about six times larger than expected for a mammal of similar body size (Jerison, 1973). The question of gradualism versus saltationism certainly applies to this case: did the evolution of human brain size from 400 g to about 1400 g occur by infinitesimally small steps; or did it mostly rely on relatively large steps as suggested by Orr; or did it involve a combination of a few large and many small steps in encephalisation?

Although human brain size is extremely well documented by dozens of fossils and discussed in various studies (Vrba, 1998; Rice, 2002a; Vinicius, 2005; Robson and Wood, 2008), any attempt to elucidate its evolution though the models of Fisher and Orr seems destined to fail. The reason is simple: although early hominins with 400 g of brain were probably under selection for increased encephalisation, it is more reasonable to assume that they were adapting to an adaptive peak (i.e. an optimal brain size) somewhere in the vicinity of 400 g than to a then distant and virtually unattainable peak of 1400 g. An increase of 1000 g in brain size would probably involve unbearable costs to early hominins in terms of energetics (the brain is a highly expensive organ to maintain; Foley and Lee, 1991; Aiello *et al.*, 2001), life history (larger brains imply an extended period of offspring dependency and later age of first reproduction; Kaplan *et al.*, 2000) and morphology (larger cranial size created an 'obstetrical dilemma' and parturition difficulties in humans; Rosenberg and Trevathan, 1996); but the costs of smaller increases would have been more acceptable. Thus, although brain size in the human lineage starts and ends with the respective values of 400 g and 1400 g, early hominins were not evolving towards the current peak: our current brain size was invisible and intangible to them, and only in hindsight can we say that they were evolving towards us. Thus, it is reasonable to propose that early hominin brain size was probably evolving towards an optimal size close to 400 g; only a hominin ancestor with a much larger brain size – perhaps close to the modern value in *Homo sapiens* – could exhibit the conditions necessary for the evolution of our brain size.

The point is that concepts of a 'maladaptive population' as a starting point and of an independent 'adaptive peak' as its evolutionary destination are easier to grasp and model mathematically; but they seem inappropriate to explain the evolution of traits that need proper elucidation such as the human brain. Under the ideal conditions of an artificial selection experiment, it may be possible to define an arbitrary adaptive peak (a given size, colour or behaviour chosen by the researcher) that populations must climb irrespective of potential costs and benefits; after all, the traits are not evolving by natural selection and therefore their potential effects on fitness are irrelevant. In this case, adaptive peaks are external to the artificially evolving population; but in the real world of energetic, developmental, ecological, social and other factors, adaptive peaks and their position also depend on the *current* state of adapting species and do not exist independently from them.

In contrast, the independence and immobility of adaptive peaks during adaptive evolution is a fundamental assumption of the models proposed by Fisher (1930: 38) and Orr (2000: 14). The concept of a fixed adaptive peak is similar to the idea of 'empty niche' used by Simpson in his historical reconstructions of horse evolution. However, the 'empty grazing niche' did not actually exist: it is an abstraction, valid only in hindsight, referring to the now existing grazing niche *before* it was occupied by the modern horse and other grazing species (niches that have never been occupied such as talking plants or flying elephants are not empty but simply non-existent; after all, an adaptive peak is an alternative name for a selective pressure in a population). Thus, although Fisher's and Orr's models refer to the idea of empty adaptive peaks at the disposal of maladapted populations, real-life adaptation is closer to the image of a bouncy castle: when no one stands on it, surfaces are smooth and featureless; but when a subject steps in, a topography with lows and highs is formed, and as a consequence a way up is defined. Walking on a bouncy castle moves the position of peaks and troughs (and the way up) at every step. This means that adaptive evolution may be gradual not because of the distribution of mutation sizes moving populations to fixed adaptive peaks, but because the current adaptive state of populations may gradually move adaptive peaks away from populations.

Dynamical adaptive peaks clearly introduce a new theoretical problem, namely whether peaks themselves move gradually or not. Although an answer to this problem is unknown and has rarely been mathematically analysed, the conclusion is that the debate over gradualism and the size of adaptive mutations becomes the empirical matter of determining how populations relate to adaptive peaks and selection pressures in the real world. If most of the time species are under stabilising selection and close to their adaptive peak, Orr's 'intermediate size' mutations will be of very small absolute size and evolution mostly gradual. But if populations are constantly adapting to moving adaptive peaks, fast environmental change, or other evolving species (i.e. in cycles involving hosts and parasites, or predators and prey), then intermediate size will mean mutations with larger absolute magnitude and fitness effects.

The conclusion is that whereas Fisher's argument cannot prove gradualism true (due to the drawbacks pointed out by Kimura and Orr), Orr's argument cannot prove gradualism wrong (due to the shared unrealistic assumption of fixed adaptive peaks). The apparent failure of Fisher to demonstrate the universal validity of Darwin's gradualist insight solely on the basis of Mendelian laws is of deep significance. Fisher's fundamental principle, which implies that adapted phenotypes cannot be transmitted verbatim and therefore must be coded and transmitted mainly in the form of additive effects, remains a powerful evolutionary generalisation. However, Fisher's claim that the particulate character of inheritance implies per se that adaptive evolution must be gradual has not been established. The reason is that the demographic and ecological background in which natural selection takes place is a factor determining the pace and mode of adaptive evolution. As discussed below, Sewall Wright was the first evolutionary geneticist to explicitly take demography and ecology into account in adaptive models.

EPISTASIS AS A MAIN LEGACY OF PARTICULATE INHERITANCE

Fisher's model, by proposing that adaptive peaks represent fixed points, suggested a rather discomforting scenario: when populations reach their adaptive optimum, there is nowhere else to go, and selection is expected to act mostly as a conservative rather than creative force. This interpretation was originally presented by Sewall Wright (1931, 1932), who argued that Fisher's 'mass selection' and the conditions it requires (large and non-fragmented populations, random mating, random recombination of loci) would necessarily trap populations onto adaptive peaks and prevent continual evolutionary change.

> In a panmictic population that has lived for a very long time under essentially the same conditions, the additive genetic variance becomes reduced to a minimum maintained by the rate of occurrence of novel favourable mutations, and evolution thus becomes extremely slow (Wright, 1977: 441).

However, Wright knew that evolution has no tendency to halt: the 'fittest' solution has been incessantly expressed in the form of countless new species and geographical varieties. For this reason, he believed that the main task of theories of adaptive evolution was to explain how species manage to escape the trap set by Fisher's mass selection.

> Selection will easily carry the species to the nearest peak, but there may be innumerable other peaks which are higher but which are separated by 'valleys'. The problem of evolution as I see it is that of a mechanism by which the species may continually find its way from lower to higher peaks in such a field (Wright, 1932).

The field of alternatives corresponds to an 'adaptive landscape' that, in Wright's unique interpretation of Mendelism, is thoroughly explored during the evolutionary process. For Wright the most important consequence of particulate inheritance is that it multiplies the number of possible genotypes, or combinations of alternative alleles; thus, genes are relevant not for their intrinsic or additive value as proposed by Fisher, but for their combinatorial potential. It is interesting to notice the similarity between Wright's original argument, which applies to combinations of alleles, and more recent interpretations of our DNA-based unlimited inheritance system.

> Given a million base pairs [and four types of DNA base pairs or nucleotides], there are 4 raised to the power one million possible structures that can be replicated, or many times the number of atoms in the Universe. It therefore provides an adequate basis for continued evolution (Maynard Smith and Szathmáry, 1999: 8).

As much as the four-letter alphabet of DNA is a source of unlimited numbers of possible new proteins, it is the virtually infinite number of possible combinations of alleles at each locus that guarantees the continued generation and evolution of new phenotypes in Wright's theory. But as much as a single nucleotide makes genetic sense only as part of a full DNA coding sequence, an individual gene makes sense only as part of a full genotype. That was the essential message from Wright: the origin of living diversity was the very large number of possible genotypes made possible by its parts – the genes or particles of inheritance.

> Estimates of the total number of genes in the cells of higher organisms range from 1000 up ... With 10 allelomorphs in each of 1000 loci, the number of possible combinations is 10^{1000} which is a very large number. It has been estimated that the total number of electrons and protons in the whole visible universe is much less than 10^{100} (Wright, 1932).

For Wright, the problem is that most of those 10^{1000} would not even be tried or tested under the operation of mass selection. To see why, let us suppose that a new mutation creates an eleventh allele at one of the 1000 loci above. Due to segregation and independent assortment, if the new allele has effects on fitness it will be exposed to competition with the other ten alleles; if deleterious, it is expected to be eliminated before it even appears in most possible genotypes. The essence of Wright's theory of adaptation is that, contrary to the common sense of mass selection, deleterious alleles may *favour* adaptive evolution.

The reason why a deleterious allele may under certain circumstances increase fitness is *epistasis*, or the interaction between the effects of two or more alleles (mysteriously named in many of Wright's works as 'pleiotropy', which as seen previously refers to genes with effects on multiple traits). Epistasis implies that not only the resulting phenotype but also the fitness effect of a combination of two genes may be different from the sum of their individual additive effects. In extreme cases, the effect of an allele may change from deleterious to adaptive depending on the genotype in which it is found; the same allele may be advantageous to me, but deleterious to my sister.

Epistasis and the combinatorial possibilities of genotypes were recognised by Fisher, but he believed that additive effects were more important. The reason would be the relatively lower inheritability of epistatic effects. Although by definition the additive effects of an allele are necessarily transmitted to offspring due to its presence, epistatic effects depend on the presence of alleles at other loci: what was an allele improving my adaptation may be neutral or deleterious to my descendants. In contrast, Wright argued that innovation in adaptive evolution would be easier to understand if we extended the idea of interaction between two genes to all of them; Wright uses the term 'interaction systems' to extend the concept of epistasis to the whole genome.

> The significant steps in evolution are shifts from control by one interaction system to control by a superior one, rather than addition or removal of single genes (Wright, 1932).

Returning to our previous example of maladapted migrating birds, let us assume that the population adapts to a diet based on a small seed type available on the island by evolving both smaller body size and bill size; let us simplify the argument by assuming that body size and bill size are regulated by two distinct genes, and that there is no growth correlation between the traits. Now imagine that a second tree species occurs on an isolated corner of the island, producing a much larger seed; in other words, it favours the opposite adaptive trend, namely the evolution of large body and bill size. Wright's argument was that if only mass selection is in operation, the second niche will never be occupied. The reason is that although large body size mutants may constantly occur in the bird population, large size is neither favourable in exploring the original small seed, nor in exploring the newly evolved large seed (without an accompanying larger bill able to crack the seed); thus, a mutant allele causing large body size is eliminated by selection. The same is true for a large bill size mutation: although it allows birds to crack the larger seed, its interaction with small body size is deleterious, and selection opposes its spread. Since neither large body size nor bill size evolve in isolation, large seeds will rot on the trees while birds fight for the small ones. For this reason, Wright argued that the correct theory of adaptation cannot be mass selection, which favours or eliminates new alleles solely on the basis of their individual (additive) values, and fails to fully explore a universe of possible epistatic interactions.

THE SHIFTING BALANCE AND THE STRUCTURE OF REAL POPULATIONS

As seen earlier, transitions between adaptive peaks or cases in which unknown intermediate states are hard to conceive or maladaptive (for example, the intermediate state between quadrupedal ancestor and bipedal descendant) were a central concern of Darwin, to the point that the first two main difficulties with the hypothesis of selection discussed in the *Origin* (the rarity of transitional forms, and the low fitness of adaptive intermediates) relate to the problem. A possible explanation for crossing between peaks is that characters may evolve 'from quite secondary causes, independently of natural selection', such as growth correlations (Darwin, 1859: 196; Huxley, 1932). Wright's solution, the 'shifting balance' theory, was an attempt at explaining how populations jump across maladaptive valleys; importantly, it was also based on secondary causes other than selection.

In the shifting balance mechanism, the secondary cause of adaptive transitions is the demographic context in which selection operates. Wright saw species as sets of small, relatively isolated and genetically diverse groups or 'demes' regularly budding off from other demes and undergoing extinction. For this reason, the aim of his models of adaptive evolution was to explain the dynamics of demes and its consequences. Variables such as levels of physical isolation, migration and gene flow between demes, and demographic bottlenecks (in summary, population structure) were introduced by Wright in order to add a more realistic dimension to genetic models, in contrast to Fisher's attempts to simplify demography with his frequent assumption of panmixia or large, randomly interbreeding populations.

The rationale behind the shifting balance theory is that it is population structuring or subdivision that allows for the long-term persistence of epistatic combinations – the key to adaptive innovation; specifically, demographic fragmentation would even allow the momentary survival of combinations engendering *unfit* phenotypes. For Wright, this happens because partial isolation can slow down mass selection. Let us imagine again our bird population; as seen, any deviations from the adaptive peak of small body and bill size will be opposed by selection. However, if the bird population is structured into relatively isolated demes, suboptimal adaptation in demes may arise and persist for some time. For example, a large bill size mutation may occur in one peripheral small group; but instead of being quickly eliminated by selection, the mutation may persist due to the reduced competition from the optimal type found only in other demes; in other words, unfit mutants may be saved from competition with the fittest purely by accidental means. Furthermore, isolation may further favour increases in the frequency of mutations reducing fitness due to drift and inbreeding in small groups. Lower levels of gene flow and migration and higher levels of inbreeding may lead peripheral demes to drift away from a given adaptive peak; by reducing the interactions between competing individuals, demography opposes the statistical bias or signal from natural selection. The consequence of relaxing selection is that populations can explore a larger set of the combinatorial possibilities: large body and small bill, small body and large bill – and even large size and large bill.

Wright proposes that a transition between adaptive peaks occurs when an accidental match happens between a lucky peripheral type on the one hand, and a potentially new niche or habitat on the other. In our example, the match is between a population carrying the two mutations for larger body size and larger bill size, and presence of the population on the isolated edge of the island where the large seed variety is found; it is only after the accidental match happens that mass selection for both larger body size and bill size can take place in the new niche. Under the shifting balance mechanism, the occupation of this new 'large seed' niche thus involves the selection of a brand new interaction system consisting in this case of only two alternative alleles, but of potentially many more. For Wright, mass selection still has a function in adaptation: once a match with a new niche is established, mass selection can operate on all other genes and traits favouring adaptation to the new habitat. Now the species occupies two adaptive peaks, and both are potential sources of relatively isolated demes connected by some level of migration and gene flow. If the new niche engenders higher rates of population growth (i.e. if the large seed niche is 'superior'), the small bird phenotype may undergo extinction. If that happens, the species makes a jump to a higher adaptive peak.

Despite his appealing use of population structure, Wright failed to convince most evolutionary biologists that the shifting balance theory represented an advance in our understanding of adaptation (Whitlock and Phillips, 2000). The main reason is that it may address a non-existing problem: the idea that mass selection traps populations and prevents continuous occupation of new niches is far from popular (Coyne *et al.*, 1997). Selective traps might work if adaptive landscapes were static: but as argued above, adaptive peaks may constantly move relative to one another, and adaptive valleys may widen or shrink. Simpson's account of horse evolution makes explicit reference to a decrease in the distance between the grazing and the browsing types during the Miocene in one phenotypic dimension: for some unknown reason, larger body size was favoured in the originally small browsing lineage. Once a single trait makes a crossing between peaks, other interacting traits (tooth crown height in that case) are no longer the cause of negative epistasis, and may be selected towards the new alternative peak (in Simpson's example higher tooth crowns evolved due to their growth correlation with body size). According to Fisher, organisms are complex and exhibit much more than two traits contributing to fitness; for this reason, it is almost inevitable that at least one of them will eventually cross the valley between two adaptive peaks, and that, although slowly, adaptive evolution never stops.

SEX AND THE ORIGINS OF SPECIES

Although the shifting balance mechanism has never been widely accepted as a theory of adaptation, it was much more influential in the development of speciation theory. Understanding the differences between the processes of adaptation and speciation requires a discussion of sex, or more specifically of one of its most important consequences: sexual reproduction (Stearns, 1987). Sexual reproduction distinguishes the mystery of speciation from the more trivial problem of population divergence, and at the same time restricts the speciation debate mostly to sexual species. To see why asexual species cannot truly speciate (or at least not in the same way sexual species do), let us consider an asexual species undergoing evolutionary changes over time. In the absence of sex, the only available source of genetic variation in evolving lineages is mutation; this also means that new mutations remain exclusively in the lineages in which they originally occur. For this reason, a purely asexual genealogy would exclusively evolve through mutation-driven divergence.

Distinct mutations may create phenotypic differentiation of various degrees between asexual lineages. In Figure 2.3, lineages A and B differ by a single mutation. In contrast, a much higher level of genetic and possibly phenotypic differentiation has accumulated between lineages A and C. In this hypothetical world of asexual reproduction, the asexual lineages A and C might be as phenotypically divergent as *Escherichia coli* and *Homo sapiens*. Thus, divergent adaptation to different environments and niches is fully compatible with asexual reproduction. The problem is that although we might be tempted to interpret the highly divergent lineages A and C as two different species, and classify the very similar pair A and B as similar varieties of the same species differing by a single mutation, the boundary between intraspecific and interspecific variation is purely arbitrary in the asexual context: there is no magic number of mutations that determines when speciation begins.

This is no longer true for sexual species, in which genealogy involves convergence instead of divergence of lineages (Fisher, 1930;

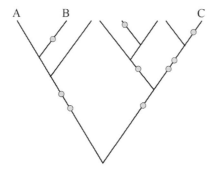

Figure 2.3   Genetic differentiation in an asexual lineage. Grey dots represent independent mutations.

Dobzhansky, 1955). For this reason, the origin of new sexual species is not just an arbitrary extrapolation of genealogical divergence: speciation must be a real evolutionary process that interrupts the convergence of genealogical lines caused by sexual reproduction, and as a consequence, produces divergent lines of phylogeny. It should be noticed that this includes 'sexual speciation' in bacteria, in which gene exchange and recombination are common (Fraser *et al.*, 2007). This is the reason why species, originally identified by early taxonomists as units of diversity in nature, have been redefined in the language of sexual reproduction. Darwin (1859: 26) was one of the first to propose that the signature of speciation was the origin of reproductive isolation between populations or the sterility of their hybrids, and that sex or 'intercrossing plays a very important part in nature in keeping the individuals of the same species, or of the same variety, true and uniform in character' (Darwin, 1859: 104). This suggestion was later formalised as the biological species concept by Ernst Mayr (1942).

As much as species, the speciation process received a new definition based on sex: it is the evolutionary process that generates barriers to previously interbreeding populations. From this perspective, it is possible to classify the various theories of speciation (for a comprehensive review, see Coyne and Orr, 2004) into two fundamental groups: one view is that natural selection directly causes speciation, so as to accelerate adaptive evolution to local conditions (as claimed by the theory of reinforcement of Darwin, Fisher and Dobzhansky); a second view is that speciation is an accident caused by the geographical distribution of species and its side effects, including local adaptation (the allopatric view of speciation by Wright, Mayr and others). The choice between the alternatives is a fundamental problem in speciation theory and one of the key controversies in evolutionary theory.

SPECIATION AS ADAPTATION: THE EVOLUTION OF XENOPHOBIA

The full title of the *Origin* contained more than one contentious statement. The first, the mutability or origin of species, seems to face opposition only from outside science in our time (Scott, 2005). His second claim that species arise 'by means of natural selection', or more precisely that speciation is a form of adaptation, remains extremely controversial. Darwin had no doubt that speciation could be an extension, rather than a mere side effect, of adaptive diversification. For this reason, the factors promoting the origin of new species would be the same that drive adaptation.

Although I do not doubt that isolation is of considerable importance in the production of new species, on the whole I am inclined to believe that largeness of area is of more importance … Throughout a great and open area, not only will there be a better chance of favourable variations arising from the large number of individuals of the same species there supported, but the conditions of life are infinitely complex from the large number of already existing species (Darwin, 1859: 105).

As seen earlier, large numbers of individuals, open areas and widespread exchange of favourable variations (i.e. panmixia or random mating) are also the conditions for adaptive evolution according to Fisher. However, Fisher recognised that the problems of speciation and adaptation were not strictly the same. Differentiation between varieties of a species does not proceed smoothly towards speciation for the important reason discussed above – sex. Sexual species can work as an interconnected genetic network diffusing mutations into areas where they are favourable, and eliminating them from regions where their effects are deleterious; sex accelerates adaptation (as discussed in more detail in Chapter 5). However, sex also means that individuals remain part of a single genetic pool or species. The theory of reinforcement, pioneered by Darwin and Fisher and later championed by Dobzhansky (1937), was an attempt to explain why natural selection, which as a rule takes advantage of panmixia to produce adaptive evolution, might sometimes produce barriers to sexual reproduction that split species into new ones.

Fisher's argument was that under certain conditions gene exchange ceases to be an advantage. If species exhibit large populations, they may end up occupying larger and more variable environments. In this case, populations may be attracted towards multiple potential niches and climb different adaptive peaks. If populations from the same species evolve divergent, or even opposite adaptations, then gene exchange between them may be mutually disadvantageous. In our example where two populations of the same bird species adapt towards smaller body size in one area, and large size in the other, interbreeding would imply introducing genes for small size into the large size population, and vice versa. According to the theory of reinforcement, if the cost of introduction of 'wrong' genes from a neighbouring population is greater than the benefit of introducing possibly favourable mutations, panmixia or non-discriminatory mating becomes a hindrance to adaptive evolution.

If adaptive divergence of populations implies low fitness of hybrids, the theory of reinforcement proposes that selection favours adaptations that directly prevent interbreeding (including pre-zygotic isolation mechanisms; Mayr, 1942). Traits capable of reducing the risk of hybridisation would include sedentary behaviour (which reduces the risk of mating with 'foreigners') and sexual discrimination based on geographical origin. In summary, Fisher believed that natural selection night lead to the evolution of sexual xenophobia: by only mating locally or with local types, hybrid offspring of lower fitness are avoided. Sexual discrimination is also predicted to include hybrids themselves, leading to their rejection as mating partners by members of either parental population.

Ultimately, reinforcement proposes that speciation evolves as an adaptive solution to conflicting interests of diverging populations. The evolution of sexual discrimination should eventually create complete reproductive isolation due to a snowball or runaway effect and produce two different species. First, a few genes cause adaptive divergence between regional populations; those few genes and traits then cause hybrids between individuals from the two populations to be maladaptive; the low fitness of hybrids favours sexual xenophobia; once xenophobia evolves by selection and gene flow is further reduced by isolating mechanisms, other genes (in addition to the few ones that caused adaptive divergence) begin to accumulate differences between the populations; increased differentiation makes hybridisation or interbreeding even less advantageous. With gene flow reduced, mutations appearing in one population cannot be transferred to another, which also generates further differentiation at other genes. Thus, what begins as gradual differentiation involving a few loci and traits may eventually become a sharp phenotypic and genotypic boundary between two populations due to the invisible barrier of assortative mating. When incompatibilities between the two gene pools accumulate to a point in which hybrids become sterile or not viable (i.e. when post-zygotic reproductive isolation evolves), speciation is complete. This runaway process bears similarity with Fisher's theory of sexual dimorphism (the peacock's tail effect, as discussed in Chapter 5).

Reinforcement has important theoretical consequences. The first is that speciation is seen as the culmination of a process of gradual accumulation of genetic diversity between populations. For this reason, even when speciation is recent, genetic differences between the new species should be observed at many genes. Second, generating hybrid offspring should be disadvantageous for all individuals. Reproductive isolation, although defined in terms of populations, evolves so as to prevent the influx of foreign genes into the individual offspring; in other words, speciation by reinforcement is not based on group selection. Finally, speciation prevents mutually negative interference during the adaptive process, so that more niches can be more quickly occupied by specialist species; speciation is therefore a necessary step in a progressive adaptive mapping of the world.

Reinforcement has caused alternating waves of scepticism and enthusiasm among evolutionary biologists (Gavrilets, 2005). The hypothesis certainly has a strong theoretical appeal, since it unifies adaptation and speciation under the single umbrella of natural selection. But even some of its supporters recognise that the strong claims by Darwin, Fisher and Dobzhansky have not been corroborated by evidence (Hostert, 1997). The most optimistic views on reinforcement argue for its compatibility with existing data and as theoretically plausible but are far from claiming a role for reinforcement as the main mechanism of speciation, in regards to either pervasiveness or evolutionary relevance (Coyne and Orr, 2004; Doebeli *et al.*, 2005). Many experimental studies of reinforcement consist of comparisons between levels of pre-zygotic and post-zygotic reproductive isolation among physically isolated (allopatric) and physically continuous (sympatric) taxa; but even those indicate that allopatry is unquestionably responsible for most cases of reproductive isolation. In conclusion, the failure of reinforcement is a challenge to the belief in the straightforward continuity between microevolution and macroevolution.

SPECIATION AS AN ACCIDENT

Despite their belief in natural selection as a direct cause of speciation, Darwin, Fisher and other proponents of adaptive speciation recognised that physical isolation very often leads to the origin of new species. One of Darwin's favourite examples was the presence of highly diverse endemic or exclusive faunas in isolated areas such as Australia. Allopatric explanations for speciation are the most parsimonious and widely accepted (Coyne and Orr, 2004), since they do not require special conditions setting natural selection against the generally advantageous process of random mating; the beginning of allopatric speciation only requires the interruption of gene flow – for whatever reason. Physical or geographical isolation is a frequent and efficient factor preventing gene flow; but since it is a demographic accident, physical isolation may imply that the 'the principal evolutionary mechanism in the origin of species must be an essentially nonadaptive one' (Wright, 1932). Under the allopatric model developed by Mayr (1963) and others, physically isolated populations evolve into separate species with the help of chance factors that gradually increase interpopulational genetic divergence, such as genetic drift and the occurrence of new mutations not shared with other populations, eventually causing hybrids to be non-viable.

Two main misunderstandings involve the idea of non-adaptive or allopatric adaptation. First, allopatric speciation does not completely deny a role to natural selection in speciation; in fact, the model assumes that genetic differentiation between populations can also be a side effect of divergent adaptation to local conditions; as much as genetic drift and new mutations, selection for different alleles will lead to genetic differentiation. What allopatric speciation denies is that speciation evolves as a product of selection for (previously non-existing) reproductive isolation itself: that is, that selection acts in cases where it has become advantageous for populations to interrupt free gene flow between them.

An example of this misunderstanding was the review of recent speciation studies by Coyne and Orr (2004: 319). They showed that genes that cause post-zygotic reproductive isolation (hybrid non-viability or sterility) do not belong to any special functional class, are not characterised by the presence of large numbers of DNA repetitive sequences or transposons (which would be expected if differentiation were mostly caused by genetic drift), and more crucially, are quickly evolving by positive Darwinian selection. They concluded that 'direct molecular data now support one of the central tenets of neo-Darwinian view of evolution – that reproductive isolation results from natural selection within species' (see also Barbash and Ashburner, 2003; Presgraves *et al.*, 2003). However, their statement delivers less than what it promises: both reinforcement *and* allopatric speciation postulate that reproductive isolation may 'result' from natural selection. The real question, not elucidated by the data presented by Coyne and Orr, is whether such genes under selection evolved so as to *directly cause* reproductive isolation and speciation as proposed by Darwin, Fisher and Dobzhansky, or as ingredients of local adaptation that *accidentally* caused reproductive isolation and speciation as proposed by Wright and Mayr.

A second misunderstanding comes from the challenge posed by sympatric models of speciation, which postulate the origin of new species without prior physical isolation (Schilthuizen, 2000; Mallet, 2001). For example, various studies have proposed that sympatric speciation can follow from adaptation to discrete niches or resources occurring in the same environment (Maynard Smith, 1966; Doebeli, 1996; Johnson and Gullberg, 1998; Kondrashov and Kondrashov, 1999) or of divergent sexual selection (Payne and Krakauer, 1997; van Doorn *et al.*, 1998; Gavrilets and Waxman, 2002; Seehausen *et al.*, 2008). The misunderstanding here is that sympatric models do not necessarily imply that pre- or post-zygotic reproductive isolation evolve in order to reduce gene flow between incipient species; they can still be seen either as a side effect of adaptive divergence to a heterogeneous (although the 'same') environment, or a side effect of differentiation in mating behaviour under sexual selection. In other words, most of the few credible cases of sympatric speciation simply reproduce the mechanisms of allopatric speciation in a microcosmos (Fitzpatrick *et al.*, 2008); they are what Coyne and Orr themselves (2004) properly call 'microallopatric speciation'. Since sympatric speciation also relies on the idea that speciation is a side effect of divergent adaptation, it represents a different model of speciation from reinforcement. Thus, although new studies may show that sympatric speciation is possible and that natural selection may cause genetic differentiation, the relevance of reinforcement, literally 'the origin of species by means of natural selection', remains unproven.

SPECIATION AND PARTICULATE INHERITANCE

It was shown above that the first condition for speciation is sex; without it, the definition of species becomes necessarily arbitrary. The second condition assumed by theories of speciation is geography. Geography means in the first place possible discontinuous distributions and physical isolation between sexual populations. And second, geographical variation is also qualitative, and engenders changes in environments and selection pressures: populations of the same species may evolve distinct, and even opposite, adaptations to distinct environmental conditions. However, adaptive evolution may coexist with the absence of speciation. *Homo sapiens* is a good example: although natural selection played a significant role in the evolution of biological differences between the Inuit and Australian Aborigines, or between African pygmies and northern Europeans (Migliano *et al.*, 2007), those are examples of within-species diversity. On the other hand, physical isolation does not necessarily promote speciation: *Homo sapiens* is again an example, with native populations from North America and Sub-Saharan Africa, or Northern Europe and South Africa and Australia being isolated from each other for thousands of years but showing no sign of hybrid non-viability or sterility.

What makes sex a necessary condition for speciation? In a sense, reproductive isolation is another consequence of particulate inheritance. Reproductive isolation is caused by the incompatibility between regionally differentiated genotypes, which in combination results in non-viability or sterility. The origin of genotypic incompatibility results from the two fundamental evolutionary consequences of particulate inheritance: the first is the possibility of individual allele replacements as proposed by Fisher, and the second is epistasis as championed by Wright. The first, allele substitution, is possible due to the modular nature of both DNA (which consists of sequences of nucleotides); the second, epistasis, follows from the modularity of genotypes (which consist of gene sets). In other words, hybrid sterility is in essence a case of negative epistasis between alleles evolving under distinct selective pressures, a phenomenon originally formulated as 'Dobzhansky–Muller incompatibilities' (Dobzhansky, 1934; Muller, 1939; Gavrilets, 1997; Brideau et al., 2006).

The level of genetic divergence (the number of gene replacements) between two regionally evolved genotypes required for reproductive isolation strictly refers to the nature of those differentiated alleles and genotypes. For this reason, whereas reinforcement implies that speciation results from various polymorphisms, the accidental allopatric view suggests that speciation might be in principle caused by a single allelic difference. Recent studies have shown that the number of genes involved in causing post-zygotic reproductive isolation in fact varies from one to more than a hundred (Coyne and Orr, 1998, 2004). However, the number of genes causing reproductive isolation may be overestimated because genetic divergence continues *after* speciation; for example, although over 70% of human and chimpanzee genes present at least one sequence difference (Coyne, 2005), most of the differences occurred after speciation over 6 million years ago.

Reproductive isolation by a single gene is exemplified by hybrid rescue mutations in the *Drosophila* genus. Crosses between *D. melanogaster* and the closely related *D. simulans*, *D. mauritiana* and *D. sechellia* generate non-viable offspring (Sturtevant, 1920; Sawamura and Yamamoto, 1997; Hutter, 1997). By genetic manipulation, it is possible to obtain hybrids that are homozygous at a few identified loci. It was found that if hybrids carry two copies of the *D. melanogaster* allele at the *Hmr* gene, viable males and females are produced (Barbash and Ashburner, 2003). Alleles from other loci (*Lhr*, *mhr*, *167.7*, *Zhr*) may also rescue hybrid viability or fertility in selected crosses (Watanabe, 1979; Davis *et al.*, 1996). Therefore, the identity and number of genes involved in reproductive isolation and speciation are highly variable.

In summary, speciation cannot be exclusively derived from the theory of natural selection; first because of the apparently stronger role played by geography and isolation in comparison with selection and reinforcement, and second because it depends ultimately on the two properties of particulate inheritance: negative epistasis and allelic replacement. The conclusion is that genes are relevant in the origin of species for being units of inheritance – not for being units of selection.

LEVELS OF SELECTION

The debate over levels of selection in evolution received much attention in the 1960s following Wynne-Edwards' (1962) reinstatement of group selection and Hamilton's (1964) theory of kin selection, which proposed that maximisation of 'inclusive' (but still individual) fitness could account for apparent examples of group selection. A central idea in Williams' *Adaptation and Natural Selection* (1966), an explicit attempt to 'purge biology' from group selection, was the argument that 'within a population, only the gene is stable enough to be effectively selected'. The reason is that whereas individual phenotypes and genotypes exist only once in sexual populations and never occur again, our individual alleles may be very ancient, jumping from our parents onto ourselves, and from ourselves onto our descendants. For this reason, although selection is a bias mediated through individual phenotypes, only alleles survive through generations (barring mutations) and are therefore the memory of such bias. Since the gene is the lasting particle of inheritance whereas its carriers are products of ephemeral genotypes, the gene must be not only the unit of inheritance, but also the unit of selection. Williams' suggestion was made even more explicit a few years later by Dawkins and the selfish gene concept.

> The fundamental unit of selection, and therefore of self-interest, is not the species, nor the group, nor even strictly, the individual. It is the gene, the unit of heredity (Dawkins, 1976: 11).

It might be argued that Dawkins simply took Darwinism to its logical consequence and that the emphasis on natural selection and particulate inheritance by Fisher, Wright and Haldane's evolutionary genetics would necessarily lead to the selfish gene. However, the view that the fundamental unit of selection is the gene is incorrect and the source of various misunderstandings (Reeve and Keller, 1999). Fisher, another critic of group selection, added a section named 'The benefit of species' to the second edition to the *Genetical Theory* in 1958 that made clear his views on the units of selection:

> The principle of Natural Selection … refers only to variation among individuals (or co-operative communities), and to the progressive modification of structure or function only in so far as variations in these are of advantage to the individual, in respect to his chances of death or reproduction. It thus affords a rational explanation of structures, reactions and instincts which can be recognized as profitable to their individual possessors (Fisher, 1930: 279).

Even to the ultra-selectionist Fisher, natural selection refers to phenotypes, not genes. It refers to phenotypes and its components as far as they affect the fitness of their carriers. Since individuals are born, die and reproduce much more frequently than species, they are the most affected by selection, but Fisher also accepts co-operative communities as a second level of selection. Some traits certainly differentiate communities among themselves and could be advantageous in cases of competition between groups. For this reason, Fisher even proposes that 'the term Natural Selection should include not only the selective survival of individuals of the same species, but of mutually competing species of the same genus or family'. However, he argued that species selection, although plausible, must be of reduced importance.

> The relative unimportance of this [species selection] as an evolutionary factor would seem to follow decisively from the small *number* of closely related species which in fact do come in competition, as compared to the number of individuals in the same species; and from the vastly greater *duration* of the species compared to the individual (Fisher, 1930: 280).

Species selection is less important because small numbers are always bad news for selection, as they increase the power of random factors such as drift; in addition, for a single episode of extinction or speciation (which we could respectively associate with species death and reproduction) there are countless rounds of individual birth and death for selection to operate upon. This does not mean that species selection has no role; although the process takes longer, selection may be restored strongly enough to make its mark on macroevolution, as exemplified by convergence.

The role for species selection in evolution points to a second important misunderstanding: the confusion between levels of selection and levels of organisation. A hierarchy of levels of selection will start from individuals and proceed to more inclusive units such as families (kin groups), groups and whole species. As seen earlier, the hierarchy of levels of organisation or complexity, however, includes different elements, such as cells, multicellular organisms, animals storing information in brains, and human societies. Thus, groups of organisms (including unicellular ones) or societies may be units of selection without being units or levels of biological organisation.

The doubts about the direct role of natural selection as the guide to the origin and fate of species suggest that macroevolution might not carry the signal of selection. That interpretation would be incorrect. The origin of species is undeniably affected by factors such as accidental isolation; but the fate of individual lineages (or to use a previous example, of an individual radiocarbon) was always assumed to involve a degree of contingency. The key contribution of evolutionary genetics to the understanding of biological complexity was the exploration of the particulate or *modular* nature of inheritance, as captured by Fisher's fundamental principle of natural selection and by Wright's focus on epistasis. As discussed in the final chapter, natural selection by itself is unable to create higher organisation simply by generating 'better' or 'higher' species given enough time, contrary to the claims by Darwin and Fisher; transitions in biological complexity require a transformation not of species, but of modular inheritance systems by natural selection. Finally, the nature of adaptive evolution in multicellular organisms cannot be deduced from natural selection and mutation sizes alone; gradualism must be understood in the context of *developmental* modularity, as discussed next.

3

Multicellularity and the developmental code

Despite the drawbacks of Fisher's argument, evolutionary gradualism remains the most accepted explanation for organic diversity. Even Orr (2001: 121), who revealed the flaw in the micromutational approach, agrees that 'alleles of large phenotypic effect (major genes) sometimes play a role in phenotypic evolution...but alleles of small effect are still more common than those of large effect'. Wright's ideas were also a direct blow against saltationist views. Under his shifting balance mechanism, the discontinuity of species results not from the discontinuity of variation (although macromutations can be accommodated within the model; see Wright, 1977), but from the geographic discontinuity of real populations and environments.

With genetics being absorbed into mainstream gradualism, saltationism had to seek refuge in what historically has been the most prolific source of anti-Darwinian ideas: developmental biology (Goldschmidt, 1940; Gould, 1977; Goodwin, 1994; Gilbert et al., 1996). Goldschmidt argued that the micromutations and allele polymorphisms studied by geneticists could only cause a limited degree of variation on a given species theme. But the origin of new species and body plans would require more radical phenotypic changes, triggered by factors exploring what he called the hidden 'potentialities of development'. For Goldschmidt, mutations were relevant only as a source of systemic changes in development; however, those were not the more trivial micromutations studied by population geneticists but highly disruptive macromutations such as those known to cause the phenomenon of 'homeosis' (Bateson, 1894). Homeotic mutations result in body structures developing in the wrong place, as exemplified by 'antennapedia' flies in which legs develop in the place of antennae, and 'bithorax' flies in which a second pair of wings replaces the halteres (Gehring, 1998).

Remarkably, it is now known that those two homeotic transformations result from mutations in single genes, respectively *Antennapedia* (*Antp*) and *Ultrabithorax* (*Ubx*) (McGinnis *et al.*, 1984; Scott and Weiner, 1984). The discovery that a single defective gene can produce a whole new bithorax phenotype, which superficially bridges the morphological gap between two-winged dipterans (flies) and four-winged insects, seemed to confirm Goldschmidt's claim that 'a single mutational step affecting the right process at the right moment can accomplish everything, providing that it is able to set in motion the ever-present potentialities of embryonic regulation' (Goldschmidt, 1940: 297). Thus, although the development of genetics was essential to the neo-Darwinian synthesis, it has also kept alive the hopes of a saltationist resistance.

The rather confrontational relationship between geneticists focusing on small mutations and developmental biologists emphasising radical morphological change has persisted for decades, but has been transformed in recent times due to a series of technical advances and discoveries. A first sign of change was a highly influential comparative study of chimpanzees and humans by King and Wilson (1975; see also Ohno, 1972), who argued on the basis of available evidence at the time that the two species exhibited almost identical proteins. Due to the similarity in building blocks or 'ingredients', they concluded that the phenotypic differences between the two species must have been caused by evolutionary changes in gene expression: that is, changes in where, when, and in which amount similar proteins are expressed during development – in other words, changes in the 'recipe' that builds organisms.

King and Wilson's genetic 'expressionism', based on the distinction between developmental ingredients (protein sequence) and developmental recipe (gene expression patterns) and on an emphasis on the latter as an important process in evolution, made an immediate impact in evolutionary biology. Gould (1977) realised that the argument could be extrapolated from the human–chimp case to species divergence in general and used as additional support for his version of heterochrony, the theory proposed by Haeckel (1896) that derives nongradual evolution from changes in developmental timing. However, at the time of the publication of King and Wilson's review very little was known about the nature of mechanisms controlling gene expression.

A better understanding of how the recipe for organisms is written in the genome and the definitive rise of developmental genetics started with the characterisation of the *Hox* gene cluster in *Drosophila* (Lewis, 1978) and of *Ubx* in particular (Bender *et al.*, 1983). *Ubx*, the first gene responsible for a homeotic transformation (the bithorax fly) to have its DNA sequenced, was shown to be a very large gene coding for a very small product. The small *Ubx* protein is neither an enzyme catalysing reactions nor a structural molecule or building block; it is instead a protein that binds to 'cis-regulatory' regions lying in the vicinity of protein coding sequences, thereby affecting the likelihood that the gene product is expressed; in other words, it is a 'transcription factor' that switches other genes on and off (Lynch and Wagner, 2008). For its role in gene regulation and in homeotic transformations, *Ubx* was soon interpreted as one of the recipe genes that developmental biologists were searching for. Since then, many other recipe, regulatory or patterning genes have been identified (McGinnis, 1994).

The role of regulatory genes in evolutionary innovation is the central question addressed by evolutionary developmental biology or 'evo-devo' (Raff, 1996; Stern, 2000; Kirschner and Gerhart, 2005; Carroll, 2008). Among other consequences, the discovery and deeper understanding of networks of regulatory genes (Davidson and Levine, 2008) required a reappraisal of the concept of homology. As seen previously, the conservation of *Pax-6* genes (members of a family of regulatory or recipe genes) suggested a deeper level of homology of existing animal eyes (Gehring, 1998); similar examples led to the radical claim that the radiation of animal body plans in the Cambrian period (the 'Cambrian Explosion') might have been a consequence of (or at least required) the origin and prior diversification of patterning genes themselves (Peterson and Davidson, 2000; Sole *et al.*, 2003; see Marshall, 2006 for a critical review). Those findings might again sound like good news for saltationist views; after all, patterning genes suggest that the basis for macroevolutionary change might ultimately rest not on the cumulative and gradual effect of small mutations, but on changes in a small set of genes with dramatic effects on body plan architecture.

Recent progress in evo-devo is, however, showing the opposite, namely that developmental biology can provide definitive evidence for gradualism. A first emerging conclusion is that, in spite of its catalysing role in the past, King and Wilson's 'expressionism' may be partially incorrect: in the following, it will be argued that although the contrast between patterning or recipe genes and ingredient or effector genes remains useful, the specific claim that changes in gene expression are the main factor behind the origin and divergence of species has not yet been corroborated (Hoekstra and Coyne, 2007).

Second, developmental genetics is close to demonstrating that the diversification of animal body plans from pre-Cambrian times can only be understood within the framework of adaptation and micro-evolution (Marshall, 2006; Conway Morris, 2006). As much as Darwin's insight showed that adaptive evolution may gradually produce new species provided a first ancestral species is postulated, recent develop-mental and fossil studies are now showing that under the assumption of a pre-Cambrian metazoan organism, diversification of body plans can be explained as a result of gradual adaptive change.

Finally, patterning genes have been crucial to our understand-ing of the origins of the first multicellular organisms themselves. The *cis*-regulatory regions (DNA sequences adjacent to coding sequences of a gene, such as promoters, enhancers and silencers, to which tran-scription factors can bind and then control the gene; Carroll *et al.*, 2001), found in virtually all genes, do not code for proteins, but store information on when and where proteins should be expressed; in multicellular organisms, this may be manifested as what is known as 'positional information' (Wolpert, 1969). Due to its role in organis-ing metazoan multicellularity, the origin of the 'developmental code' represented one of the most important steps in the evolution of bio-logical complexity. Multicellularity is the only unequivocal example of an evolutionary transition *sensu* Maynard Smith and Szathmáry (1995), by representing both the origin of a super-unit by aggregation of pre-existing unicellular organisms, and of an underlying new system of biological information consisting of transcriptional factors and regu-latory sequences with exclusively informational roles.

The evolution of multicellularity from single cells required a series of gradual steps including three main innovations: reproduc-tion, regulation of gene expression, and in some cases the clear dis-tinction between germline and somatic lines that characterises full multicellularity as defined by Weismann (1889). The three innovations emerged as adaptations to unicellular life, but later became the foun-dation of animal development and its defining feature: the modular organisation of multicellular super-units.

REPLICATION AND REPRODUCTION

Development can be defined as the origin of a new phenotype from a newly formed genotype; inversely, reproduction is the origin of new genotypes from developed or mature phenotypes. The alternation of these two complementary processes defines life cycles, which attained their most elaborate forms in multicellular organisms (Bonner, 1998). The origin of life cycles is synonymous with the origin of life itself and predated multicellularity; they represent the transition from a pre-biotic world of self-replicating molecules to our current world of living organisms that develop and reproduce (Hazen, 2005). The immediate pre-biotic ancestor to life and life cycles is widely believed to have been the RNA World (Gilbert, 1986) of self-replicating ribozymes (Cech, 2002), or RNA molecules able to catalyse reactions including replication (like protein enzymes) and to store information in its own nucleotide sequence (like DNA).

The RNA World and its ribozymes are, however, pre-biotic instead of alive. The reason is that they lack a universal feature of all current life forms: the distinction, at the physical or molecular level, between genotype and phenotype. Ribozymes are good hypothetical ancestors to life exactly for not displaying such distinction; the nucleotide sequence of a ribozyme represented both hereditary information and catalytic function, and for this reason its replication was at the same time reproduction or the origin of a new genotype, and development of a new phenotype. In summary, life, our DNA World and cycles of development and reproduction are all aspects of a single process: the origin of the genetic code (Crick *et al.*, 1961; Crick, 1970), which established separate functions for DNA (genotype or information), proteins (phenotype or function), and RNA (mediation between DNA and RNA and their regulation).

As the immediate ancestor to life, the RNA World was the very stage where the evolution of the genetic code took place. Some hypotheses for the origin of the genetic code postulate associations between RNA and amino acids (acting as co-factors) available in the primitive Earth (Wong, 1991; Szathmáry and Maynard Smith, 1997); in this case, the association enhanced structural or catalytic properties of ribozymes and had no informational role. The 'genomic tag hypothesis' (Weiner and Maizels, 1987) by contrast postulates that ancestral ribozymes exhibited a specific 3′-tRNA-like terminal motif working as a simple telomere, similar to what is observed in some contemporary bacterial and plant RNA viruses (Rao *et al.*, 1989). In the RNA World, basic (positive) amino acids would be able to bind to the negatively charged tRNA-like terminal tags, thereby increasing their affinity for ribozymes performing replication.

Some ribozymes found in extant organisms can cleave such 3′-terminal tags (Guerrier-Takada *et al.*, 1988), and if their ancestors did the same in the RNA World two consequences would follow. First, untagged ribozyme molecules would lack an initiation site for replication, and be limited to an exclusively catalytic role; this would imply an original division of labour between genomic (tagged) and catalytic (untagged) subpopulations. Second, a by-product of tag cleavage would be free, small tRNA-like sequences bound to basic amino acids; those would be the precursors of current tRNAs. The origin of the genetic code would follow from the evolution of complementary base-pairing between ribozymes and tRNA precursors, eventually leading to elaboration of codon assignment and protein synthesis. At that point, hereditary material would be in fact coding for protein molecules. In other words, the genomic tag hypothesis implies an informational origin for the associations between amino acids and RNA. Finally, duplex DNA would eventually replace single-stranded RNA as a more efficient genomic template, perhaps as a strategy developed by ancient viruses to invade the first cells (Forterre, 2006).

Whatever its origin, the association between amino acids and ribozymes was the precursor of the genetic code and of true life cycles. Current mechanisms of development are distant descendants of the first nucleic acid templates coding for a phenotypic skin of amino acid sequences; whereas reproduction evolved from early forms of protein-assisted template replication.

However, with the known exception of viruses, genetic material does not reside in simple protein skins but in cells. Although the origin of cellular organisation is controversial (Woese, 2002), compartmentalisation created an extended genetic space under the exclusive influence of enclosed replicators. This brought about important consequences for the evolution of development: within an enclosed compartment or cytoplasm, encoded proteins and other phenotypic structures may evolve functions directly or indirectly contributing to successful replication. In unicellular organisms, those functions collectively constitute metabolism and reproduction; to what extent one may talk of proper development in unicellular organisms can only be understood in the light of the process of gene expression.

GENE EXPRESSION

Whereas in the pre-biotic RNA World the same self-replicating molecular entity performed the functions of genotype and phenotype, in our DNA World genotypes must be expressed or materialised as phenotypes. Under the condition of particulate gene inheritance, controlling how and when the materialisation of phenotypes occurs involves the control of expression of each particle of heredity; in other words, it takes the form of gene regulation. For decades, the standard example of gene regulation was the lactose operon of *Escherichia coli* (Jacob and Monod, 1961). In this bacterium, glucose is the most commonly used source of energy, but lactose is an alternative when glucose is not available. The use of lactose is possible because *E. coli* also carries the gene for the enzyme β-galactosidase, which cleaves lactose into galactosidase and glucose, which can then be used. The lactose operon, a small cluster of genes including β-galactosidase, functions in such a way that the enzyme is synthesised only when lactose is present.

This is achieved through an efficient feedback mechanism. When lactose is absent, a repressor protein (a transcription factor produced by another gene in the operon) continuously binds to the β-galactosidase gene operator. The operator is a binding site in a gene (or part of its DNA sequence with affinity for regulatory proteins) that overlaps with the RNA polymerase binding site (the DNA sequence to which the polymerase binds so as to express its coding sequence as messenger RNA). When the operator is occupied by a repressor, the RNA polymerase cannot bind to its site and gene expression does not happen; in the lactose operon, a repressor therefore continuously silences or switches off the β-galactosidase gene.

But when lactose is present, this arrangement changes. Lactose is converted into allolactose, which has the property of attaching to the repressor and releases it from the operator; RNA polymerase can then bind to its site, so that messenger RNA and then multiple copies of the β-galactosidase enzyme are synthesised. As a result, lactose molecules are cleaved and produce glucose molecules. The feedback is then established: as the active β-galactosidase enzymes cleave lactose molecules, the latter decrease in number and can no longer inactivate the repressor. This eventually causes the β-galactosidase gene to be switched back off again. Despite its simplicity, the lactose operon provides the metabolism of *E. coli* with the ability to respond efficiently to environmental variation.

The regulation of 'housekeeping' genes such as β-galactosidase is required to maintain life in all species, but gene regulation gained the additional role of 'housebuilding' in developmental processes. As seen above, development is the process through which individual phenotypes are rebuilt from genetic scratch every generation. But species cannot be easily classified as either developers or non-developers; the reason is that they differ in the extent to which phenotypes are rebuilt from ancestors. In other words, phenotypic organisation in descendants may not be completely derived from a new genotype, and is often inherited (at least partially) from the parental phenotypes; this can be exemplified again by E. coli and its reproduction (Lewin, 2007).

Bacteria reproduce by fission into two similar descendants (and by other forms of fission such as budding or size-asymmetrical fission, and fragmentation or simultaneous fission into multiple descendants). Although the products of binary fission are conventionally called daughter cells, from a genetic perspective the two resulting cells are not true sisters: they are in fact mother and offspring. The reason is that one of the cells (the mother cell) keeps the original chromosome or DNA molecule that existed before reproduction, whereas the other cell (the daughter cell) inherits a new copy of the chromosome and is therefore the true descendant. New mutations caused by incorrect replication of DNA can only be expressed in the daughter cell. This distinction at the genetic level holds even when cell division is perfectly symmetrical, or when the phenotypes of mother and daughter (and by extension the phenotypes at 'birth' and 'maturity') cannot be distinguished.

If bacterial phenotypes barely differ between 'birth' and 'adulthood', to what extent do bacteria develop? To answer this question, let us consider a new mutation in a hypothetical gene coding for a cell wall protein. Immediately after division, the new mutation will be transferred to the daughter cell in a newly replicated chromosome; however, the daughter cell also inherits all its cellular structures from the maternal cell through fission, and indirectly from the maternal chromosome that synthesised them. The presence of parental products in the descendant organism is one example of what is known as a 'maternal effect' (Mosseau and Fox, 1998). However, with time and the expression of the mutant gene in the daughter cell, mutant cell wall proteins replace the fixed stock of proteins inherited from the mother cell. Thus, development in bacteria is nothing more than the gradual expression of new mutations against a background of inherited maternal effects; if the daughter chromosome carries no mutation, no proper development occurs, nothing new is built from genetic scratch, and a whole new phenotype is virtually inherited as a maternal effect; we would observe some housekeeping but no extensive housebuilding.

MULTICELLULARITY AND THE DEVELOPMENTAL CODE

Unicellular organisms such as yeast (Queller, 2008; Smukalla et al., 2008), slime moulds (Strassmann et al., 2000; Bonner, 2008) and some bacteria (Galperin, 2008) may exhibit social behaviour and more sophisticated life cycles than *E. coli*, but development is most frequently studied in multicellular organisms and animals in particular. A main consequence of multicellularity was the evolution of cell types operating as disposable phenotypic entities. Disposable proteins are phenotypic units adopting various functions (enzymes, antigens, hormones and others) that can be replaced during the life cycle. Multicellularity engendered an additional division of labour between germline, the cells that give rise to gametes and perpetuate the units of inheritance, and somatic line, the class of all disposable cell types responsible for the functioning of the multicellular whole (Weismann, 1889); in humans, for example, the number of somatic cell types may exceed 400 (Vickaryous and Hall, 2006).

All somatic cells derive from a single zygote (or from a single unfertilised egg in the case of asexual or parthenogenetic species), and this implies that despite their phenotypic and functional differences they are genetically identical in the same individual (with some exceptions; Vickaryous and Hall, 2006). If somatic cells do not differ in the genes they carry, they must differ mostly in the way their genes are expressed. We can think of all somatic cells as carrying a full encyclopaedia of genetic and developmental information; all animal cells must necessarily 'read' common volumes of the encyclopaedia (for example, the volume 'How to be an animal cell'); but volumes such as 'How to be a brain cell' or 'How to be a skin cell' are read only by specific cell types, and this would explain how the differentiation between neurons and skin cells occurs. The essence of multicellularity is therefore the fragmentation in the use of genetic information by somatic cells. Fragmentation is possible because inheritance is particulate or encoded in individual genes (or discrete volumes of information) and because mechanisms of gene regulation (or control of genetic reading) had already evolved in unicellular organisms.

How did gene regulation in unicellular organisms become developmental regulation in multicellular organisms? Multicellular development requires differential gene activation and regulation among cell types; but as Huxley and de Beer suggested in their classic *Elements of Experimental Embryology* (1934), this points to a logical dilemma. Their question was: how is the *first* or original asymmetry in gene expression established in a developing multicellular organism? We know that brain and liver cells are distinct because they express distinct genes (specific 'brain cell' genes and 'liver cell' genes), or express common genes in different ways; but what drives the expression of a brain gene exclusively in the future brain cells? A possible answer is simply a recipe or regulatory gene, whose function would be to switch a brain gene on and a liver gene off in a brain cell gene. The problem is that such a regulatory gene (like all others) is present in all cells; this raises the question of what activated the activating gene exclusively in brain cells in the first place. Appealing exclusively to genes as causes of cell differentiation leads to an infinite recursion, and for this reason Huxley and de Beer argued that asymmetrical gene expression cannot be explained by genes alone. At some stage, gene expression must be influenced by 'epigenetic' factors; their favourite examples were gravity or the entry point of sperm in the egg that might potentially cause an uneven distribution of substances or localised chemical change in a previously symmetrical egg.

Time and genetic research have shown that Huxley and de Beer were only partially correct. Some genes do have an exclusive function of regulating other genes during development; they were also correct in pointing out that at some stage in embryonic development even regulatory genes need to be regulated. From the starting point provided by the *Ubx* gene a few decades ago, whole arrays of regulatory genes whose exclusive function is to manage other genes have now been characterised (Istrail and Davidson, 2005). We now know that an important source of original asymmetries in zygotic and embryonic gene expression are parents themselves; in various multicellular organisms, maternal effects establish the first co-ordinates of gene expression through the products of *parental* patterning genes, and this is how genes responsible for early development are placed out of the loop of infinite recursion.

It should be noticed that the field of developmental genetics is highly dynamic and has recently witnessed a potential revolution with the discovery of RNA interference (RNAi), the process of gene regulation based on the direct binding of RNA molecules to target messenger RNAs (Siomi and Siomi, 2009; Carninci, 2009). RNAi is changing even our textbook examples of developmental regulation (for example, it is now known that *Ubx* itself is regulated by non-coding RNAs; Sanchez-Elsner *et al.*, 2006). Besides, developmental regulation may also depend on processes such as genomic imprinting via DNA methylation (Reik and Walter, 2001). With this in mind, the patterning of the antero-posterior body axis in the fruit fly *Drosophila* is used below to exemplify (in a simplified way and excluding some important genes and developmental steps) the building of a multicellular body plan from a few initial molecular cues.

A classic case study of how genes organise multicellularity in animals is the patterning of the antero-posterior (A-P) axis in *Drosophila melanogaster* (Lawrence, 1992). The formation of the *Drosophila* A-P axis is a parade of key patterning genes and a window into the elaborate flow of information between cells in the developing embryo. The A-P axis is established very early in fruit fly development. The *Drosophila* egg contains an oocyte (the zygote after fertilisation) and 15 nurse cells (which produce yolk and other nutrients transferred into the oocyte) and is surrounded by follicle cells derived from the maternal ovary. In the first minutes after deposition of the fertilised egg, endoreplication (nuclear division of the zygotic cell without the formation of cell membranes between the new nuclei) occurs. Due to the presence of yolk, the new nuclei float towards the surface of the egg to form a syncytial blastoderm (or monolayer of nuclei). At this stage, the egg is similar to a rugby ball, with a rigid corion membrane as the outer surface, the syncytial blastoderm as the internal surface, and yolk at its centre.

When it reaches the blastoderm stage, the *Drosophila* egg begins to show the answer to the question posed by Huxley and de Beer. The original source of asymmetry in gene expression of the developing embryo will be the structural asymmetry of the egg itself, anteriorly occupied by the 15 nurse cells, and posteriorly by the fertilised oocyte. Due to this arrangement, the posterior follicle cells (but not those at the anterior end of the egg) receive the protein *gurken* produced by the oocyte. This protein is a signal protein that polarises the egg microtubule array, a system connecting anterior and posterior follicle cells that transports gene products across the egg. The polarised (i.e. 'one-way') microtubules then keep the messenger RNA from *bicoid* (a gene expressed by the maternally derived nurse cells) at the anterior end, whereas the messenger RNA from genes such as *nanos* and *caudal* (also produced by the nurse cells) are moved to the posterior end. The *bicoid* messenger RNA and *bicoid* protein are then present in higher concentration at the anterior end of the egg; *nanos* and *caudal* concentrate at the posterior end. Additionally, anterior *bicoid* codes for a transcription factor that inhibits translation of the posterior *nanos* maternal RNA, sharpening the differences in concentration. Thus, embryonic nuclei at the two ends of the egg end up surrounded by distinct chemical environments, and an asymmetry between 'anterior' and 'posterior' nuclei is established.

It is from the positional cue established by oocyte and maternally expressed genes that the embryonic A-P axis is derived. The maternal cues are translated into embryonic architecture because *nanos* and *bicoid* regulate a set of early expressed zygotic genes, collectively known as 'gap genes'. For example, the *hunchback* gap gene is expressed only when anteriorly found *bicoid* transcription factor is present, but is repressed by the posteriorly found *nanos*; therefore *hunchback* is observed only at the anterior end of the egg. Other gap genes respond to different concentrations of the maternally expressed genes, and are expressed at particular positions along the A-P axis. As a result, the embryonic map gains additional elements: in addition to the anterior and posterior poles, it develops four major gaps or broad territories. Another way of describing the pattern is to say that nuclei or cells from different territories are expressing different combinations of gap genes.

Gap gene products are messenger molecules too, and regulate the expression of other target genes. Based on the particular combination of gap genes that they express, embryonic cells activate one of a few downstream targets known as 'pair rule' genes; the most important ones are the *even skipped* (*eve*) and *fuji tarazu* (*ftz*) genes, which are never expressed by the same cell. The result is an elegant pattern of 14 alternating stripes of *eve* and *ftz* or genetically differentiated cellular territories along the A-P axis. Whereas the seven *eve* stripe rules are defined independently (i.e. by a different combination of maternal and gap gene products), the seven *ftz* stripes are produced by an out-of-phase duplication of the *eve* pattern (Rivera-Pomar and Jackle, 1996).

At this stage of embryonic development the boundaries between the 14 stripes are not sharply defined; in other words, some cells between *eve* and *ftz* stripes are in 'nowhere land'. The fourth level of patterning gene expression, represented by 'segment polarity' genes such as *engrailed*, refines the pair rule pattern to establish clear boundaries between cell territories, eventually defining 14 adjacent segments. As a result, all cells of the embryo are given a clear regional identity in the embryo, or a cell territory address along the A-P axis.

The processes described above do not have a clear counterpart at the cellular or phenotypic level. Artificial staining techniques are normally required to make cell territories visible in pictures, since the different identities of embryonic cells up to that stage mostly refer to the sets of invisible developmental genes that they express. It is the next set of patterning genes that initiates the translation of abstract genetic individuality into particular developmental fates and the structures that we see in the adult fly. This is the role of the well-known *Hox* genes: to activate genes directly responsible for the morphological identity of segments in the *Drosophila* embryo, and directly or indirectly for the identity, number and location of cells types, organs and appendages (Akam, 1998). For example, the interactions between the *Hox* genes *Abdominal-A* (*Abd-A*) and *Ubx* restrict the expression of the gene *Distal-less* (*Dll*) to three segments that eventually become the adult thorax (Vachon *et al.*, 1992); the result is that legs develop only in those segments. Wing primordia in their turn are formed under high concentrations of the *Hox* gene *Decapentaplagic* (*Dpp*), whose expression is determined by a combination of the *Hox* genes *Sex combs reduced* (*Scr*), *Ubx* and *Abd-A*. *Ubx* also regulates genes responsible for the position of wing veins and leg bristles, among other structures.

It is only at the stage when *Hox* genes and their targets are expressed that structural or functional genes specific to cell types or structures (or effector genes) are mobilised. Thus, leg or eye genes are expressed in the proper place only after a virtual scaffold or map of the adult body is drawn with the invisible ink provided by patterning genes. Similar mechanisms and various homologous genes explain the formation of the dorso-ventral axis in *Drosophila* (Carroll *et al.*, 2001).

REGULATORY REGIONS AND GENE BUREAUCRACY

A-P axis specification in *Drosophila* exemplifies the nature and operation of the developmental code of multicellularity: it is a system that subordinates effector genes (the functional or efficient side of the genome) to a class of managerial genes. As a result, a positional map with the co-ordinates of a given body plan is established, and organs, territories and cell types develop in their specified addresses. A measure of the amount of information required for cells to process developmental instructions, and therefore commit to a specific developmental fate, is revealed in one important example: the determination of the second *eve* stripe in the *Drosophila* embryo (Small *et al.*, 1992). As in the case of the A-P axis formation, a simplified description is presented below.

Upstream to the coding region of the pair rule gene *eve*, a *cis*-regulatory region of 480 base pairs was found with multiple binding sites for the transcription factors *nanos*, *hunchback* (maternally expressed), *giant* and *Krüppel* (gap genes). It was also revealed that those two gap genes repress *eve* expression; however, when *nanos* and *hunchback* are present and bound to their sites, they neutralise the effect of the repressors and *eve* is expressed. This is why the *eve* stripe 2 is expressed at the parasegment 3, since the cells in this territory express all four genes. In summary, transcription factors coded by four different regulatory genes and more than a dozen binding sites are required to determine a single *eve* stripe. The other six *eve* stripes expressed at the odd parasegments of the embryo are independently specified by a different combination of repressors and activators. A total of seven distinct regulatory regions are required to determine the seven *eve* stripes, including an autoregulatory region that responds to the *eve* product itself (Ludwig *et al.*, 2005).

The determination of *eve* stripes is another example of the role of regulatory proteins and regions in multicellular development. It has been known for some time that genomes do not contain only 'meaningful' sequences that code for proteins; they also include large amounts of junk or selfish DNA (Doolittle and Sapienza, 1980; Orgel and Crick, 1980). However, this distinction between coding and non-coding regions did not take regulatory regions into account; only recently, with the completion of whole genome sequencing, is the size and distribution of regulatory regions beginning to be estimated. The *eve* gene in *Drosophila*, for example, occupies a stretch of about 16 000 DNA base pairs, but its coding region extends for less than 1500 base pairs; less than 10% of the gene codes for protein. The seven regulatory regions on the other hand are about three times larger and comprise over 3500 base pairs. Although it is still true that most of the *eve* locus may be characterised as junk DNA, 70% of the 5000 base pairs of information stored by the gene *eve* refers to regulatory or developmental information rather than coding information.

The same is true for our species, where at least 2–3% of the genome consists of *cis*-regulatory regions – more than the 2% coding for protein. In yeast, while 70% are represented by coding regions, about 15% represent *cis*-regulation (Kellis *et al.*, 2003); but crucially, yeasts are unicellular and do not develop like multicellular organisms. In *Drosophila* the average size of regulatory regions is about 10 000 base pairs while the average coding region is only 3000 base pairs long (Levine and Tjian, 2003). This means that genes, especially in multicellular organisms, are more than their protein coding sequences (interspersed with parasitic or meaningless non-coding sequences): they are more properly described as information processing units whose output is not just a protein, but more exactly the location, quantity and timing of protein synthesis. In addition to *cis*-regulatory sequences, it is estimated that 5–10% of genes are regulatory proteins or transcription factors in metazoans; they amount to about 1000 genes in flies and worms, and 3000 genes (or 10% of the total), possibly controlling as many as 100 000 enhancers and silencers in humans (Pennisi,

2004). Other examples are given by the first mappings of regulatory networks: for example, the expression of no less than 65 transcription factors and 26 other signalling molecules is required in the zygote of *Ciona intestinalis* (the sea squirt) only to take the embryo to the stage of gastrulation (Imai *et al.*, 2004; Lemaire, 2006). Even more signs of regulation may be found in apparently junk DNA as the mechanisms of RNA interference are further elucidated.

In summary, a whole dimension of genomes consists of 'white collar' genes and *cis*-regulatory regions that respond to them: downstream genes must 'listen' to positive or negative commands (induction or repression) from their superiors, and then make their own calls to subordinates. In analogy with historical human societies, a class of bureaucratic genes had to evolve so as to cope with the public or collective dimension of the multicellular society.

IS EVOLUTION MOSTLY THE EVOLUTION OF REGULATORY REGIONS?

The discovery of a hierarchy of patterning genes with the role of regulating the expression of downstream effector genes seems to confirm King and Wilson's (1975) distinction between developmental recipe and ingredients. Whereas King and Wilson pointed to the high conservation of macromolecules or effector genes between humans and chimpanzees and by extension between other species, conservation is now known to characterise patterning genes themselves (Gehring, 1998; Kirschner and Gerhart, 2005; Carroll, 2006). Transcription factors may remain extremely similar across widely divergent taxa: for example, the *Pax-6* sequence is nearly similar in flies and mice (and still functional when transferred between the species; Quiring *et al.*, 1994), and identical in humans and chimpanzees. Since both effector and patterning gene products tend to be conserved, the most obvious alternative to metazoan diversification would be the evolutionary diversification of *cis*-regulatory regions and gene regulation. This was the new form adopted by the expressionist hypothesis after the discovery and characterisation of the developmental code. However, despite the support of many evo-devo researchers (Wray, 2007; Carroll, 2008), and with the technical means for properly testing the hypothesis being now available, King and Wilson's expressionism has not been fully vindicated (Hoekstra and Coyne, 2007).

Technical advances occurred in two fronts. Whole-genome projects have supplied complete sequence data for various unicellular and multicellular species, while DNA microarray techniques materialise the seemingly impossible task of comparing expression levels of homologous (i.e. the 'same') genes in related species (that amounts to almost 30 000 genes in the case of the human–chimpanzee pair). A first problem with the expressionist argument was identified in the genome sequences of humans and chimpanzees. Data confirmed a value of 99% similarity in DNA sequences between the two species; however, this result can be misleading since it cannot be extrapolated to gene identity (Coyne, 2005): a 99% similarity in the DNA of two species is in principle compatible with *all* of their genes being different by about 1%; in this case, *all* ingredients would differ between the species. In the real case of humans and chimpanzees, data indicate that 71% of the human genes exhibit at least one base pair change compared with chimpanzees (Mikkelsen *et al.*, 2005), which frontally clashes with the claims of King and Wilson that most protein coding sequences would be conserved.

A likely explanation for why they overestimated levels of protein conservation is that their sample of macromolecules was biased towards ancient genes under strong selection: enzymes such as haemoglobin, cytochrome *c* and DNA helicase are highly conserved among mammals in general, and not only between humans and chimpanzees (Miranda, 2006; Becerra *et al.*, 2007). The conclusion is that phenotypic differences between humans and chimpanzees may well be the cumulative effect of a few substitutions in 71% of encoded proteins or ingredients, rather than in the developmental recipe or levels of expression of similar building blocks.

However, microarray analysis has also shown that genes do differ in expression between the two species. Based on the study by Enard *et al.* (2002) revealing that 30% of genes show interspecific differences in expression levels, Carroll (2003) claimed that evidence was now available to suggest that regulatory changes are the main cause of phenotypic divergence between humans and chimps. Microarray analysis has also been applied to the particularly informative case of eusocial insect polyphenism (or discrete morphological variation among workers, soldiers, queens and other castes). Polyphenisms involve genetically similar organisms and are induced by environmental factors such as diet, revealing the existence of alternative developmental pathways within the same genome. The microarray technique might be able to reveal what patterning genes activate a 'queen recipe', a 'worker recipe' or a 'soldier recipe' depending on environmental inputs. However, studies have so far produced disappointing results. As a rule, the genes that stand out in comparisons of expression levels are low in the hierarchy of development (Miura *et al.*, 1999; Sumner *et al.*, 2006; Weil *et al.*, 2009). In honey bees (Evans and Wheeler, 1999), five of seven genes showing highest divergence in expression among castes are ingredient genes; for example, genes involved in ovarian development and metabolism were obviously expressed at high rates in queens but not in the non-reproductive workers. The other two genes are not clearly involved in developmental regulation.

Rather than bad luck, those results reveal a conceptual flaw in the use of microarrays to test King and Wilson's expressionist hypothesis. As shown by the example of the A-P axis in *Drosophila*, developmental pathways may be controlled by very subtle variations in the timing, location and amount of a single or a few transcription factors; but when applied to the case of polyphenisms, those subtle signals are likely to be overwhelmed by large variation in effector genes coding for structural proteins or enzymes needed in larger quantities. While the microarray technique is undeniably useful in medical genetics, for example by identifying gene products expressed at levels in cancer cells as preferential targets for drug action (Li *et al.*, 2008), so far it has not revealed much about the patterning genes that control morphological variation between castes.

Returning to the case of interspecific variation, this means that although we predict differences in gene expression between humans and chimpanzees, the identity of the genes may disappoint. We know that hair proteins must be expressed at higher levels and in relatively more skin cells in chimpanzees because their bodies are fully covered; we can also predict that various genes coding for brain proteins must be expressed at higher levels in humans simply because our brain is larger and grows for longer (Vrba, 1998; Rice, 2002a; Vinicius, 2005). However, their specific claim of the expressionist argument is that changes in gene expression and not in protein sequence were the key or even single explanation for adaptive divergence. Recently Khaitovich *et al.* (2005) have investigated this claim in detail, with results that offered further reasons for scepticism.

First, their study compared gene expression in organs that diverged the most (the brain) and the least (liver or heart) in phenotype between humans and chimpanzees. The results were unambiguous: contrary to the expressionist model, most variation in gene expression is found in the organs that evolved the *least*. Khaitovich *et al.* concluded that changes in gene expression are mostly neutral and less likely to occur in genes responsible for phenotypic divergence (although there are exceptions to this rule, such as genes related to the X chromosome). In conclusion, microarrays may fail to identify the basis for developmental reprogramming between species for two reasons: because adaptive changes in gene expression are more pronounced in effector genes than in key patterning genes, and because changes in gene expression may not be adaptive at all.

Secondly and more importantly, although the distinction between coding versus regulatory sequences makes fundamental sense, the question of which is the main stage of adaptive evolution may not have one straightforward answer. The reason is that Khaitovich *et al.* have also shown a strong correlation between changes in gene sequence and gene expression: genes whose expression diverges the most between humans and chimpanzees (probably in their *cis*-regulatory regions) are also those that differ the most in coding sequence. In a sense, this finding is far from surprising: for example, selection for darker skin pigmentation may lead both to the evolution of increased expression of an already existing dark pigment *and* to the evolution of an even darker pigment by changes in its gene sequence. Inversely, if selection is weak or absent, neutral variation is expected to accumulate in both *cis*-regulatory and coding regions, causing changes in gene expression *and* coding sequence.

In contrast, Pollard *et al.* (2006) have identified a region of an RNA gene (*HAR1*), which is expressed in the human neocortex during early development, as the region with the most accelerated evolution in the human genome relative to chimpanzees; the gene probably regulates protein-coding genes required for brain development (through RNA interference rather than transcription factors). Prabhakar *et al.* (2006) have recently generalised their results, and emphasised the relevance of *cis*-regulation in trait evolution. However, it should be noticed that those studies focused on regulatory proteins and *cis*-regulation; other studies focusing on ingredients have even discovered a protein exclusively found in the human brain and not present in the chimpanzee genome (Hayakawa *et al.*, 2005). The apparently contradictory results certainly indicate the need for further studies, but the conclusion seems to be that both *cis*-regulation and coding mutations are relevant during adaptive divergence, although some traits may be more likely to evolve through the former and others through the latter (Hoekstra and Coyne, 2007; Wray, 2007).

In conclusion, although the distinction between *cis*-regulation and protein sequence is fundamental to genetic and developmental studies, there is not enough evidence for the hypothesis that *cis*-regulatory changes are the only or most important cause of phenotypic divergence between closely related species such as chimpanzees and humans (Hill and Walsh, 2005). This is not the same as concluding that changes in regulatory mechanisms are not relevant; it means that the relationship between gene expression and microevolution is not necessarily the one portrayed by the expressionist argument. As seen below, the interaction between genetic and developmental informa- tion is important and implies why evolution in multicellular organ- isms may essentially be gradual.

MODULARITY AND MICROEVOLUTION

Consider a winged insect species under strong selection pressure to evolve terrestrial locomotion and lose its wings. Now suppose the existence of a mutation that enlarges the size of all appendages includ- ing wings and legs. It is easy to see that this mutation would be on the one hand advantageous for increasing leg size and favouring ter- restrial locomotion, and on the other hand deleterious for increasing wing size instead of reducing it; in other words, the mutation causes 'antagonistic pleiotropy' (Williams, 1957). In this case, the fate of the mutant allele depends on its net effect on fitness: if the advantageous effect on leg size is stronger, the mutation may spread despite the asso- ciated deleterious effect on wing size. As seen in the previous chapter, Fisher's argument for micromutations implied that the likelihood of a mutant phenotype being deleterious increases with the number of traits that it involves. Possible antagonistic pleiotropy may be also part of what Orr called the cost of complexity: in a more complex organism (which in Orr's sense means an organism with more traits contribut- ing to adaptation), it is more likely that a mutation increasing adap- tation in one character may cause deleterious fitness effects on many other traits. If that is true, why has adaptive evolution not come to an absolute halt?

The answer to that question is 'developmental modularity' (Wagner and Altenberg, 1996; Wagner et al., 2007), another conse- quence of patterning mechanisms. Development via specification of cellular modules, as exemplified by antero-posterior segmentation in *Drosophila*, is important in evolution for significantly reducing the cost of complexity discussed by Fisher and Orr. The main reason is that developmental modularity can neutralise one type of antagonistic pleiotropy, namely *spatial* pleiotropy. In simple terms, gene regulation may evolve so as to switch on or up-regulate a mutation in a module, organ or cell where its effects on fitness are positive, and at the same time switch off or down-regulate the gene in places where its effects are deleterious. For this reason, patterning genes and *cis*-regulatory regions may facilitate the evolution of effector genes by controlling their expression levels, location and timing. Wagner and collaborators (2008) have offered further empirical corroboration to those conclusions, by studying pleiotropy in mice through quantitative trait loci (QTL) and showing that most mutations affect few traits in modularly organised animals.

Developmental modularity thus explains the joint evolution of *cis*-regulatory and coding regions of genes identified by Khaitovich *et al.* (2005). Returning to the example of the winged insect under selection for terrestrial locomotion, we can imagine how a mutation causing appendage overgrowth might eventually evolve into a mutation causing only leg overgrowth (i.e. the mutation may lose its pleiotropic effects). For example, the gene involved may evolve a new binding site for a repressor in its *cis*-regulatory region; as exemplified by the *eve* stripe 2 mechanism, a repressor protein may be expressed only in the cell territory that develops into adult wings, but not in legs. In this case, the overgrowth mutation would in practice only 'exist' in leg cells; it would become an effector gene never used in the wings.

An important conclusion is that due to developmental modularity the origin, evolution and disappearance of countless effector genes, signalling cascades and metabolic pathways may have taken place in a single body segment or organ, or a single cell type. Brain cells, bone cells or skin cells require particular subsets of genes, but those genes are likely to have disastrous effects on any other cell type. This means that both genes and phenotypic traits in multicellular organisms are to a certain extent fragmented into a series of developmentally independent units; each of those units responds for a fraction of the phenotypic dimensions of the whole organism, and for a fraction of the genome. For this reason, body plans, organs and cell types are less constrained to evolve and adapt (Wagner *et al.*, 2008). Thus, if phenotypic change is slow and gradual as proposed by Fisher, it may be for reasons different from phenotypic 'integration' or complexity; as seen in the previous chapter, it may relate to ecological conditions such as the constant proximity of populations to adaptive peaks; when the conditions for adaptive radiations (or 'adaptive revolutions') are present, species seem able to evolve fast (Harmon *et al.*, 2009).

The role of developmental modularity in the microevolution and diversification of multicellular animals is exemplified in many ways; an interesting case is variation in bilateral symmetry. Whereas the left and right body sides frequently mirror each other in arthropods, vertebrates and other bilaterian taxa, in male fiddler crabs one of the two claws is enlarged and used in courtship of females and male contests (Rosenberg, 2001). Most fiddler crab species are antisymmetric, with half the population being right-handed and the remaining half left-handed. The claw that develops the larger size is randomly determined: soon after claw growth starts, one of the claws is lost, and the other develops large size. However, all species of the genus *Gelasimus* are right-handed, meaning that genetic determination of handedness has somehow evolved in the group. Nothing is known about the genetic or developmental mechanisms involved but it is believed that differential growth is achieved through mutual inhibition between the cell territories from which the two claws derive; this is only possible due to the modular nature of appendage development in crustaceans.

Another example is morphometric diversification in vertebrate skeletons. Mammals typically exhibit seven cervical (neck) vertebrae, including giraffes where individual neck vertebrae grow much larger than thoracic (rib-bearing) vertebrae and larger than neck vertebrae in other mammals (Galis, 1999). The yet unknown genes behind the giraffe's neck phenotype may be growth factors responding to the same patterning genes that induce morphological differentiation between neck and thoracic vertebrae early in development; those genes may be the vertebrate *Hox* gene homologues that specify the identity of vertebrate somites, the antero-posterior modules giving rise to vertebrae in chordates (Burke *et al.*, 1995).

The machinery of developmental modularity may have even evolved to perform a purely decorative function in some species. Intricate colour patterns in butterfly wings are produced by some patterning genes (*Distal-less*, *Hedgehog*) also involved in building the arthropod body plan (Brakefield *et al.*, 1996; Keys *et al.*, 1999). In panther chameleons, the coloured radial patterns, stripes, spots and even individual scales are to some extent a visualisation of the positional map of skin cells. Although the genes involved in the evolution of chameleon colouration are unknown, the patterning genes that organise body plan axes (antero-posterior, dorso-ventral, left–right) and morphology of appendages may have been deployed in skin cells to control pigment deposition in individual scales. The chameleon palette is extremely rich, including various shades of yellow, blue and red; these colours may have required both the evolution of exquisite pigments unique to chameleons (new ingredients and coding sequences) and changes in the expression of pigment genes (new recipe or binding sites in *cis*-regulatory regions of pigment genes). The mechanism determining colour pattern in chameleons is highly sophisticated, including various cell types (some containing yellow and red pigments, others containing melanin, others reflecting blue light), besides the possibility of neurologically and hormonally regulated changes in colour (Schwab, 2001).

Developmental modularity has thus contributed to the adaptive microevolution of multicellular body plans, as exemplified by an ever-growing list of examples (for summaries, see Kirschner and Gerhart, 2005 and Carroll, 2006). As seen below, it also offers an explanation for cases, most dear to the old mutationists, of apparent discontinuities in macroevolution.

THE GRADUAL EVOLUTION OF HOMEOTIC MUTATIONS

Can the adaptive microevolution of modular body plans be the only or main source of their *macro*evolutionary diversity (i.e. the differences between arthropods and vertebrates, dipterans and four-winged insects and other cases of discontinuities)? A first look at the more than 30 extant animal phyla, most of them modularly organised (Gerhart and Kirschner, 1997; Carroll, 2006), might suggest that metazoan body plans are alternative combinations of the same structural elements (body axes, segments, appendages); even within the same phylum (arthropods being a clear example), variation in number and position of wings, legs, eyes and body segments explains a significant fraction of diversity (Raff, 1996).

This means that the origin of new body plans may have relied to a large extent on the reshuffling of a small set of structural elements or modules. Etienne Geoffroy Saint-Hilaire originally proposed that new body plans had evolved by single-step mutational jumps, but as seen earlier it was due to Bateson (1894) and Goldschmidt (1940) that homeotic mutations, which replace or multiply whole body parts or segments, were postulated as possible agents of macroevolution. Given the analogy between homeosis on the one hand, and variation in number of body segments, wings, legs and eyes observed among dipterans, butterflies and spiders on the other, they could not avoid the conclusion that homeotic mutations were behind the sudden, although infrequent, origin of new body plans.

Contrary to those expectations, developmental genetics has provided evidence that not only denies a role to homeotic mutations in macroevolution, but incorporates them into a fully gradualist view of evolution (Budd, 1999). This has occurred mostly due to a deeper understanding of the phenomenon of 'meristic' variation, or changes across taxa in the number of similar structures such as vertebrae and appendages (Bateson, 1894; Stern, 2000). The repeated insect legs, arachnid eyes or dragonfly wings in a given species are more than just similar; they are in fact 'serially homologous' units derived from duplication of an original set of structures (Carroll *et al.*, 2001). An example of meristic variation observed in the wild was given earlier by the variable segment numbers in British centipedes (where meristic variation is, however, derived; Arthur and Kettle, 2001); a case produced in laboratory conditions was the induction of extra eyes in *Drosophila* through the ectopic (i.e. misplaced) expression of the eye-inducing *Pax-6* gene (McGinnis *et al.*, 1984).

The findings above are helping to clarify the macroevolutionary role of mutations able to change the number and position of body structures. The main conclusion is that meristic and homeotic variations are distinct, although related, phenomena. The familiar homeotic mutations discussed by geneticists must be meristic: by affecting segment identity, they also change numbers of at least two distinct structures (the *bithorax* mutation, for example, changes both leg and haltere numbers). However, meristic variation is not necessarily homeotic: there is no proper homeosis in British geophilomorph centipedes, since their middle segments vary in number but not in identity (the exception is the rarer example of homeosis affecting the terminal segments; Kettle *et al.*, 1999).

Furthermore, evidence from developmental biology, phylogenetic studies and palaeontology suggest that meristic variation and duplication of homologous structures or modules often *precedes* their differentiation; in other words, whereas meristic variation is primitive, homeosis seems to be a derived feature of the history of many animal lineages (Carroll *et al.*, 2001). For example, instead of 'horizontal' (homeotic) links among wing morphologies of extant flies, butterflies and beetles proposed by mutationists, insect wing diversity is now seen as the result of gradual divergence from a common ancestor bearing two pairs of undifferentiated wings (Carroll *et al.*, 1995).

Phylogenetic analyses have shown that dragonflies, which display two undifferentiated wing pairs, retain the primitive morphology of this common ancestor (Carroll *et al.*, 2001). Despite retaining a primitive undifferentiated pair of wings, the posterior wing pair in dragonflies develops in a segment already regulated by the homeotic gene *Ubx*, a feature also present in the more derived flies, butterflies and beetles. The reason is that *Ubx* is responsible for other functions such as controlling differentiation between the second and third thoracic segments in general (Warren *et al.*, 1994; Carroll *et al.*, 1995).

The fact that the posterior wing pair in all those taxa develops in *Ubx* territory is the key to revealing how distinct wing morphologies evolved. The differentiation of anterior and posterior wings in dipterans, butterflies and beetles occurred under the influence of effector genes under the control of *Ubx*. In other words, selection favoured genes taking a lift on *Ubx* or *Antp*, and causing the gradual differentiation between the originally similar wing pairs. This probably required the origin of new binding sites to *Ubx* and *Antp* in many low-order patterning genes and effector genes (for another gradualist scenario, see Budd, 1999). Thus, the same process of progressive modularisation of effector gene expression that explains the gradual evolution of elongated giraffe necks, asymmetrical claws in crabs, chameleon colours and many other cases of microevolutionary differentiation is also behind the differentiation of a primitive undifferentiated wing pair into the specialised structures found in derived winged insect groups.

Fossil evidence revealed that even the dragonfly body architecture is a relatively derived arthropod body plan. The ancestor to all winged arthropods is now believed to have exhibited a series of similar segments along the A-P axis, produced by repeated duplication events (similar to what is observed in current British centipedes), each one bearing a pair of ventral legs and dorsal appendages (Kukalová-Peck, 1983); in other words, its morphology probably resembled that of a centipede with the addition of dorsal appendages. Dorsal projections are likely to have originally evolved to perform a respiratory function (Carroll *et al.*, 1995), but in the extant winged insects they evolved into wings and appear in no more than two segments.

Thus, the histories of body plan evolution and patterning gene diversification were closely connected in arthropods. Since the control of segment differentiation is a function of *Hox* genes, levels of segment differentiation should correspond to differences in spatial patterning of *Hox* gene expression (Akam, 1998; Gellon and McGinnis, 1998). For example, *Hox* gene expression should display a simpler spatial pattern in crustaceans (in which most A-P segments are fairly similar) than in the highly derived dipterans or butterflies with their highly specialised body segments and appendages. This was demonstrated by studies in the crustacean *Artemia franciscana*, in which *Antp*, *Ubx* and *AbdA* are expressed along most of the A-P axis in approximately the same developmental modules (Averof and Akam, 1995). In dragonflies, which exhibit a differentiation between thoracic segments (which carry wings and legs) and abdominal segments (with no append-ages), one expects *AbdA* (which represses wings and legs in *Drosophila*) to be expressed only in abdominal segments; no data are available to test the prediction. Finally, in flies, butterflies and beetles, which show an even more elaborate differentiation between segments and appendages, the map of *Hox* gene expression is even more intricate, as revealed by the studies cited above.

There is another consequence to the evolution of more derived body plans and differentiated appendages in arthropods: the gradual evolution of homeotic mutations. Based on the conclusions above, mutations in *Ubx* are unlikely to have a homeotic effect on dragonfly wings, since they are not differentiated. But in flies, where *Ubx* speci-fies the development of halteres only in the third thoracic segment, change in segment identity may – and does – occur due to mutations that inactivate *Ubx*. In other words, the homeotic mutations such as those creating the *bithorax* flies are a consequence rather than cause of body plan 'individuation' (Haldane and Huxley, 1927). It is also expected that those mutations become more deleterious, and therefore more difficult to be observed in viable organisms, as serially homolo-gous segments and appendages of a body plan become more differenti-ated. This is the case of homeotic mutations in the number of cervical vertebrae in humans, which are associated with major morphological abnormalities and strongly opposed by selection for causing death before reproduction in almost all cases; this result is consistent with the strong conservation of cervical vertebrae number in all mammals except sloths and manatees (Galis *et al.*, 2006).

As homeotic effects become more likely in body plans display-ing more differentiation and specialisation of segments and append-ages, meristic variation is prevented and body plan architecture tends to 'freeze'; for this reason, variation in segment number is found in natural populations of geophilomorph centipedes but not in flies or but-terflies species. Thus, we may reanalyse the cost of complexity in the context of modular evolution: developmental modularity also means that the adaptive and gradual transformation of a given body plan is much less constrained than implied by Fisher's and Orr's 'universal plei-otropy', and eliminates the need for scenarios of evolutionary saltation between derived body plans – for example between four-winged insects as dipterans. In fact, it shows that such jumps are unlikely to happen.

In summary, the evolution of developmental modularity was crucial to the organisation and evolution of metazoan multicellularity.

It opened the doors to the origin of differentiated segments, organs and other structures; to meristic variation and repeated deployment of structures once they emerged; and finally to further differentiation and specialisation of structures on physiological, morphological and adaptive grounds.

As a final example, the cephalocordate *Amphioxus* may provide an idea of what the ancestral vertebrate looked like (Holland *et al.*, 1992): the lancet presents the same pattern of antero-posterior segmentation and many repeated undifferentiated segments observed in crustaceans, geophilomorph centipedes and snakes (although in the last two groups the presence of many undifferentiated segments is derived). Basal vertebrates such as lampreys still preserve a body plan resembling this pattern, and it would be no surprise if meristic variation were observed in those groups. Meristic variation in fins is still observed in fish species (Angus and Shultz, 1983). Finally, the specialisation of individual vertebrae and vertebral regions in limb-bearing tetrapods has certainly limited meristic variation in vertebrae number (Narita and Kuratani, 2005). If it is true that appendages induce segment specialisation and conservation in antero-posterior segment number, snakes should be an exception to the rule. In fact, snake species are the only group of tetrapods displaying highly variable numbers of vertebrae across species (Cohn and Tickle, 1999), with some species having more than 500 vertebrae (Vonk and Richardson, 2008). Not surprisingly, snakes emulate centipedes and also present *intraspecific* variation in number of vertebrae (Peabody and Brodie, 1975).

THE ORIGIN OF ANIMAL PHYLA

Developmental genetics has also thrown light on a mystery that has intrigued biologists for almost two centuries. Geoffroy Saint-Hilaire proposed that vertebrates and arthropods presented a fairly similar arrangement of structures and tissues along the dorsal-ventral (D-V) axis, namely a linear sequence of extra-embryonic epidermis, body coelom, gut, muscle wall, neural tube and ectodermic epidermis, except for an *inversion* of the axis; in other words, he interpreted chordates as arthropods sitting on their backs. Geoffroy postulated a deep homology of dorso-ventral organisation in the two taxa and claimed that only a hopeful monster (in current terminology, a macromutation) could explain the rare inversion event.

Geoffroy's hypothesis may be discarded on the basis that the structural elements being compared cannot be proven to be homologous (for the same reason nobody suggests an inside-out inversion between the vertebrate endoskeleton and the arthropod exoskeleton). Surprisingly, studies showed that Geoffroy's hypothesis cannot be simply dismissed. It was discovered that not only antero-posterior but also dorso-ventral structures in arthropods and vertebrates are derived from developmental modules controlled by homologous patterning genes. More dramatically, homologous patterning genes display inverted territories along the D-V axis in the two groups, suggesting an actual inversion of the axis (de Robertis and Sasai, 1996).

However, demonstrating the existence of inverted gene expression is not the same as demonstrating a sudden axis inversion (Gerhart, 2000). Formulating an alternative gradual explanation is an equally difficult task, because the two phyla are evolutionarily distant and not much is known about their common bilaterian ancestor. For this reason, comparisons of vertebrates with their closer deuterostome relatives (especially echinoderms, urochordates and cephalochordates) should be more informative.

The cephalochordate *Amphioxus* in particular displays various characteristics in common with the vertebrate body plan and is a good model for the general architecture of their common ancestor (Garcia-Fernández and Holland, 1994). Urochordata (which include ascidians and sea squirts) on the other hand are highly distinctive (Stach *et al.*, 2008). They are classified as chordates on the basis of similarities during the larval stage, which presents chordate defining characteristics such as dorsal notochord and neural tube. But adults drastically depart this pattern and as a rule do not display bilateral symmetry (Swalla *et al.*, 1999). Ascidians adopted a sessile lifestyle based on filtering, so that the larval mouth attaches to a substrate before metamorphosis takes place; as a result, the D-V axis cannot be clearly identified in the adult. Finally, echinoderms (which include sea urchins and starfish) are also known to relate to chordates due to similarities at larval stages but adults also depart from bilateral symmetry and in this case adopt a pentameric or fivefold radial pattern, and no proper dorso-ventral axis can be identified (Peterson *et al.*, 2000).

The conclusion is that instead of one sudden episode of inversion, the D-V axis may have not existed at some point of the chordate lineage; an absent D-V axis characterises two of the three deuterostome groups described above. The three deuterostome groups also exhibit *Hox* gene clusters, but in echinoderms *Hox* genes are only expressed after the larval stages (Lowe and Wray, 1997; Martinez *et al.*, 1999) and play a role different from the absent A-P axis organisation. For similar reasons, it is possible that the inverted D-V axis in vertebrates relative to arthropods was derived from an ancestor where the axis, but not the D-V molecular machinery shared with arthropods, was already absent (Gerhart, 2000; Matus *et al.*, 2006). Thus, a combination of phylogenetic analysis and developmental genetics suggests a scenario where a radical body plan reorganisation occurs gradually rather than by a sudden mutational jump.

THE CHALLENGE OF MULTICELLULARITY

The discovery of patterning genes, *cis*-regulatory regions and developmental modularity opened a window to a clearer understanding of how animal body plans evolve and are moulded by selection. Although the existence of a regulatory dimension in the genome (Davidson and Erwin, 2006) has changed our views on biological information, changes in regulation are not the only or predominant basis for evolution as implied by King and Wilson's expressionist hypothesis. Patterning mechanisms are relevant for catalysing and facilitating evolutionary change, beginning with the very microstructure of the gene: developmental regulation led to the co-evolution of transcription factors coded by patterning genes on the one hand and of *cis*-regulatory regions and coding sequences of countless effector genes on the other; this implies the co-evolution of the genetic code and developmental code, and of developmental recipe and ingredients. This means that the evolution of multicellularity and its dependence on the developmental information did not imply that genetic information lost importance; on the contrary, multicellularity demonstrates that more complex organisms require the simultaneous contribution and joint evolution of multiple levels of biological information.

Developmental genetics has also made a fundamental contribution to microevolutionary theory by showing how developmental modularity helps in overcoming the cost of complexity implied in Fisher and Orr's concept of universal pleiotropy (Stern, 2000). Modularity has facilitated the evolution of new genes and proteins on the basis of their potential effect on a single structure (wing or eye genes) or cell type (brain cell or liver cell genes). Thus, the possibility of gradual evolution in animals cannot be easily derived from particulate inheritance (or genetic modularity) alone; it is more clearly understood as a consequence of both genetic and developmental modularity.

At the macroevolutionary level, patterning mechanisms have revealed how the origin of extant animal body plans may have taken place without need for hopeful monsters (Akam, 1998). The derived animal architectures found in flies and butterflies, for example, seem to have evolved not from each other by major homeotic rearrangements, but from ancestors displaying less differentiated modules and weaker selection against meristic variation. It was the subsequent moulding of modular body plans that gradually led to the freezing of animal body plans and selective resistance to sudden structural change, and to the deleterious character of homeotic mutations observed in vertebrates and arthropods. Thus, the important role of changes in regulatory mechanisms do not mean, as potentially implied by the expressionist argument, that changes in ingredient genes are less relevant; it implies that macromutations are essentially unnecessary, and that the evolution of ingredients has extensively accompanied the evolution of derived body plans and disposable somatic cells.

Finally, patterning mechanisms and developmental modularity provide key hints to the evolution of animal multicellularity itself. Multicellularity is ultimately an extension of the Principle of Order; from an original distinction between genotype and phenotype (or informational genes and functional proteins) that emerged with the DNA World, multicellularity evolved as a new form of phenotypic order (the soma or modular whole consisting of disposable somatic cells) derived from a new form of microscopic order (the developmental order mediated via informational proteins or transcription factors and cis-regulatory regions). Gene regulation via interacting transcription factors and cis-regulatory regions had their precursors in direct regulation by molecules present in the environment and simpler feedback mechanisms (such as the lac operon in E. coli), and then evolved towards regulation by molecules coded by organisms themselves: patterning genes and their products. Those products, the transcription factors, represented a fundamental evolutionary innovation: they are proteins that have no enzymatic or structural function and serve the sole purpose of connecting genes into networks of information.

Developmental modularity therefore rests on the pillars set by genetic modularity; genetic inheritance is fragmented into independent genes, and genes themselves present modular cis-regulatory regions carrying binding sites able to arise, disappear and independently evolve (Carroll et al., 2001). It is important to notice that mechanisms of RNA interference do not invalidate the argument; regulatory RNA molecules act side by side with protein regulators, and since genes coding for regulatory RNAs must be stored in DNA molecules, they may be regulated via *cis*-regulatory regions and transcription factors like other genes (Holbert, 2008).

In the following chapter, further consequences of the distinction between somatic and germline cells to the life cycle are discussed: especially, the processes of ageing and death that characterise multicellular organisms are shown to have evolved as the ultimate expression of somatic disposability.

4

Life cycle evolution: life and death of the soma

The hypothesis of natural selection presented by Darwin in the *Origin of Species* offered a new solution to old mysteries such as adaptation and the origin of species and also offered breakthrough analyses of new mysteries such as male ornamentation and facial expressions in animals. It is surprising that Darwin, aware of the far-reaching consequences of natural selection, has thoroughly neglected a virtually universal feature of life: the inevitability of senescence and 'natural' death. The silence about the topic in Darwin's writings is even more unexpected as we realise that ageing satisfies all conditions for evolutionary treatment. Senescence and death can be estimated both at the individual and population level through life tables, and measured in its physical or behavioural aspects (Stearns, 1992; Austad, 1993). Rates of ageing and individual longevity within species are influenced by genes and are partially inheritable, which means they are potential targets of selection (Korpelainen, 2000). Longevity is also highly variable across species (Carey and Judge, 2002); many of us are aware of the differences between longer-lived (cockatoos, elephants, humans) and shorter-lived species (warblers, mice, fruit flies). Finally, longevity is likely to affect fitness for obvious reasons: other things being equal, longer-lived individuals in a population are expected to leave more descendants (Stearns, 1992). If other inheritable traits affecting fitness such as body size, shape or behaviour have evolved by natural selection, longevity should be no exception.

Perhaps the reason for Darwin's neglect is the difficulty of considering death or senescence as adaptive and a product of natural selection in any palpable sense; after all, death is the final defeat in the struggle for survival. From this perspective, all we should know about ageing and death is that organisms are expected to evolve features to avoid or postpone them at any costs. However, species have failed to extend life indefinitely and are all mortal (although exceptions are possible in theory and perhaps even in nature, with ageing in bacteria being a particularly controversial issue; see Rose, 1991 and Stephens, 2005). Why has natural selection apparently failed to avoid senescence and natural death in almost all species?

A first step towards the answer is to understand that there is more to biological ageing than wear and tear, and more to death than ultimate damage caused by extrinsic factors. Twenty-first-century humans, for example, have managed to create safe, almost disease-free environments in which life of some individuals is everything but a struggle for survival, and yet death inevitably happens. Of the healthiest 100-year-old human beings living in Western societies, one third has a likelihood of dying before turning 101, and the likelihood of any of us surviving to age 140 is now still close to zero despite observed increases in life expectancy. The same is true for other animals as life in captivity rarely doubles the maximum longevity of a species in the wild (Carey and Judge, 2002).

Death and senescence are inevitable because they seem to follow not only from accidents but also from 'natural causes' or intrinsic functional decay. Intrinsic or biological decay increases the likelihood of accidental death itself to occur: for example, diseases or infections that organisms can easily fend off at earlier ages become lethal at old age because of immunosenescence, or ageing of the immune system (Ginaldi *et al.*, 2001; Palacios *et al.*, 2007). In summary, the deleterious changes associated with senescence at old age seem to be as natural and important as the developmental changes that occur early in the life cycle. This suggests that genes may store not only the information guiding development from a fertilised egg to an adult organism, but may be responsible for the changes that make death more likely with increasing age. The fact that genes are behind the adaptations that help us in the struggle for survival, and at the same time seem to set us up for natural death, defines the evolutionary paradox of ageing.

Based on the original insights of Weismann, the evolutionary theory of senescence built step by step by Fisher, Medawar, Williams, Hamilton, Kirkwood and others is seen as a solution to the paradox of natural death. Understanding the theory requires a change of perspective: while senescence explains the inevitability of death in development, in evolution it is the inevitability of death that explains senescence. Life history theory (Harvey and Nee, 1991; Stearns, 1992; Charnov, 1993) has extended evolutionary theory of senescence to the understanding of other key landmarks of animal life cycles such as birth, weaning, sexual maturity and menopause in animals (Harvey and Purvis, 1999; Hawkes and Paine, 2006). Together, the evolutionary theory of senescence and life history theory provide an explanation for why natural selection produced organisms that inevitably age and die, despite the apparent advantages of eternal youth.

Finally, natural death is a product of evolution in an even more fundamental sense. Ageing and natural death in animals are intrinsically linked to the evolution of animal multicellularity, since they are the physiological expression of the somatic disposability. The origin of disposable multicellular phenotypes had another important consequence: the origin of a new evolutionary law, namely that the power of natural selection decreases with individual age.

WEISMANN'S TWO INSIGHTS

The starting point of the evolutionary theory of senescence was August Weismann's (1889) remarks on the division of labour between somatic cells and germline cells in multicellular organisms. Weismann's argument can be better understood if a parallel is drawn to another key principle in biology, the 'central dogma of molecular biology' proposed by Crick (1970). The central dogma postulates a one-way flow of information in biological entities: information can only flow from DNA, through an RNA intermediate, to proteins. The fundamental dogma elucidates the distinction between genotype and phenotype at the molecular level, and is therefore a mechanistic rather than evolutionary principle.

Weismann's contribution was to propose that the germline versus soma distinction implies that the functional part of multicellular organisms (the soma, or different cell types, tissues and organs) is meant to die, so that another part (our germ cells and gametes) may replicate and survive across generations. Somatic cells were therefore an evolutionary extension of proteins: they evolved as purely functional units of the multicellular whole, and like proteins, may be as a rule continuously replaced by new ones. Germline cells are in contrast the eternal link between generations (Surani, 2007). For this reason, only mutations occurring in the germ cells can be transferred to descendants; mutations in somatic cells such as those causing cancer do not go beyond the individual and the generation in which they occur.

Weismann correctly grasped the mechanistic distinction between informational germ cells and functional somatic cells, but there is a crucial difference between the germline versus soma theory and the central dogma. In addition to the division of labour between DNA and protein, in multicellular organisms one finds a further division of labour among DNA molecules themselves: whereas the DNA molecules carried by germline cells store information required for reproduction, most DNA molecules are present in somatic cells. Despite being informational entities, somatic DNA is relegated to the same disposable and purely functional role of proteins and somatic cells. Thus, whereas disposable proteins cannot produce further copies of themselves, somatic cells (either differentiated cells such as skin cells or brain cells, or the stem cells that give rise to the former) carry their own DNA hard copy and can in principle rebuild themselves, replace proteins with new ones, and produce new copies typically by mitosis (cell cloning) during the whole life cycle or at least during development.

The fact that somatic cells are disposable despite carrying DNA leads to a question: if a soma can continuously generate new somatic cells and rejuvenate itself, why do organisms die? Is it not expected that an organism that constantly replaces cells in the skin, muscles, liver or brain before organs show any sign of ageing can be an everlasting or potentially eternal source of gametes, and therefore fitter than any mortal competitor?

According to Weismann, the reason for senescence and natural death in multicellular organisms was selection against old individuals. To understand his argument, consider a population with ages ranging from newborn to 'old'. Natural selection is in action, so that all individuals compete against each other for survival; this includes competition between the young and the old. According to Weismann, the victory of the old in the struggle for survival would be a tragedy for the species, since it would mean diverting resources away from potentially more fertile individuals (the young) towards the less vigorous (the old). That would bring about an obvious cost to the group in terms of total offspring number and fitness. Weismann argued that senescence and natural death evolved as adaptations that eliminate the old, clearing the way for the youngest generations; the younger can do a much better job at successfully reproducing and transmitting genes into a new generation than senile individuals. Thus, for Weismann natural death occurs as a form of deliberate genetic homicide and implies the existence of 'killer' genes that specifically eliminate the selfish elderly who want to perpetuate themselves.

Weismann's argument was shown to be wrong (Medawar, 1952). Firstly, the argument appeals to group selection: it proposes that specific old-age killer genes would evolve due to a hypothetical advantage to the group, despite being unfavourable to (old) individuals. But as previously seen, there are more individuals than groups, and since the individual life cycle is faster than group cycles, natural selection operating on individuals is generally more effective (Williams, 1966). For this reason, even if Weismann were correct and old individuals were a liability to populations, selection would not necessarily lead to the evolution of senescence and natural death via killer genes. Secondly, Weismann's logic was intrinsically circular: it tries to explain senescence and natural death by characterising the old as being less fit than the young, and therefore assumes as a starting point what it is trying to explain.

In summary, Weismann's two insights contributed in important but distinct ways to the development of evolutionary theory. The first (the germline versus soma distinction) ranks alongside Crick's central dogma of biology as one of the crucial axioms of biology. The second insight (that senescence is the product of natural selection), although incorrectly explained by Weismann, inspired evolutionary biologists to find better explanations for ageing and natural death.

FISHER'S SECOND FUNDAMENTAL PRINCIPLE

It took over 30 years until the first solid argument for natural death based on individual selection was formulated by Fisher (1930) in his *Genetical Theory of Natural Selection*. The breakthrough was his definition of fitness as a measure of the total or overall reproductive success of an individual during its life, a variable currently known as 'lifetime reproductive success' (Stearns, 1992); it is therefore a sum over the whole individual life cycle.

At any given point of the individual life cycle, a fraction of the reproductive output has already been expressed as past reproduction, while a remaining fraction is yet to occur as future reproduction. The fraction of reproduction expected from an individual in the future was defined by Fisher as its 'reproductive value' at that age, and is the key variable to his argument. For example, the reproductive value of an individual at the start of sexual maturation must be relatively high since all its reproduction is yet to happen, while the reproductive value of a postmenopausal woman on the other hand is nil; reproductive value thus decreases as individuals approach the end of their life cycle.

From the idea of age-dependent reproductive value, Fisher made a crucial statement about adaptive evolution by arguing that the power of natural selection to distinguish between fit and unfit must also vary with age. The argument is clear if we use the language of allele competition. Suppose the existence of a wild-type or common allele at a given locus, and the occurrence of a new lethal mutant allele that when expressed causes immediate death. Let us assume that this mutant allele is expressed soon after birth. In this case, since the lethal mutation kills all its carriers at an early age *before* they reproduce, it simply cannot make it to a second generation: by killing an organism before its reproduction occurs, the mutation is virtually committing suicide. For this reason, selection will strongly oppose the spread of any lethal mutant that is expressed at early stages of the life cycle, when all of or most reproduction is still expected to occur (i.e. when reproductive value is high).

Now let us assume the occurrence of the same lethal gene, with one single difference: it only manifests its deadly effect at older age, when most reproduction has already occurred (i.e. when reproductive value is low). In this case, individuals carrying the mutation may still have their fitness lowered since death interrupts reproduction. But the fact is that selection acts too late in this case. Since most of individual reproduction has already taken place, copies of the lethal mutation make it to the next generation before it kills its original carriers. Humans provide an extreme example of this process: in the case of a mutation that only manifests its lethal effect in women over the age of 50 (i.e. after menopause in most women), there is virtually no difference in reproduction between a carrier and a non-carrier of the lethal mutation. Since death occurs after the end of reproduction (i.e. when reproductive value is zero), the lethal mutation replicates as successfully as the wild-type allele.

The conclusion is that the same lethal mutation may be strongly opposed in one case, and pass totally unnoticed by selection in another, purely as a function of its early or late timing; specifically, the power of selection to eliminate lethal or deleterious mutations decreases with individual age and reproductive value. This statement was a second fundamental contribution of Fisher to evolutionary theory. Based on that, Fisher derived a relationship of far-reaching consequences between the decrease with age in reproductive value, and the increased risk of death (senescence):

> It is probably not without significance that the death rate in Man takes a course generally inverse to the curve of reproductive value (Fisher, 1930: 29).

The evidence for this relationship has since then been observed in many species: as a rule, life tables show that mortality rates do

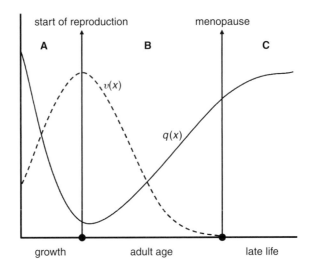

Figure 4.1 Schematic representation of life cycle stages in women. Horizontal axis represents age; vertical axis is a generic continuous scale. (Area A) After birth, reproductive value or $v(x)$ (dashed curve) increases continuously, reaching a maximum when reproduction begins; mortality rates or $q(x)$ (solid curve) decrease to a minimum due to parental care and increasing body size. (B) During adult age or reproductive life, reproductive values decrease and mortality rates increase; the power of natural selection decreases and senescence takes place. (C) After menopause, reproductive value and strength of selection are zero, and mortality rates stop rising; the 'rate of ageing' stabilises, although at high values.

increase after reproduction starts, whereas fertility rates and reproductive value decrease. The picture is more intricate, however: mortality rates both *before* and *after* the reproductive phase in many species need special explanation (Figure 4.1). For the sake of his argument, Fisher focused on the reproductive period and relied on data for post-industrial Australian women from the early twentieth century. Although the data are far from ideal for evolutionary studies (due to cultural and technological influences on mortality, fertility and reproductive value in Westernised societies), they clearly showed that from the moment human reproduction begins and reproductive value begins to decrease, mortality rates and the likelihood of natural death for each individual starts to increase; other studies have confirmed the relationship also in traditional human societies (Weiss, 1973; Hill and Hurtado, 1996; Migliano *et al.*, 2007).

What is then the reason for senescence? The decrease in reproductive value means that old age contributes relatively less to the total lifetime reproductive output of an individual. Old age, being less relevant for fitness, must therefore be overlooked by selection; and so will be deleterious mutations that are expressed late. The consequence is the accumulation of deleterious genetic effects late in the life cycle, causing an overall reduction in 'health' and 'vigour' that we associate with senescence, and ultimately with natural death.

Although Fisher proposed that senescence is progressive and genetically determined, his argument does not require the existence of killer genes implicit in Weismann's argument. Senescence and natural death would instead be caused by multiple deleterious genes expressed at later ages, rather than by genes specifically evolved to eliminate the elderly. In other words, ageing occurs because the power of natural selection decreases with age, both to eliminate deleterious genes and to fixate favourable ones.

Unfortunately, Fisher's argument also presents the problem of circularity. He postulated more than a link between reproductive value and mortality: he also proposed the former as the cause of the latter. In other words, mortality (which reflects senescence and the likelihood of natural death) increases with age *because* reproductive value decreases, and not the other way round. But why is there a decline in reproductive value with individual age in the first place? Reproductive value must certainly decrease with age in an organism that is finite (i.e. where natural death is present) and where physiological measures including fertility decay with age (i.e. where senescence is present); but why life cycles are limited and senescence occurs were the original questions posed by Fisher. In summary, whereas the correlation between reproductive value and ageing represented a fundamental advance to the evolutionary theory of senescence, the causal link between them remained beyond Fisher's grasp.

MEDAWAR AND ACCIDENTAL DEATH

A first successful explanation for the cause of genetically determined senescence and natural death was proposed by Medawar (1952). The starting point of his argument was the distinction between accidental and natural death. Medawar was aware that the two concepts are difficult to distinguish in practice; as pointed out above, cases of natural death are likely to involve an interaction with accidental factors.

In order to disentangle the two factors, Medawar proposed a thought experiment with a population of eternal test tubes that neither 'age' nor 'die'. The example works equally well for a hypothetical population of non-ageing and immortal humans. Although the eternal test tubes or immortal humans are not affected by natural death, they are still exposed to external causes of destruction or death: collisions or falls in the case of test tubes, predation, wars or infectious disease in the case of immortal humans. To add numbers to the experiment, let us suppose that the rate of accidental destruction of test tubes or accidental death in humans is 1% per year. This means that after 20 years, only 82% of them still exist, 37% after 100 years, and only 1% after 458 years – despite the fact that the surviving tubes do not look old but exactly like brand new ones.

It was the appeal to the effect of accidental death rates that allowed Medawar to avoid the circularity of Fisher's argument. Although a 20-year old, a 100-year old and a 458-year old immortal human are similar regarding vigour and health, accidental death still poses a limit to individual lifespans, and still causes a reduction in reproductive value with age. Accidental death is therefore the ultimate and evolutionary reason for the decrease in the power of natural selection with age. For Medawar, this is what causes the moulding of genetically determined ageing and natural death.

To understand how, let us now assume that a deleterious mutation occurs and spreads in our population of immortal humans, which has the same rate of accidental death of 1% per year. If the mutation expresses its deleterious effect at age 20, it affects the reproductive performance of 82% of all individuals carrying it; 18% will be already dead before age 20 from accidental causes. The fraction of 82% is certainly a fraction large enough for selection to penalise its carriers and prevent further spread of the mutation.

However, if the same mutation expresses its deleterious effect at age 458, only 1% of its carriers will survive to pay the price: most of life and reproduction has already occurred, and 99% of its carriers will not be affected by the deleterious effects. The mutation thus causes a small effect on fitness when expressed at an age when individuals are already dead for accidental reasons; as a result, carriers and non-carriers will exhibit very similar fitness, and selection may not be strong enough to eliminate the deleterious mutation from the gene pool. The same is true for an advantageous mutation: it will not be strongly favoured if it occurs too late due to its low effect on fitness, and may be lost by genetic drift.

How does the decrease in the power of selection explain the evolution of senescence? Medawar clarified the process by considering different alleles of the same gene, producing the same deleterious effect but differing in the timing of its expression. Let us consider a human population where various individuals carry different alleles and therefore manifest the deleterious effect at different ages; for example, let us assume a normal distribution with a mean onset age at 40 years. It is clear that individuals expressing the deleterious effect earlier than average (say at age 38) pay a higher price than those that express them later (say at age 42), since a larger fraction of their reproductive life will be impaired. Selection will be stronger against alleles causing earlier onset, and as a result the mean age at expression of effects moves beyond 40 years; Medawar named that process 'gene recession'. The opposite effect ('gene precession') is expected in the case of favourable mutations: the same fitness-increasing mutation is more favourable when expressed earlier, and selection will favour an increase in frequency of alleles with early expression.

In principle, gene recession and precession may occur in all genes. As a result, as individual age increases we expect a reduction in the frequency of fitness-enhancing genetic effects, and an increase in frequency of deleterious effects. There is no circularity in Medawar's rationale: populations face externally imposed mortality curves; those external factors are the cause of a finite lifespan and of necessarily declining reproductive values with age; selection expedites the effects of favourable alleles and delays the onset of deleterious alleles; senescence evolves due to the accumulation of deleterious or lethal effects of genes late in life, meaning that the population gains a genetically determined mortality curve that mimics the effect of external mortality rates; as a result, senescence and natural death persist even if external or accidental mortality is eliminated.

Senescence and natural death are genetic processes, but they are not adaptations: they are a consequence of the decrease in the power of selection with age, and of its power to eliminate deleterious mutations expressed at ages when individuals are likely to be dead due to chance factors.

WILLIAMS AND THE LOGIC OF TRADE-OFFS

Medawar's concepts of gene recession and precession have other important consequences. Let us consider the human genome consisting of over 25 000 genes. Any alleles at these loci may potentially present variation in timing of expression, and for this reason they may be subject to selection for gene recession and precession. There is, however, a basic difference between the two processes. First take gene precession: given two mutations with the same fitness-increasing effect but differing in timing, selection is expected to favour the allele with the earliest expression. Now take gene recession: given two deleterious alleles, we expect stronger selection against the 'early' allele, and a possible survival of the 'late' allele due to the weakness of selection to eliminate it. However, there is an alternative to gene recession: the complete loss of the locus (i.e. the silencing or deletion of the gene), since eliminating both deleterious alleles is better than choosing the least deleterious one. If elimination of gene loci makes theoretical sense, why are genes causing diseases such as cancer (Greenman *et al.*, 2007), diabetes (Zeggini *et al.*, 2008) and other typically late-life diseases still present in the genome of humans and other animal species?

A first answer is that 'bad' alleles entered the genome because they were once advantageous, and then became deleterious due to evolutionary changes in other genes (the genetic background). In this case, one would expect those alleles eventually to undergo gene recession or deletion. The presence of alleles with late deleterious effects is therefore explained by Medawar's logic: they are only present because selection is weak at later ages and takes longer to act.

A second answer, originally proposed by Medawar (1952) but championed by Williams (1957), is *temporal* and *antagonistic* pleiotropy. As seen earlier, spatial pleiotropy means that genes may have different effects in different modules or cells; temporal pleiotropy occurs when multiple effects occur at different stages of the life cycle. For example, insulin-like growth factors (IGF) in mammals control the differentiation of neural cells early in embryonic development (Taupin, 2006), affect birth weight and regulate post-natal body growth (Stratikopoulos *et al.*, 2008). Antagonistic pleiotropy occurs when some of the phenotypic effects of a gene are deleterious while others are favourable; the same IGF alleles that stimulate cell proliferation and are required for normal growth are also risk factors for diabetes and cancer in adult life (Lindsay *et al.*, 2003; Canzian *et al.*, 2006).

Williams argued that when an allele with temporally antagonistic effects occurs, 'natural selection may be said to be biased in favour of youth over old age whenever a conflict of interest arises'. The antagonistic pleiotropy theory therefore proposed a different explanation for the evolution of senescence: it implies that alleles with late deleterious effects exist because of their early advantageous effects – not because of the weakness of selection to eliminate them. The hypothesis also explains why gene loci are not eliminated altogether: they are maintained because alleles are supposed to have early advantageous effects.

It should be remembered that pleiotropy is a genetic property that may evolve itself (Cheverud, 1996; Wagner *et al.*, 2008). If an allele produces both positive and deleterious phenotypes with different timings, it may be under selection to undergo *both* precession (of the positive effects) and recession (of the deleterious ones). In this case, selection would be able to maximise positive effects and minimise the deleterious ones, and therefore oppose antagonistic pleiotropy. But senescence would still evolve due to an accumulation of deleterious late effects of alleles; the only difference is that those alleles originally had strongly pleiotropic effects, and Williams' theory becomes just a special case of Medawar's. However, if antagonistic pleiotropy *cannot* be modulated by selection, then organisms are forced to live with deleterious effects of alleles if the positive effects are strong enough. This means that Williams' model is an explanation of senescence relying on the existence of pleiotropy as a genetic constraint to selection.

Recent studies have compared the two theories, and evidence seems to favour the mutation accumulation hypothesis of Medawar (Hughes *et al.*, 2002; Keller *et al.*, 2008). Although evidence points against pleiotropy as a genetic link between early vigour and senescence, the case for a *selective* link or 'fitness trade-off' is much stronger (Stearns, 1992; Barnes and Partridge, 2003). For example, species enjoying the advantage of earlier reproduction pay the price of faster senescence and death (Kirkwood and Rose, 1991); species that gain from higher fertility pay the price of higher offspring mortality (Charnov and Ernest, 2006; Gillespie *et al.*, 2008); species and individuals that grow larger to take advantage of higher survivorship and mating success pay the price of delaying their first reproduction (Charnov, 1993); and so on. However, although trade-offs do have a genetic basis (Pettay *et al.*, 2005), they do not necessarily depend on pleiotropic genes (Zera and Harshman, 2001). Williams' main contribution to the evolutionary theory of senescence was not antagonistic pleiotropy, but the idea that natural selection is often forced to strike a balance or compromise between opposite functions such as reproduction, growth or body maintenance; as seen below, not only the senescence phase but the whole life cycle in animals evolve as the result of those trade-offs.

The rationale developed by Fisher, Medawar and Williams showed that the inevitability of accidental death must cause a decrease in reproductive value with age, and therefore the evolution of genetically determined senescence and natural death. However, there is still a problem with the argument. It is true that external mortality and the inevitability of death imply that reproductive value decreases every day an organism lives: the more you live, the less there is still to be lived, and less future reproduction is expected from you. Thus, if reproductive value continuously decreases with age, selection should get continuously weaker, and mortality rates should constantly *increase* with age.

Intriguingly, this is not what always happens. Take the mortality curve of humans and other species such as lions or baboons: instead of showing continuous increase, those curves are typically U-shaped with equally high rates of mortality *before* reproduction starts. A first ad hoc explanation by Medawar (1952) was that 'there are clearly special reasons why baby animals should be more vulnerable' and therefore excluded the pre-adult stage from his model. Before that, Fisher (1930) believed that there was no need for special reasons. His argument was that mortality rates are U-shaped because reproductive value peaks at the point where sexual maturity occurs. In other words, reproductive value *increases* from birth to sexual maturation, and then decreases with age.

To understand Fisher's argument, consider two girls aged 4 and 14; let us also assume that sexual maturity occurs on average at age 15 in this human population. Since they are both pre-adult, all their reproduction is yet to occur. But according to Fisher, the 14-year-old girl has a higher reproductive value, because it is only one year away from sexual maturation and potential reproduction. The risk that she will not reach maturity is only the mortality rate between ages 14 and 15. In the case of the 4-year-old, the risk of death before the start of reproduction is much higher, and includes not only the risk of death between ages 14 and 15, but also between ages 4 and 14.

Fisher's argument is, however, incorrect. Younger pre-adult individuals are indeed less likely to reach maturity than older ones, but that is only because we are dealing with cumulative probability. Each one of us is more likely to survive for one year than for another two years, but this is true whether mortality rates increase or decrease from year one to two. For the same reason, a person who pays a given tax for two consecutive years necessarily pays more than another who does it for the first year only, independently from the tax rates in year one and two. Thus, the likelihood of surviving from age 14 to sexual maturation must be higher than the likelihood of surviving from age 4 to sexual maturation (which involves surviving from age 4 to 14 *and* from age 14 to sexual maturation); this would be true under the observed condition of decreasing mortality rates in humans, or with hypothetically increasing or constant rates. Thus, although Fisher's explanation is compatible with U-shaped mortality curves, it cannot explain why mortality rates decrease from birth to sexual maturity in species such as humans.

Hamilton (1966) was one of the first authors to argue that the initial falling stage of U-shaped mortality curves could not be explained by the principle of decreasing power of selection with age. We know that natural selection strongly opposes a lethal mutation affecting 30-year-old women (who can still reproduce), but weakly opposes lethal mutations affecting post-menopausal women aged 50 or over (who have already ceased reproduction). However, if the comparison only includes pre-reproductive individuals, age *does not* matter. If a lethal mutation kills female humans at birth, at age 14, or one day before sexual maturation occurs, the result is the same: they were all killed before reproduction, and no copy is transmitted to the next generation. Therefore, the power of selection to eliminate deleterious mutations is highest at *any* point before reproduction, and mortality should therefore be at their lowest point throughout the period.

What then is the explanation for high but decreasing death rates between birth and the start of reproduction in some species? Hamilton realised that the problem could be solved with a double change in perspective: from senescence theory to *social* theory, and from offspring fitness to *parental* fitness. We know that a lethal mutation has maximal deleterious effects on its carrier at any point before reproduction, but what is the effect on the fitness of the parental generation? If a lethal mutation kills offspring before they reach sexual maturation, the investment in reproduction is lost. But if in addition to their genes mothers and fathers also dispense parental care between fertilisation and sexual maturation, the timing of expression of lethal or deleterious mutations becomes relevant.

To see why, suppose there is a lethal gene that kills a human baby at birth; in this case, the mother wastes all the reproductive investment made during pregnancy. Now, take a second mutation that kills the offspring at age 15: in this case, the mother wastes the investment during pregnancy, all investment in lactation up to weaning, and all investment between weaning and age 15. It is clear that the latter alternative is the worst possible scenario: although both mothers lose their offspring, selection is expected to favour a mother that actively expedites the lethal effect and terminates pregnancy earlier, so as to minimise the investment loss and to proceed more quickly to a new pregnancy.

Hamilton's explanation is that selection should favour the evolution of 'alarm' mechanisms able to sense problems or handicaps in offspring, and to induce early discarding of developing offspring at any sign of trouble. For this reason, the high mortality rates of pre-reproductive offspring cannot be explained by deleterious genes of the Fisher–Medawar–Williams type, which persist due to the weakness of selection to eliminate them; on the contrary, selection on the offspring is strong enough to oppose deleterious mutations in pre-reproductive individuals. Instead, the death of pre-reproductive individuals must be caused by killer genes of the Weismannian type, which evolved as a defence against the waste of *parental* reproductive effort. But instead of old age assassins, Hamilton proposed the existence of baby killer genes.

In summary, species with high levels of parental care such as social mammals and monogamous birds are expected to exhibit U-shaped mortality curves: in the case of viviparous species, mortality should be high during pregnancy and at the beginning of life due to the interest of parents in discarding potentially unfit offspring, and higher again at the end of life due to the accumulation of deleterious mutations with late onset. Mortality rates are at their lowest around the age at which reproduction starts, because organisms are too old (or close to the start of reproduction) for offspring rejection to be advantageous for their parents, and because they are too young for senescence to have started.

Hamilton's hypothesis also implies that the higher the level of parental investment observed in a species, the more 'demanding' parents should be, and the higher the pre-adult mortality rates should be. This would explain why child mortality rates are so high in species such as humans, and why more than half of all human pregnancies end up as miscarriages (with upper estimates reaching 78%; Roberts and Lowe, 1975; Forbes, 1997). The hypothesis also implies that the more parents have to lose (i.e. the highest the level of parental investment), the earlier the mechanisms of offspring rejection should be operating; it is not surprising that most human miscarriages occur at embryonic phases before pregnancy is even detected.

The strategy of giving up on a potentially problematic offspring is only valid if parents have the option of conceiving 'better' offspring; otherwise, it is still better to keep the offspring that is potentially available. Two main ways of achieving this aim are offspring competition (Mayhew and Glaizot, 2001) and offspring replacement (Forbes *et al.*, 1997). In offspring competition, litter or clutch sizes are larger than the optimum (the value that maximises offspring survivorship), which leads to increased competition between siblings and to the survival of the fittest offspring. In offspring replacement, additional or marginal offspring are not even able to compete with the chosen ones; they are mere back-ups that only survive if the core offspring die and need replacement. In either case, Hamilton's conclusion was that 'mother nature never remotely intended all of her embryos conceived to be born, not even intended that all human babies should be raised' (Hamilton, 1996: 90).

In summary, there should be two very distinct forms of natural death: one is senescence and the accumulation of deleterious effects late in ontogeny, and the second is the early death of potentially unfit and disposable descendants in the interest of parents. The seemingly paradoxical consequence of Hamilton's argument is that species in which parents may conceive offspring only to let them die are those that we associate with good parenting – those species that provide higher levels of parental care. In the particular case of *Homo sapiens* and having in mind the rate of over 50% of embryo disposal in our species, Hamilton's explanation implies that human mothers with their extended pregnancies and sophisticated mechanisms of parental care are at the same time the best and the worst in nature. This is a consequence of investing too much in a given offspring: you have too much to lose if things do not go as planned.

GROWTH AND FITNESS

A consequence of Hamilton's explanation is that gradually decreasing mortality rates in pre-adults should only be observed in combination with parental care. In the absence of parental mechanisms evolved to interrupt the development of potentially problematic offspring, the power of natural selection on offspring survival should keep mortality rates at their lowest values at any point before the start of reproduction. However, Hamilton's hypothesis is convoluted and involves interpreting parental investment as a cause of high offspring mortality, besides assuming the existence of killer genes targeting their own carriers (as they are shared by parents and offspring).

An alternative explanation to early decreases in mortality can be outlined if attention is given to a property of life cycles that, despite being conspicuous, is neglected by Hamilton's argument: namely that the period between conception and reproduction is also the period required for adult size and shape to be attained; in other words, the process of pre-adult mortality decrease coincides with growth and development – and as argued by authors such as Kaplan and Robson (2009), that must be more than coincidence. First, growth certainly evolved in connection with its end result – adult size and all its implications for reproductive success. Adult size affects adult survival; this may, for example, cause an arms race or escalation in body size of predators relative to their prey (Reynolds and Reynolds, 1977; West et al., 1991; Vermeij, 1994). Body size also has direct effects on reproductive success, and explains the large size of dominant males among elephant seals, gorillas and other species (Andersson and Iwasa, 1996). Body size may also affect female reproduction due to its positive correlation with fertility and with levels of metabolic energy that can be potentially invested in offspring (Charnov, 1993). Larger size also involves costs (the most obvious being higher absolute maintenance costs; West et al., 2001), and a balance is achieved, as discussed later.

It is also clear that growth during the pre-reproductive phase may reduce mortality rates of developing offspring. The reasons are not very different from factors operating in adults: growing offspring may become less susceptible to predation, infection, or to accidental death in general. The possibility that rates of accidental death may be influenced by growth and developmental stage was not taken into account by Medawar when he presented his fictional race of eternal test tubes. In fact, his 'eternals' differ from real organisms not only by avoiding senescence; as importantly, they do not grow or develop. If eternal glass test tubes were born small, thin and fragile, and took a year to grow to their final size and thickness, external mortality rates would probably decrease during development as they do in real organisms. In other words, mortality would reach a lowest point at the start of maturity not because it represents the beginning of reproduction as assumed by Fisher, Medawar, Williams and Hamilton, but because it is the end of growth and development.

Distinct from Hamilton's hypothesis, the argument above should not hold only for species with parental investment: if growing from birth size to a larger adult size is advantageous, individuals should invest available energy into growing from newborn size to a given adult size. The existence of parental care itself may contribute to the process of growth: parents may be interested in reducing mortality rates of offspring and to help offspring grow fast and attain a larger adult size. They may be expected to invest in offspring growth, thereby reducing mortality rates during the pre-reproductive phase. This idea is expressed in recent models that attempt to explain U-shaped mortality curves based on the concept of 'intergenerational transfers' (Lee, 2003; Kaplan and Robson, 2009). In summary, decreases in mortality are not necessarily caused by selfish parents trying to minimise losses with potentially problematic offspring, do not necessarily demonstrate the presence of killer genes, and should not be observed exclusively (although more often) in species with parental care; decreases in pre-adult mortality rates are therefore the other side of growth and development. There is still no solution to the problem of U-shaped mortality curves and new hypotheses and models are expected to emerge.

Finally, if larger size has the potential of reducing mortality and increasing reproductive success, why is the duration of growth (and adult size itself) limited in so many species, in particular among high vertebrates? Why is indeterminate growth frequent or predominant in groups such as lower vertebrates, fish or amphibians, but not in *all* animal species (Sebens, 1987)? The most accepted answer to those questions is that indeterminate growth may not be an option for certain species because its two main ingredients – *energy* and *time* – are available in limited quantities. As seen below, the finite nature of those variables has important effects on the moulding of life cycles.

THE REPRODUCTION OF SOMA: ENERGY, TIME AND TRADE-OFFS

Animals cannot allocate an infinite supply of energetic resources to themselves; a first consequence of this fact is a trade-off between metabolic investment in growth and reproduction (Stearns, 1992). Animal growth and reproduction are competing processes that require energy for the synthesis of additional biomass – respectively in parents and descendants. Determinate growth is a particular solution to the dilemma, whereby somatic growth occurs first, and then at the point of maturity or adulthood, metabolic resources are directed towards reproduction or growth of a descendant soma (Charnov, 1993). The trade-off between growth and reproduction defines a variable of crucial importance in life cycles: the age of maturity, the moment at which the shift from growth to reproduction takes place.

While energy availability is a constraint behind the very existence of the trade-off, a second one plays the fundamental role in determining *when* it occurs; that factor is time. The availability of time defines a second trade-off, that between reproduction and longevity, and explains differences in maturation rates across animal species (Williams, 1957). The amount of time organisms have at their disposal, or their life expectancy, differs widely across species. Those characterised by high mortality rates or a short life expectancy are under pressure to start reproduction faster, otherwise they run the risk of not reproducing at all; the opposite is true for long-lived species (Charnov, 1993). The Virginia opossum (*Didelphis virginiana*), a North American marsupial, is a good example of the effects of mortality rates on the timing of reproduction (Austad, 1993). Two main populations of this species have been isolated for a period of over 10 000 years: an original mainland population, and a more recent island population facing much lower rates of accidental death due to the absence of natural predators on the island. Austad predicted that the lower rates of accidental death faced by the island population should lead to two main consequences. The first, a slower rate of senescence on the island, was confirmed by physiological studies; the second would be an earlier age at first reproduction in the shorter-lived mainland population. This prediction was also confirmed, both by the earlier reproduction and by a relatively higher investment in the first breeding season in comparison with island females, which took longer to start breeding and spread their reproductive effort across two years.

Together, the ecological constraints imposed by energy and time are the background against which opposite selective forces determine age at first reproduction, termination of growth, and adult body size. On the one hand, the advantages of larger body size in terms of higher survivorship and reproductive performance favour *late* termination of growth and beginning of reproduction. On the other hand, due to the finitude of real life cycles, selection also favours an *early* start of reproduction, which minimises the risk of death before reproduction and increases the duration of reproductive life. The relative strength of the constraints of energy and time determines the balance between selection for early reproduction and for extended growth. The rationale also explains why age at reproduction and body size are positively correlated among mammals: stronger selection for early reproduction implies earlier growth termination and smaller body size, whereas late reproduction implies extended growth and increased size (Charnov, 1993).

The links between mortality rates, age at first reproduction and adult body size can be found in our species too. Migliano *et al.* (2007)

have argued that the extremes of body size in traditional human societies, represented by tall East African pastoralists and pygmies from Africa and Asia, can also be explained by a trade-off between growth and reproduction. Human pygmies exhibit much higher mortality rates than other hunter-gatherer populations, and on average start reproduction earlier. Interestingly, taller pygmy women showed higher fertility than shorter ones, demonstrating that larger body size carries advantages even among pygmies. Thus, as in other mammalian species, body size in humans seems to be the result of a balance between selection for larger size and extended growth on the one hand, and for earlier maturation and reproduction on the other, with the balance tending towards the latter in pygmies due to higher mortality rates prevailing in the marginal environments they occupy. The hypothesis proposed by Migliano *et al.* (2007) differs from previous explanations that assumed that small body size in pygmies was adaptive by itself for reasons of thermoregulation, food scarcity and locomotion in forests (Diamond, 1991). It would be important to test the same trade-off hypothesis in other species exhibiting pygmy forms such as hippos and elephants (Fernando *et al.*, 2003; Weston and Lister, 2009), or to apply the idea to extinct species such as the small-sized fossil hominin *Homo floresiensis* found on the Pacific island of Flores (Brown *et al.*, 2004; Lahr and Foley, 2004).

The idea that adult body size is the outcome of a complex balance involving various selective pressures and constraints is relatively new in evolutionary studies. In previous decades, attempts at explaining life cycles as integrated wholes frequently postulated body size as the main cause of variation in life history (Huxley, 1932; Lewontin, 1979; Western and Ssemakula, 1982). The main reason was the discovery that body size correlated with a large range of variables such as brain size, social group size, home range, pregnancy duration, lifespan and others, suggesting that most adaptive features of species could be consequences or by-products of a given body size (Shea, 1983).

However, a series of studies demonstrated that interpreting life history simply or mostly as a side effect of body size is incorrect. Correlations among life history variables such as pregnancy duration, weaning age, age at sexual maturation and longevity remained significant after controlling for body size (Harvey and Purvis, 1999). Charnov (1993) even claimed that body size is the consequence rather than cause of those life history traits. However, the evidence and arguments above indicate that body size is neither the ultimate cause nor a mere by-product of adaptation. Being a key element in the trade-offs involving growth, reproduction and longevity, adult body size is certainly more than a side effect: it is a target of selection itself due to its potential effects on fitness such as reduced mortality and higher fecundity. Contrary to the views of Huxley and others, body size is, however, not the single or key variable in animal life history: since termination of growth conflicts with the start of reproduction, adult body size evolves as an element of a fitness-maximising equilibrium.

The determination of adult body size in animals with finite growth is only one example of the compromises characterising life cycles. Contrary to Williams' original hypothesis, the fact that certain adaptations bring about both advantages and disadvantages is not a consequence of the genetic phenomenon of pleiotropy; it is a consequence of the selective phenomenon of trade-off management.

THE END OF REPRODUCTION: MENOPAUSE AND SENESCENCE

If vigour and body size increase until the beginning of reproduction, and if reproduction marks the start of senescence, animal life cycles may be seen as the rise (development) and fall (senescence) of individual somas. The timing of the inflexion point results from a balance between opposite selection pressures. Life history trade-offs may also be responsible for another turning point – menopause or the end of reproductive function in females. Menopause used to be seen as a recent historical phenomenon exclusive to humans and caused by the extension of life by cultural and technological means. However, recent studies show that menopause is observed in other species and has probably evolved in humans well before historical times (Walker, 1995; Packer et al., 1998; Cohen, 2004; Shanley et al., 2007). Although it is now generally accepted that menopause is an old piece of the human life history jigsaw, various questions remain. The two main challenges of evolutionary accounts of human menopause are first to explain how a trait that apparently reduces reproductive success could have evolved; and second, why reproductive cessation is exclusive to females.

A straightforward answer would be to interpret menopause simply as an aspect of senescence or physiological decay; ovaries may stop functioning like other organs do when we get old. But if this explanation were correct, reproductive cessation should also be observed in males and in all other species in which senescence is observed. The favoured adaptive hypothesis for menopause is that it results from another trade-off, this time involving the advantages of current versus future reproduction.

Williams (1957) proposed that reproductive cessation is not the same as senescence, but instead an adaptation to a human life history already characterised by it. He argued that at some point in human evolution it became advantageous for senescent women to avoid 'increasingly hazardous pregnancies' and focus on raising current offspring; at that point, selection began to trade late for early reproduction, until an originally gradual decline in reproductive value became the abrupt shutting down represented by menopause. Since reproductive value is zero after menopause, there should be no selection against deleterious mutations after its onset: that is, post-reproductive life expectancy should be zero too. For Williams, the reason why women survive well past menopause is that although they no longer produce new offspring, they are still reproducing in the sense of raising current offspring to adulthood. Since old age can still make a contribution to fitness, selection can therefore oppose mutations that cause senescence and death; that would have caused the extension of post-reproductive life in humans.

Williams' hypothesis was criticised by Hawkes and collaborators (1998) for implying that menopause was caused by a shortening of the reproductive span in humans. Comparative data from closely related primates show instead that the length of our reproductive span is that expected for a primate of our body size. Female reproduction in humans does not end early: women simply live longer than expected after reproduction has finished. The 'grandmother hypothesis' proposed by Hawkes also states that the reproductive value of postmenopausal women is not zero; but while Williams proposed that this happened due to assistance provided to daughters, the grandmother hypothesis suggests that this happens because senescent women are helping their *grand*children. A study by Lahdenperä *et al.* (2004) has recently shown a positive effect of grandmothers on the reproductive success of their daughters (i.e. on their grandchildren number).

Both Williams' and Hawkes' hypotheses imply that the evolution of menopause requires a combination of parental care and senescence; parental care means that reproduction goes beyond conception or birth and is only properly finished when offspring become independent, whereas senescence implies that at some point of the life cycle the contribution to fitness resulting from assisting existing descendants becomes preferable to generating additional offspring. Whether postmenopausal survival is associated with the survival of children or grandchildren may depend on the combination of parental care and the senescence rate in a given species. More recently, Cant and Johnstone (2008) have added reproductive competition between females from different generations to the list of possible causes of menopause, but stressed that the mechanism may occur in parallel with the kin-based explanations proposed by Williams and Hawkes.

In summary, theories of menopause disagree both on whether post-reproductive life evolved due to selection for mothers' or grandmothers' longevity; and on whether it arose from inter-generational co-operation between related females or from competition between unrelated females. What they have in common is the idea that termination of reproduction may evolve species characterised by high levels of parental care. Rather than just a dimension of senescence, menopause is the outcome of a trade-off; the question is whether menopause is the late cost of parental care received early in life (the mothers hypothesis) or the cost of reproductive assistance from grandmothers in the early stages of reproduction (the grandmothers hypothesis). They also have in common the belief that humans are long lived because of selection on women rather than men. Only recently have males been considered a possible factor in the extension of human life (Tuljapurkar et al., 2007).

FREE RADICALS AND MOLECULAR SIGNALLING

The evolutionary theory of senescence and life history theory suggest that ageing evolved as a consequence of adaptive processes moulding the life cycle so as to maximise total reproductive success; thus, despite not being an adaptation, senescence has an evolutionary reason to exist. This conclusion apparently clashes with a competing perspective that interprets senescence as the outcome of specific physiological mechanisms that could be prevented. In particular, it is argued that free radicals or highly reactive chemical agents released by common metabolism are the actual cause of mutations in somatic cells, the accumulation of which eventually produces senescence (Harman, 1956; Hughes and Reynolds, 2005). Further findings followed from the discovery of other possible mechanisms such as the increase in the rates of telomere breakage in somatic cells (Blasco, 2005; Herbig et al., 2006). Given their differences, are the evolutionary and physiological perspectives complementary or do they propose alternative explanations for ageing?

The answer begins with the realisation that the evolutionary and the free radical theories of senescence differ regarding the nature of the alleles behind ageing. Consider the evolutionary theory: either due to accumulation of deleterious effects late in life as proposed by Medawar, or due to pleiotropic effects as proposed by Williams, alleles that cause ageing are assumed as present in an organism since conception or zygotic formation. Huntington's chorea, Medawar's chosen example, is caused by an expansion in the number of a nucleotide triplet (CGA) in the autosomal *HD* gene, and leading to the production of a protein with a longer tail of the amino acid glutamine (Walker, 2007); the mutation that expands the gene occurs during gamete formation and is therefore present in the germline and in the zygote.

In contrast, the free radical theory is based on mutations that occur in *somatic* cells after conception – especially at old age. The occurrence of somatic mutations is expected: somatic cells evolved as disposable units that carry equally disposable copies of genes. Evidence has accumulated that many late-life diseases (such as cancer) are almost exclusively caused by somatic mutations (Stratton *et al.*, 2009) rather than germline mutations. The knowledge of the genetic basis of certain diseases occurring late in life was not available to Medawar and Williams when they proposed their evolutionary models.

Whereas organisms are in principle powerless against germline mutations (as they are already present in organisms and simply need time to manifest their effects), somatic mutations must be induced during the life cycle by accidental factors (either present in the environment or produced by cell metabolism, such as free radicals). Moreover, the somatic nature of certain mutations does not imply that diseases such as cancer are not partially inheritable (the reason is that certain alleles are more likely to mutate into the deleterious types that cause disease).

Despite their mechanistic differences, the two perspectives are not contradictory. If ageing results at least partially from somatic mutations, natural selection is expected to favour the evolution of repair mechanisms preventing them from happening and causing disease. As an example, no skin cell in the human body is older than two months, and the telomeres in those cells are much younger, being constantly checked and repaired by enzymes (telomerases and DNA polymerases; Gilson and Géli, 2007).

If somatic mutations can in principle be avoided, why do they accumulate late in life? The reason is that higher frequency of telomere breaks and somatic mutations at old age in multicellular organisms results not from a higher activity or accumulation of mutagens, but by a lower efficiency of repairing mechanisms. This happens because of the ageing of the immune system itself, which can only be explained by the evolutionary theory of senescence: immunosenescence occurs because selection is weaker to oppose telomere breaks and somatic mutations at old age (Franceschi *et al.*, 2000). This is the core of the 'disposable soma theory' (Kirkwood, 1977), which reconciles the evolutionary theory of ageing with the acceptance of the role of somatic mutations.

Finally, it is clear that ageing caused either by mutations already present in the zygote or occurring in somatic cells could in principle be postponed, and this has given rise to a series of studies focusing on the specific mechanisms causing late-life decay. Recently, the possibility of avoiding or postponing ageing has been further stimulated by the discovery of 'mortality plateaus' in various species ranging from *Drosophila* to humans (Rose *et al.*, 2005); in short, such plateaus would exist because mortality rates seem to stabilise, although are at high levels, after the end of reproduction (as the power of natural selection, having reached a minimum value after the end of reproduction, cannot decrease any further). The possibility of artificially postponing ageing is, however, a recent product of human culture; in the world of multicellular organisation produced by natural selection, senescence is the price that the soma must pay for the perpetuation of the germline.

CONCLUSION: MULTICELLULARITY AND THE LIFE CYCLE

Based on the original insight proposed by Weismann, evolutionary theory is now able to explain why individual life is manifested as a cycle from birth to death, or why no metazoan seems to be blessed with eternal youth. The ultimate reason for the existence of life cycles is a property defining life itself: the distinction between genotypes bearing hereditary information, and phenotypes required for the survival and perpetuation of genotypes. The disposability of phenotypic entities has been a price paid for the potential immortality of genetic information; but while an original distinction between DNA and proteins dates to the very origin of life, the division of labour between somatic lines and the germline in multicellular species represented a later step in the evolution of biological organisation.

Multicellularity also meant that even DNA becomes disposable – if it happens to be present in a disposable somatic cell. For this reason, mutations that eventually lead to death may only be expressed in somatic cells. They are either present from conception and are expressed late (as the alleles causing Huntington's disease for example), or they are somatic mutations occurring during the life cycle due to DNA-damaging factors.

Disposable somatic cells thus represented a first form of 'extended' or emerging phenotype in relation to encoded proteins. The emergence of multicellularity engendered a new mode of operation of natural selection; this mode, the decrease in the power of natural selection with individual age, is the explanation for why eternity is not adaptive in multicellular organisms and is the key to the understanding of life cycles. Multicellular super-units are not eternal because natural selection loses its power with individual age, and death is the logical conclusion to somatic existence. The understanding of the mechanistic basis of senescence may lead to therapies that prevent or postpone natural death in humans; but, paraphrasing Hamilton, mother nature never remotely intended humans to remain young and live forever.

Mortal somatic bodies evolved in some evolutionary lineages ultimately to perform the function of reproduction, or perpetuation of information-storing molecules carried by germ cells. For this reason, it is not surprising that sex, a fundamental ingredient of reproduction in most species, is also seen as a major transition in the evolution of biological complexity (Maynard Smith and Szathmáry, 1995). In the following chapter, it is argued that sex was neither a transition in evolution nor a late evolutionary addition to originally asexual life forms: sex is in fact as old as life itself.

5

Sex and its consequences: the transition that never happened

Sex has been a key player in the unfolding of evolutionary history. The most diverse and successful taxa are sexual (among bacteria and eukaryotes, single-celled and multicellular, animals, plants and fungi). In some species sex even gives the impression of being more important than survival, as exemplified by males that sacrifice their lives to females as payment for mating (Prenter *et al.*, 2006), or mothers that feed their descendants with their own flesh (Hamilton, 1967). The exceptional status of sex in evolutionary theory has been formalised in two particular ways. First, the concept of a 'paradox' or 'cost' of sex (Maynard Smith, 1971) points to the fact that sex seems to be too complicated and risky in comparison with the simpler mechanism of asexual reproduction; but the fact that sexual species are much more common than asexual ones implies that sex must offer some exceptional adaptive advantage. Second, sex has been elevated to the status of a major transition in evolution by Maynard Smith and Szathmáry due to its significance to organic history. They argue that sex involved the origin of meiotic or reductional division, recombination of parental genes, the need for gametes that transfer hereditary information across generations and other innovations, which together would represent the origin of a new method of transmission of biological information.

The high status of sex as a microevolutionary paradox and a macroevolutionary transition certainly seems to be justified, but at closer examination some problems can be seen with both arguments. First of all, what we call 'sex' is usually a series of traits widely differing in their occurrence. To understand this, let us picture to ourselves the couple represented by Rodin's sculpture *The Kiss*, an archetypal representation of human sexuality. We can immediately capture the passion and infatuation of the couple and their apparent and reciprocal attraction to beauty; those features are certainly known to characterise mate choice in humans. But although present in various species such as peacocks, guppies and others, mate choice is absent in many others and far from universal. Despite reproducing sexually, many individuals (typically females) in species exhibiting harems neither chose nor are chosen, and are in fact monopolised by dominant males. In those species, sexual selection is only expressed in the form of contests between males. In other species, sexual selection is virtually absent. Reproduction in many species of fish, for example, simply consists of the synchronised release of gametes by the two sexes. In other words, sex may exist without sexual selection.

Rodin's representation of human sexuality also features a biunivocal or one-to-one relation uniting the loving couple; underlying that relation is the similarity in numbers of males and females in populations (including humans where monogamy is not the rule; Goldsmith and Zimmerman, 2001). Not only in human groups but also in most animal species are sex ratios close to a balance. Interestingly, even in species such as elephant seals (where harems may include a single breeding male for up to about a hundred females) there are still as many males and females in the population; in other words, polygamy should not be taken as evidence for unbalanced sex ratios, a mistake made by Darwin (1871) himself. An explanation for the occurrence of balanced sex ratios, characteristic of most traditional human societies and other species, was first offered by Fisher (1930) and is discussed below. But in a few species, sex ratios are truly biased and found in values of tens of females to a single male (Hamilton, 1967). This means that although sex generally requires a member of each sex (with exceptions; see Whitfield, 2004), males and females do not necessarily come in pairs or similar numbers; sex is not the same as a balanced sex ratio.

The Kiss also represents gender roles in our species, with a larger, muscular male holding a lighter and apparently more passive female; said otherwise, sexual dimorphism is part of our view of human sex and probably characterises humans, our hominin ancestors and many other animal taxa (Reno, 2003; Lockwood *et al.*, 2007; Gordon *et al*, 2008). However, morphological differentiation between males and females is not a universal feature in sexual species. In many avian species such as the colourful neotropical parakeets, males and females are so similar that they can only be distinguished by DNA genotyping (Cerit and Avanus, 2007).

In addition to the absence of sexual dimorphism, in many species there is sex without sexes. Hermaphrodites produce two types of gametes and are in a sense both male and female (Ghiselin, 1969; Schärer, 2009) whereas bacteria, which are known for being 'promiscuous' and showing highly dynamical patterns of gene transfer (Fraser *et al.*, 2007), lack permanent male and female sexes altogether.

Bacteria are crucial to elucidate a final distinction between sex and its consequences: they show that sex is not the same as sexual reproduction. In bacteria, sex in the form of the exchange of genetic material between two individuals is not required for the replication of the haploid genome itself. Conjugation is not required for the generation of offspring or cell fission, and simply corresponds to horizontal transfer of genes between two individuals, rather than vertical transfer to the next generation observed in sexually reproducing species. Bacteria exchange genes for the same reason that humans exchange words: it corresponds to an exchange of potentially useful information, but it is not a condition for reproduction. In summary, obligatory sexual reproduction (a mechanism that uses genetic exchange as a necessary condition for reproduction and the generation of offspring), is not the same and not as universal as sex, but another important consequence of it.

The conclusion is that there seems to be only one feature common to all sexual species: from viruses and bacteria to humans, sex involves interchange of genetic information (Williams, 1975). This definition clarifies the advantages of sex and the reason why it evolved: whereas in asexual species the only source of new genes or alleles is mutation (apart from possible vertical transmission by viruses), in sexual species an alternative source exists: another organism. For this reason, the evolution of sex or the exchange of genetic material can only be understood once it is distinguished from its evolutionary consequences (Stearns, 1987). Rodin's *Kiss* more than clearly exemplifies the distinction between sex and its consequences in our species. It portrays human sexuality as an amalgamation of characteristics including separate sexes, sexual dimorphism, a balanced sex ratio and sexual selection. Interestingly, very few of us would immediately interpret the scene as having any relation to exchange of genetic information: that is, with sex itself.

The distinction between sex and its consequences is relevant because each consequence of sex is likely to have evolved for a different reason; and those should not be confounded with the reason for the evolution of genetic exchange in the first place. As seen below, this is the key to the solution of the apparent paradox of sex: the paradox in fact relates not to sex itself but to its consequences.

We will discuss the possibility that some evolutionary consequences of sex may have even evolved under the selective pressure to *oppose* sexual reproduction altogether (and not just among diverging populations as claimed by models of speciation by reinforcement), and with it, sex or genetic exchange itself. This implies among other things that asexuality should not be seen as the ancestor of sex, but another item on the list of its consequences. The common temporal precedence of sex over asex in evolutionary lineages has been shown in at least one context: existing asexual species tend to be recent offshoots of sexual species rather than survivors from an old asexual world (Rice, 2002b). Recently, more radical arguments have been presented in favour of the view that sex predates asexuality: there is growing interest in the hypothesis that both DNA and genetic exchange are as old as life (Raoult and Forterre, 2008) and shaped the origin of the major living groups (bacteria, archaea and eukaryotes).

This leads to the second argument – the macroevolutionary one – for the importance of sex in evolution: sex was one of the major transitions in evolution (Maynard Smith and Szathmáry, 1995) because it represented the origin of a new system of transmission of biological information (namely the transfer of haploid sets of genes via gametes). This view assumes that sexual organisms evolved from less complex asexual ones. In contrast, if sex was a feature present in the ancestor to all extant organisms and asexuality was mostly a consequence of sex, sex must be reinterpreted as the major transition that never happened. In the following, it will be argued that the basic problem with Maynard Smith and Szathmáry's argument is that it confounds sex with one of its less universal consequences – obligatory sexual reproduction based on meiosis.

If sex is neither an adaptive paradox nor a major evolutionary transition, does it follow that it has played a minor role in evolution? That conclusion would be equally incorrect: one of the reasons for distinguishing between sex and its consequences is to emphasise that it was more important to evolution than any of its consequences. Exchange of genetic information was important because it allowed for a more thorough exploration of the modular nature of inheritance. All known life forms are based on modular genomes consisting of discrete genes, and on genes consisting of discrete functional modules (coding and regulatory) and ultimately of modular nucleotide sequences. With a few (and mostly recent) asexual exceptions, the evolution of life has depended on the nearly infinite combinatorial potential of modular DNA-based genetic inheritance, which can only be efficiently explored through sex.

THE MISLEADING COST OF SEX

The idea that sex is paradoxical followed from a theoretical argument developed by Maynard Smith (1971, 1978). To understand the concept of the twofold cost of sex, let us imagine a sexual species, characterised by dioecy (the existence of separate male and female sexes); diploidy (with adults carrying two copies of each gene, and gametes only one); females either getting pregnant or laying eggs and bearing most of the metabolic costs of reproduction; a stable population, meaning that each female generates two individuals in their lifetime; and a balanced sex ratio. Let us assume a population of 100 individuals, 50 of which are males and 50 females. Now consider the origin of an asexual mutant, similar to other females but for one respect: it generates descendants by mitosis (or cloning) without requiring fertilisation by a male gamete. Let us say that this parthenogenetic female founds a lineage that eventually results in a population of 100 parthenogenetic females. The question posed by Maynard Smith was: how would the sexual population fare in comparison with the mutant asexual descendants?

Faced with the challenge from asexuals, the sexual population would exhibit a series of handicaps. The first is a demographic one. In the sexual population, it takes two individuals to generate one descendant (a 'reproducing' female that must necessarily bear the costs of pregnancy or the production of an egg, and a fertilising or 'mating' male that provides offspring with a haploid set of genes but no parental care). Thus, the 100 sexual individuals reproduce as 50 pairs, and only 50 individuals (the females) get pregnant or lay eggs. In contrast, all the 100 asexual females are able to generate offspring amounting to a twofold advantage, or a twofold cost of sex.

It is important to understand that the demographic cost comes directly from the existence of the exclusively 'mating' and 'non-reproducing' males. But as seen earlier, sex is not the same as dioecy; in sexual populations in which sexes are not separate, such as hermaphrodites (Michiels and Newman, 1998), all individuals can get pregnant or lay eggs. Thus, on closer examination it seems that the demographic handicap of sexual populations may follow from this reason: not sex or genetic exchange itself, but the occurrence of males and dioecy.

The same argument applies to a second reason for the demographic handicap: a balanced sex ratio. Instead of 50 offspring of each sex, suppose that the same sexual population generates offspring that is 99% female and only 1% male. In this case, the sexual population with 99 females would be very similar to a population of 100 parthenogenetic individuals: since the demographic handicap is proportional to the number of males in the population, a female-biased sex ratio could single-handedly reduce the twofold cost of sex to a mere 1%. Thus, the twofold cost of sex is also a cost of the prevalence of balanced sex ratios in sexual populations.

But even in this case a *genetic* cost of sex can still be defined. Consider the two female populations, the sexual and the parthenogenetic, and assume that there is virtually no demographic cost due to a reduced small number of males (i.e. let us assume that 99 females are fertilised by a single male). Even in this case there is a cost of sex: while the asexual females transmitted all their genes to clonal offspring, a sexual female only contributes half their genes, the other half being supplied by the male. In other words, due to reductional division the sexual female produces offspring that are genetically shared with a male, and is only 50% related to her from a genetic point of view. Thus, the genetic cost (which is also twofold, since sexual females lose half of offspring genes to males) does not strictly follow from sex or genetic recombination either, but from diploidy and obligatory sexual reproduction.

We can also define an *ecological* cost of sex, which in contrast is not necessarily twofold. For example, sexual reproduction involves an extra cost in the form of mating investment (Kokko and Jennions, 2003) required for copulation and fertilisation to occur; this includes various forms of sexual selection, such as the sometimes deadly battles between males, or the processes of sexual display and female choice (Andersson and Simmons, 2006). A second cost following from copulation is a risk factor: sexual organisms may fail to reproduce simply for not being able to find a mating partner; in other words, reproduction and fitness of sexual females become dependent upon males (and vice versa). Needless to say, all those costs and risks are not present in asexual females, which do not waste energy selecting males, competing against other females for male partners, and never fail to reproduce due to the absence of a match with a male. However, as in the case of demographic or genetic costs it is clear that the ecological costs of sex are derived from consequences of sex such as mate choice and other forms of sexual selection.

To sum up, the paradox of sex and its twofold cost do not follow from the process of genetic exchange, the only definition of sex that universally describes all sexual species; the cost of sex, in particular the twofold cost described by Maynard Smith, follows from some of the consequences of sex, such as dioecy, diploidy and a balanced sex ratio. Due to its widespread occurrence, this means that sex itself must carry with it some advantage able to overcome the various costs associated with its consequences. In order to understand what the adaptive advantage of genetic exchange is, we must first realise that sex is not for reproduction: sex is for evolution.

ADVANTAGES OF GENETIC EXCHANGE

Why is genetic exchange, observed in so many taxa from bacteria to most multicellular species, so advantageous? It is easier to see the reason for the prevalence of sex if we compare genetic exchange with simple genetic *change* – that is, mutation. Given the modular nature of DNA and genomes, the primary source of genetic change consists of mutations in genes (via changes in base pairs and in regulatory or coding modules) or gene sets (via duplication or loss of genes or whole chromosomes). Sex is by definition the exchange of such novelties across individuals; through sex, an individual bacterium may share a mutation originally occurring in another individual, and a diploid mother may generate offspring carrying genes from a second individual (the father). In other words, sex complements the primary sources of genetic change to generate more variation in individuals or descendants. The problem is therefore to explain why additional genetic variation is an advantage.

The first classic answer states that sex accelerates the speed of adaptive evolution; and this advantage would lead in the long run to the prevalence of sexual species over asexual lineages (Maynard Smith, 1978; Goddard *et al.*, 2005; Paland and Lynch, 2006). This argument was originally proposed by Weismann (1889) and developed by Fisher (1930) as one of the consequences of his fundamental principle that establishes the link between rates of adaptive evolution and genetic variance. Let us again suppose the existence of two competing populations, one sexual and one asexual. In the asexual population, consider the occurrence and spread of two favourable mutations A and B, in two distinct individuals and genes. What is the expected result? One sees that a competition must occur between three types of individuals: those carrying the mutation A, those carrying mutation

B, and those carrying neither mutation A nor B. It is expected that individuals carrying one of the two mutations will outcompete individuals carrying neither. However, clones carrying A and B would also compete against each other; eventually, only one favourable mutation survives (the most favourable one), and the other is wasted. The only way the asexual species could possibly evolve a genome carrying the two favourable mutations A and B is if they both occurred in the same lineage (i.e. the high-fitness individual AB will only exist if mutation A occurs first, and then mutation B occurs in the same lineage, or vice versa). Since the occurrence of either A and B is a relatively rare event, the occurrence of both A and B in the same lineage must be even rarer. In conclusion, since adaptive evolution in asexuals is under the control of mutation rates, it must be a relatively slow process.

Now consider a sexually reproducing species and the same two mutations A and B (which for the sake of simplicity are assumed to be dominant). If an individual A and an individual B mate, a descendant AB can in principle occur only one generation after the mutations occurred. In other words, sexual species can put together different advantageous mutations in a same descendant lineage much more quickly. This means that evolution towards increasing adaptation is accelerated by genetic exchange. For this reason, if sexual and asexual populations were given the same mutations A and B and competed against each other, one expects a sexual mutant AB to occur first and to beat the asexual opposition in the adaptive race. It should be noticed that the argument, based on the rationale presented by Fisher and Maynard Smith, demonstrates the advantages of sex independently from obligatory sexual reproduction; it would also hold true for a comparison between a strictly asexual bacterial lineage and a sexual one (which would exchange genes via conjugation without needing it for reproduction).

While the explanation for sex outlined above appeals to the spread of advantageous mutations, a second class of theories focuses on the effect of sex on deleterious mutations (Kondrashov, 1998; Otto and Lenormand, 2002). Their original and most popular version is known as 'Muller's ratchet' (Muller 1932, 1964). The ratchet points to the fact that a mutation, once it has occurred, has only one likely way out in asexual populations: the extinction of its carrier and all its descendants (as back-mutations are unlikely). In contrast, in sexual populations there is an alternative way out for deleterious mutations: the generation of genetically diverse offspring due to recombination (Keightley and Otto, 2006). Thus, whereas an organism descending from a carrier of a deleterious mutation necessarily carries that burden, sexual carriers can produce genetically clean offspring. Thus, even if asexual populations have an advantage over sexual organisms for not bearing the costs of males, asexuals must pay a high adaptive or fitness price due to the accumulation of deleterious mutations. It could be argued that the accumulation of mutations in the lineages would also happen in the case of *advantageous* mutations. However, Muller's ratchet is based on the well-known fact that deleterious mutations are much more frequent than advantageous ones (Fisher, 1930; Kondrashov, 1984; Denver *et al.*, 2004), and for this reason, the accumulation of the former would be a more important factor.

How could asexual organisms avoid the cost of deleterious mutations? In an asexual species, selection could reduce the time required for the advantageous mutations A and B to occur in the same lineage by favouring increased mutation rates and reproductive rates; in this way, at a cost of a huge fraction of low-fitness descendants, mutation could replace recombination as a way of exploring the combinatory potential of modular genomes. The problem with this solution is that only simple organisms with small genomes (virus-like or bacterium-like ones) could potentially rely on this strategy – and they actually do. However, in larger genomes the likelihood that a given mutation is deleterious increases, and the strategy would handicap species by limiting genome sizes (Eigen, 1971).

We may conclude that sex or genetic exchange is adaptive because individuals can share advantageous mutations occurring in lineages other than their own, and because they oppose the accumulation of certain deleterious mutations. Thus, even when there is a short-run advantage in asexuality due to the extra females, sexual lineages normally do better in the long run because sex more efficiently explores the modular nature of genetic inheritance to create advantageous combinations. The conclusion is valid both for an individual and its descendants, and for this reason, it would not be a surprise if selection favoured the evolution of mechanistic links between sex and reproduction. The familiar outcome, the evolution of obligatory sexual reproduction and diploidy (Hadany and Beker, 2007), consolidated sex as a requirement for reproduction. Diploidy and sexual reproduction evolved in unicellular eukaryotes and is observed in ciliates, yeasts and other protozoans, but those taxa can switch to clonal or asexual reproduction during their life cycles (Otto and Gerstein, 2008). Among multicellular organisms, plants and even some metazoans such as aphids (Simon *et al.*, 2002) can alternate between sexual and asexual cycles, but in most metazoans sexual reproduction is obligatory and dependent on equal genetic contributions from two distinct sexes. However, the evolution of separate sexes and in particular the evolution of males had its own adaptive and evolutionary reasons.

THE ORIGIN OF SEPARATE SEXES

As much as sex may exist without sexual reproduction, sexual reproduction might also exist without separate sexes. The cycle of adult diploid organisms, haploid gametes and finally their fusion into a new diploid zygote does not require the two gametes to be differentiated into egg and sperm, or the two parents to differ as female and male. If sexual reproduction only requires haploid gametes and their fusion, why do parents normally differ as male and females? First of all, why did gametes evolve their differentiation into egg and sperm?

The answer is natural selection at the individual level; although both diploid parents can take advantage of sexual reproduction by simply partaking in it, it is easy to see that sexual reproduction, which may be naïvely seen as a mechanism of reproduction based on co-operation between parents, also engenders new forms of competition between them. Take first the case of gamete fusion. If the success of a gamete depends on its fusion with another one, adaptations increasing the likelihood of fertilisation will be favoured by selection. For example, gametes that move towards others would have an advantage over immobile ones; if they all move, those that move faster may be favoured. Such considerations are used to explain the origin of the smaller, mobile sperm cells as gametes that maximise the likelihood of fertilisation; they also explain the differentiation of the larger, female egg that typically contributes resources (nutrients and cell organelles such as mitochondria) to the zygote. Anisogamy, or the differentiation between male and female gametes, has been explained by various hypotheses (Bulmer and Parker, 2002; Kokko *et al.*, 2006), but they are all variations on the theme of parental conflict of interests, and the frequent evolution of two stable solutions (small and mobile sperm, large and resource-rich egg) to the problem of fertilisation.

Anisogamy is the feature that defines the two sexes in most sexual species; however, even when two distinct gamete types exist, different sexes do not necessarily follow. This solution is hermaphroditism, where organisms may produce both male and female gametes. More than that, hermaphroditism with reciprocal exchange of gametes is arguably another possible solution to the paradox of sex (Maynard Smith, 1978; Grober and Rodgers, 2008). Each individual can donate and receive genetic material from mating partners and generate genetically variable offspring; all individuals can be fertilised or lay eggs, meaning that pure males that only mate but do not invest in reproduction (responsible for the demographic cost of sex) do not exist; finally, self-fertilisation is possible in some hermaphroditic species as a short term solution (Braendle and Felix, 2006) which minimises the ecological risk of death without reproduction. Thus, hermaphrodites seem to reap the benefits of both sexual and asexual reproduction, and the paradox becomes why hermaphroditism has not evolved in more animal lineages.

A dramatic explanation for the non-universality of hermaphrodites is the phenomenon of 'penis fencing' in the marine flatworm *Pseudoceros bifurcus* (Michiels and Newman, 1998). In this species cross-fertilisation seems to bring advantages for both individuals involved as they are both internally fertilised. But there is a problem: in sexual reproduction, whether in dioecious species or hermaphroditic ones, we saw that the two processes of mating and reproduction can be separated in principle. The mating component of sexual reproduction involves parental actions that precede and lead to the formation of a zygote; the reproduction component involves parental processes that lead from a fertilised zygote to a reproductive offspring. In a hermaphroditic species such as *P. bifurcus*, each parent should be involved in both; however, a form of cheating is possible.

Let us imagine two flatworms engaging in sexual reproduction: they can fertilise eggs and have their eggs fertilised at the same time. They share half the genes both in their eggs and the eggs carried by the partner; they both reproduce and exchange genes; in summary, they both win. That solution seems to be ideal by avoiding the demographic, genetic and ecological costs of sex. The only problem with this solution is that there is an even better one: to impregnate your partner without having your own eggs fertilised. This is the aim of penis fencing in *P. bifurcus*: instead of reciprocally exchanging gametes, individuals try to inject sperm cells into each other's bodies by force. Mating is therefore a battle in which the strongest individual acts as a sperm donor. What is the advantage associated with this behaviour? If sperm is smaller and cheaper than eggs (as predominantly happens), and if mating is faster and less costly than reproduction (which is also true in many cases), it pays to export the cost of reproduction to other individuals and to become a mating specialist; after all, weaker organisms would have to carry genes from the mating specialist in their fertilised eggs. In other words, it seems that the dream of all hermaphrodites in *P. bifurcus* would be to become a male.

It is clear that not all individuals can be winners in this case. If some individuals are destined to bear the burden of fertilised eggs for being less efficient at mating, their option is to do the best of a bad job and specialise in reproduction; that means to give up attempts at sperm donation and focus on increasing the chance of success of their fertilised eggs (for example, by adding more nutrients to the fertilised eggs). Thus, losers would be left with the option of evolving female characteristics.

A formal version of the argument above was offered by Charnov *et al.* (1976) who demonstrated that hermaphrodites are not more common because, under most ecological scenarios, male and female specialists do better than hermaphroditic generalists that invest in both mating and reproduction. Charnov and collaborators argued that if the average fitness of mating specialists (males) and reproductive specialists (females) is higher than the average fitness of hermaphrodites, then separate sexes should evolve. The fact that hermaphroditism is not more common in animals shows that this may often be the case (perhaps because except under exceptional circumstances mating is cheaper than reproduction). For example, in species with low population density, the opportunistic male strategy of investing in mating success and exporting the costs of reproduction to other individuals may not pay off (Ghiselin, 1969; Eppley and Jesson, 2008). Thus, when finding a partner (and a partner of the right sex) is a potentially costly process, hermaphroditic species may have an advantage over dioecious species.

In summary, the existence of separate sexes is one of the consequences of obligatory sexual reproduction and diploidy. Sexual reproduction means that reproduction cannot be separated from sex or genetic exchange; but it also means sex as mating may be separated from sex as reproduction regarding investment in offspring. It should be noticed that existing hermaphroditic animals are often descendants from dioecious species (Jarne and Auld, 2006; Grober and Rodgers, 2008). For this reason, the example of penis fencing in *P. bifurcus* is not an attempt to explain why species with two separate sexes evolved from hermaphrodites, but a way of explaining why hermaphroditism may derive from dioecious species if the cost of mating is too high; in other words, hermaphroditism is another adaptive strategy that evolved as a consequence of sex.

TOO MANY MALES

As seen earlier, the mere existence of males does not necessarily imply a twofold demographic cost to sex; one of the additional conditions for it is the widespread occurrence of balanced sex ratios in natural populations. The cost of sex is proportional to numbers of males or non-reproductive individuals in populations: if the ratio of males to females is 1:1, males cause a twofold cost. If all males were converted into females, the number of pregnancies, eggs and offspring would in principle rise by a factor of two; or (number of males + number of females)/females = 2. If males outnumbered females by a ratio of 9 to 1, the cost of males would be tenfold (or 10/1 = 10). The cost of sex can thus be minimised under the condition of a small number of males. Let us think of a population with a ratio of 1 male to 100 females: males evolved by definition as mating machines and are able to fertilise many females; even in small numbers, they would still make recombination and genetic exchange possible; and the numerical predominance of females would guarantee no loss in terms of reproductive efficiency in the population (in this hypothetical case, the cost of sex would be only 101/100 = 1%). Thus, the evolution of sex ratios biased towards females would at the same time preserve the advantages of sex and eliminate the demographic handicap relative to asexuals.

However, this is not what happens: animal species frequently exhibit balanced sex ratios and pay the twofold cost of sex. A classic argument by Fisher (1930) explains why males and females frequently appear in similar numbers: the reason is natural selection operating on individual fitness. As in the case of green or yellow peas in Mendel's experiments, let us interpret male and female sexes as phenotypes controlled by a single gene (or a sex chromosome). Now let us assume again a population with a female-biased sex ratio of 1:9, where a few males fertilise all the females. Fisher showed that this sex ratio is not at equilibrium and cannot be maintained by natural selection. To see why, notice that with obligatory sexual reproduction the *total* reproductive success of the male sex and the female sex must be similar: a thousand descendants imply that male fertilisation occurred a thousand times; thus, carriers of the male allele (i.e. all the fathers) left a total of 1000 descendants, and carriers of the female alleles (all mothers) also left 1000 descendants. Total reproductive output or fitness of each allele and sex is therefore 1000 (or alternatively 500, if we consider that each descendant is equally shared between the parents; we use the value 1000 for the sake of simplicity).

In contrast, the *average* or expected fitness by individuals of each sex is not necessarily similar in sexual populations. In our example, since females outnumber males by a factor of nine whereas the total reproductive output is the same in the two sexes, average female fitness is nine times *smaller* than male fitness. In other words, an average newborn male is expected to leave nine times more descendants during his lifetime than an average female; the male allele confers higher fitness than the female allele and should spread. The opposite would hold if males were more numerous; in this case, they would exhibit lower average fitness. Fisher thus argued that biased sex ratios are rare because of frequency-dependent selection, meaning that the rarest sex is the fittest until it is no longer the rarest; selection favours an equilibrium between the sexes and a balanced sex ratio.

Fisher's argument also explains exceptions to balanced sex ratios. We can understand exceptions if we analyse in more depth the concept of 'average' or 'expected' fitness used above. Fisher assumes that the expected fitness of an individual in a generation is based on the average fitness of the previous one; similarly, when prospective university students chose to study for a degree in law or medical studies, they expect to earn the same as current lawyers or medics (the previous generation of law and medicine students). Fisher's argument assumes that sexual reproduction relies on a public market of reproduction in which all individuals compete for their share in the next generation. Random mating or panmixia, constantly assumed by Fisher, are other names for those natural free markets in which individuals measure their fitness against each other.

Sex ratios may deviate from equilibrium when free competition is absent. The reason is a form of protectionism. Returning to our comparison, if professional success in law or medicine is based not on merit but on factors such as family background or friendship with hospital managers, then average and expected success in the career may not be the same. This may be true for reproduction too. Hamilton (1967) argued that 'local mate competition' represents situations in which offspring are granted a reproductive market reserve and saved from open competition. For example, parasitoid wasps lay eggs inside a caterpillar, where they develop into sexually mature individuals (Werren, 1980). Mating occurs inside the host before wasps emerge from it. In this case, a single male can fertilise his various sisters without having to compete against other males. Notice that although male average fitness is higher than in females, there is no selection for increase in male number: mothers gain no advantage by producing brothers that compete for their own sisters, and extra males would cause a reduction in the number of females or potential eggs laid. As a result, some parasitoid wasp species exhibit sex ratios of about 1:25 (Putters and van den Assem, 1985). Interestingly, if a second female lays eggs inside an already infested caterpillar, she adjusts the sex ratio of her offspring by producing more males than the first, which is expected due to the increase in competition; the second female is in fact trying to fight the local monopoly and restore conditions closer to random mating, and sex ratios move closer to an equilibrium between male and female numbers in the offspring (Burton-Chellew *et al.*, 2008).

Another example is given by mites of the genus *Adactylidium*, in which offspring are viviparous, develop into sexually mature adults inside their own mother, and mate before birth (Gould, 1980); once mating occurs, offspring feed on the mother's flesh (meaning that females can get pregnant only once). Due to local mate competition, sex ratios are biased towards females (Hamilton, 1967). In this case, a question must be asked: why are males even born? If all females are fertilised inside the mother, incest is the rule and there is no true outbreeding or admixture of genes from different lineages. Given that females die after a first pregnancy, they cannot generate genetically variable offspring from a second non-incestuous mating. The same is true for males: although they are forced to commit incest, mating after emergence from their mother could represent true outbreeding but is not possible (all other females are either pregnant or dead). In other words, there seems to be no true sex or genetic exchange in those mites. Why have they not evolved towards asexual or parthenogenetic reproduction? A possibility is that some females may fail to be fertilised inside the mother (for example, if the male dies inside the mother); those would emerge from mothers as virgins, and might be able to mate with unrelated males. Those few cases of outbreeding would be enough to keep some level of genetic exchange in those species, and explain the maintenance of sex in those species.

In conclusion, the existence of similar numbers of males and females in most animal species follows from competition between the two sexes. In species such as parasitoid wasps and mites of the genus *Adactylidium* where competition is limited, males are close to elimination – and together with males, sex itself. Thus, not only hermaphroditism but also asexuality may be a tempting adaptive alternative to some sexual species.

A first contribution of Darwin's *Origin of Species* was to explain adaptation as the outcome of a struggle for survival; another equally important contribution was to show that adaptation could be more than that. By presenting *sexual* selection as an alternative to natural selection, Darwin planned to include apparently maladaptive traits such as extreme male ornamentation or costly behaviours as components of individual fitness. The difference between the two forms of selection can be more easily understood if we appeal to the most commonly used measure of fitness, the Euler–Lotka equation that gained prominence in evolutionary theory due to Fisher (1930):

$$\int_{0}^{x} e^{-rx} l(x)m(x)dx = 1.$$

The equation depends on two main functions, the survivorship curve $l(x)$ and the birth rate or fertility function $m(x)$, and defines the fitness r as their product over the whole lifetime (corrected by the exponential demographic parameter). A modified and simpler version of the Euler–Lotka equation is the total lifetime reproductive success:

$$R_0 = \sum_{x-0}^{\infty} l(x)m(x).$$

The equation means that the fitness of an individual can be measured as the total number of descendants generated in its lifetime. Assuming that this organism lives for a number of years, this total value can be easily calculated as the number of descendants the organism produces during the first year of life (the fertility rate in year one) times the probability of surviving to the end of the first year, plus the fertility rate in year two times the probability of surviving to the end of year two; and so on, until the last year of life.

If this is true, what are the ways that fitness or reproductive output may be maximised by selection? The equation shows two options: more offspring may follow either from longer survivorship or higher fertility. In the case of sexually reproducing species, this conclusion is particularly relevant. On the one hand, adaptations that maximise fitness of sexual individuals by increasing their survivorship or $l(x)$ are the product of *natural* selection, and literally relate to the struggle for survival. On the other hand, adaptations that maximise fitness by increasing fertility or $m(x)$ are the result of *sexual* selection, as defined by Darwin in the *Descent of Man*:

In such cases…males have acquired their present structure, not from being better fitted to survive in the struggle for existence, but from having gained an advantage over other males…It was the importance of this distinction which led me to designate this form of selection as sexual selection (Darwin, 1871: 257).

The most dramatic examples of differences between natural and sexual selection occur when maximisation of one component of fitness occurs at the expense of the other: that is, when survivorship (health) and fertility (attractiveness) are forced into a trade-off (Brooks, 2000). Under the hypothesis of sexual selection, apparently superfluous ornaments such as the peacock tail gain a new explanation (they are useful by increasing male fertility), but also inspire new questions. The first is: why are apparently superfluous traits able to increase fertility? Second, Darwin's formulation appeals to the familiar fact that sexual selection seems to produce morphological effects mostly in one sex; for example, why are males the most common carriers of sexual ornaments? Those aspects of sexual selection, another consequence of sex, are discussed below.

WHY SEXUAL DIMORPHISM?

Although separate sexes follow from the existence of two distinct gamete types (by definition, females produce the larger gamete), the differentiation between males and females very often goes beyond anisogamy. Animal species with separate sexes are frequently dimorphic in various phenotypic aspects (Muller and Wrangham, 2002).

Both the non-universality of hermaphrodites and the processes of sexual selection point in one direction: the driving force behind the differentiation between male and female phenotypes is their asymmetry in reproductive investment. As seen earlier, wherever sex is an obligatory step in reproduction, males often evolve as mating specialists in order to maximise their chances of fertilising eggs, at the same time exporting the cost of reproduction to females that often invest resources required to transform a fertilised egg into offspring. The resources that males deny to offspring (such as time and energy) are channelled into the very traits evolved by sexual selection that converted males into efficient mating machines, namely secondary sexual traits responsible for attractiveness to females (ornaments or display behaviours directed to female choice) or reproductive supremacy over other males (horns, body size or other biological weaponry used in contests).

According to Trivers (1972), it is the possibility of asymmetrical investment in reproduction that determines sexual differences in their interest in their own offspring; because males invest less in a given offspring, they are more concerned with their quantity than with their quality, as they have less to lose if an offspring fails to survive. Females in contrast invest more in a given descendant and have more to lose if it perishes. Differential parental investment is expressed in various ways, beginning with anisogamy itself: the male gamete is not only often smaller and lighter, but also cheaper and produced in larger quantities than the more costly female egg loaded with nutrients. As a note, the larger known gametes are in fact sperm cells, such as the 6-cm-long sperm cells in the fruit fly *Drosophila bifurca* (Bjork and Pitnick, 2006); the explanation in this case is sperm competition (Parker, 1970) in species where females may copulate with multiple males, rather than higher levels of male investment in offspring.

Species with internal fertilisation add the next dimension of differential investment in offspring. First, internal fertilisation involves higher parental investment by females before offspring are even born, especially in the case of viviparous species. Second, internal fertilisation favours higher pre-birth investment by females due to paternity uncertainty: contrary to mothers, males cannot be sure that they really sire the offspring (Queller, 1997; Kokko and Jennions, 2003). As a result of higher investment by females and the limitation of resources, an individual female is able to produce fewer offspring than a male. Variance in reproductive success also tends to be much greater in males, with a few successful males siring a large number of offspring, while others sire none (Shuster and Wade, 2003). Finally, differential investment in offspring also extends to parental care dispensed to offspring after birth: males care for offspring in less than 10% of mammalian species, and even in birds (where biparental care is present in over 90% of species) females bear most of the burden of reproduction (Clutton-Brock, 1991).

The conclusion is that the optimal reproductive strategy, from the point of view of males, consists in favouring quantity of fertilisation over quality of offspring, and investing in ways of obtaining reproductive supremacy over male competitors. In other words, the ideal male world is a large female harem kept by force. Females on the other hand should favour quality over quantity of offspring. Since sex is compulsory, they should also be more interested in the genetic and phenotypic quality of their male reproductive partners. The ideal female world is therefore a combination of provisioning husbands, and freedom to choose male partners with the best genes (Krebs and Davies, 1987). The opposite interests of males and females generate an explicit conflict over reproductive strategy: the existence of a harem goes against the interest of the female in choosing the male that best assists her with reproduction and rearing of offspring, whereas males do not want to be chosen by females but to monopolise them reproductively.

A given mating system or solution to the conflict, such as polygamous systems in which a few males monopolise females by outcompeting other contestants, as in red deer or elephant seals (Kruuk et al., 2002), monogamous systems in which females choose males based on their qualities as good husbands or their genes (Kirkpatrick, 1987), or combinations that involve males competing against themselves so as to influence female choice (Wong and Candolin, 2005) is a result of the particular ecological conditions in which the conflict takes place (Royle et al., 2002). For example, if females depend upon good food sources for reproduction, males may be able to monopolise territories offering those characteristics and to force females into harems. Mammals, with their long pregnancies, high investment in offspring and long dependency of the infant on the mother, favour the emergence of female harems. In groups such as passerine birds, where females are not as dependent on territoriality and are more mobile, a more likely outcome is female choice; males are forced to evolve ways of convincing females of their qualities. Not surprisingly, mammals are predominantly polygamous, whereas birds are predominantly monogamous (Clutton-Brock, 1991).

For the same reason, it is not surprising that monogamous birds are frequently sexually monomorphic. When female choice prevails in a species, selection favours the evolution of males that share the costs of rearing offspring in the form of foraging and protection; in other words, the evolution of 'provisioning husbands' tends to occur, and males can no longer invest in weaponry or behaviours useful in male-to-male contests. This has been the case of various species of birds such as neotropical parakeets mentioned earlier. More dramatically, females sometimes manage to obtain both resources from a good husband and genetic variation in offspring, by cheating and mating with other males (Foerster et al., 2003).

However, sexual dimorphism is frequent in birds and other animal groups. One reason is that sexual conflict does not always result in female choice and provisioning males or good husbands. An alternative reason is that females are not always looking for good husbands: in some species 'beauty' is what matters, and sexual conflict leads to the evolution of male ornamentation.

MALE ORNAMENTS AS ACCIDENTS

The advantages of choosing a male on the basis of his potential contribution towards reproductive costs are obvious; why are females in many species mostly interested in aesthetical features such as ornaments and courtship behaviours? Fisher (1930) offered an explanation for male ornaments as results of the interaction between sexual selection and natural selection; this explanation is known as the 'runaway' model. Let us imagine a mutation in a gene controlling a male trait that is both adaptive and potentially visible to females; a hypothetical example would be a mutation producing brighter feather colouration and offering more efficient camouflage and defence against predators. Let us also assume that some females carry genes that determine preference for those males. Although controversial when originally proposed by Darwin (1859), it is now accepted that females in various species are able to choose males on the basis of their size, colour, smell, vocalisations and other traits (Collins and Luddem, 2002).

If there is a match between the two conditions, namely genes that cause adaptive changes in the male trait, and other genes that produce female preference for those extreme traits, a selective process may be set in motion. On the one hand, males exhibiting brighter feather colouration enjoy better defence mechanisms, and consequently higher survivorship and fitness; this predicts by itself an increase in the frequency of males displaying brighter feather colouration as a result of natural selection. On the other hand, females that prefer males with the brightest colouration are also favoured, since their sons inherit genes conferring higher fitness; in other words, females are rewarded for being able to 'read' male fitness from male phenotype.

Fisher's argument for runaway selection is that natural selection will *not* be able to maintain the average feather colouration at the adaptive peak; the reason is interference from sexual selection. In our example, the mutation for brighter colouration confers an advantage over other alleles due to its effect on survivorship: but the allele that causes the preference of females for brighter males adds another advantage to it, namely the effect on fertility of the attractive males. In other words, males carrying brighter colouration are more successful both because of its direct effects on survivorship and its effects on attractiveness and because bright males are chosen by more females. The allele for male brighter colour also leads to a spread of the allele commanding preference for brighter colours in females; they are both present in the offspring of bright males. This creates a feedback loop between the allele for brightness in males, and for preference for male brightness in females.

As a result of the feedback loop, female preference for brighter males may continue to operate even if the average male phenotype evolves past the brightness level corresponding to highest male survivorship (the levels favoured by natural selection). This may occur if the loss in survivorship caused by excessive brightness (caused, for example, by high energetic investment in its maintenance) is more than compensated by an increase in male fertility due to sexual selection; in other words, males may trade survivorship for fertility in some species (Brooks, 2000). For this reason, new mutations causing even brighter colouration, and alleles determining even stronger preference for brighter males, may be favoured by sexual selection.

According to Fisher, male feathers stop getting more brightly coloured because the runaway process runs to a check. At some point, the fitness gains from a more exuberant ornament are equal to the fitness loss derived from lower survivorship. An equilibrium value for brightness therefore results as a balance between two opposite forces: natural selection on male survivorship and sexual selection on male fertility.

It is interesting to notice that the model of runaway selection depends on an underlying or hidden assumption about the nature of female choice. In Fisher's formulation, female preference must be directional and never stabilising for the runaway process to occur; in other words, females must prefer brighter males, instead of males of a given (or optimal) brightness. Why would natural selection be unable to fine-tune female preference, and favour female preference for the male phenotype conferring highest survivorship to males? If this were possible, equilibrium values would be at the optimum for both natural and sexual selection, and male traits would not evolve into pure ornaments such as the peacock tail. In fact, some studies have revealed that there is variation in the shape of female preferences (Ritchie, 1996) within the same species, whereas others showed that runaway selection can occur even when female preference is stabilising (Lande, 1981).

This means that female preference does not necessarily misread male fitness and lead to exaggerated traits. A second class of theories thus proposes that male ornaments have evolved as honest signals that help females to read fitness from male phenotypes, and most importantly, also throws light on the very reasons for the predominance of sexual over asexual species.

ORNAMENTS: ANIMAL SIGNALS OF FITNESS

As seen earlier, females are expected to choose males on the basis of their potential contribution to offspring whenever possible. However, mating choices may take both nature and nurture. Whereas various aspects of nurture provided by males, such as protection and resources, are visible to females, some aspects of male nature may be less perceptible. It has been proposed that male ornaments and other 'display' adaptations evolved as 'fitness flags' that allow features such as general health, the condition of the immune system and other features to be perceived by females. Due to their cost, the peacock tail, courtship dances and other costly traits would be more than symbols of beauty: they evolved as symbols of health and 'good genes' (Zahavi and Zahavi, 1997; Westneat and Birkhead, 1998; Andersson and Simmons, 2006).

Those good genes are clearly not the ones responsible for male ornaments or fitness flags themselves; on the contrary, they are genes for health and fitness increasing survivorship both in males and females. For this reason, in the fitness flag models sexual selection does not oppose natural selection. If a given mutation confers a fitness advantage due to its effect on the immune system, it is likely to be eventually fixed in the population – with or without sexual selection. According to fitness flag models, genes that control male displays simply advertise those invisible fitness genes (Kodric-Brown and Brown, 1984), and therefore accelerate the speed of adaptive evolution.

It has been argued that a main reason that species are under pressure to evolve fast, and individuals are under pressure to generate variable offspring, is the continuous arms race between hosts and parasites that virtually no species can avoid (Hamilton, 1980; Hamilton et al., 1990). If this is true, pathogens are the factor tying together the two ends of the evolution of sex. On the one hand, pathogens explain the maintenance of sex as genetic exchange, due to the pressure they create on immunological variability. On the other hand, immune systems become a cause of evolution of fitness flags (Hamilton and Zuk, 1982) and thus contribute to sexual dimorphism. Various studies have shown a positive relationship between immunity to pathogens, overall individual condition and level of ornamentation in males (Read, 1988; Møller, 1990; Garvin et al., 2008; Solis et al., 2008). This contradicts the runaway hypothesis that as seen above is partially based on evidence for a trade-off between attractiveness and survivorship in some species. Thus, more than one process may have been behind the evolution of male ornamentation; a possibility is that whereas the runaway process is set in motion by mutations that increase fitness exclusively in males, the pathogen theory states that ornaments signal the existence of genes that are adaptive for both males and females.

What is important about fitness flag views is that sex may have led to the transcendence of genetic information itself. Sex seems to have allowed genetic information to evolve at higher rates. However, certain aspects of genetic information in sexual species, such as the 'quality' of alleles, can only be transmitted in the form of 'beauty' and other signals. At least in vertebrates, the signalling of genetic qualities may have been an important factor behind the evolution of higher cognitive skills. Dunbar and Shultz (2007) have recently shown, using data from birds, carnivores and artiodactyls, that monogamous or pair-bonded species tend to be more encephalised than polygamous species. Given the links between female choice and monogamy, a possible extrapolation is that the signalling of male qualities may have been one of the reasons for the evolution of larger brains, as their analyses seem to exclude the possibility that higher encephalisation in monogamous species was related to levels of parental care.

THE PHYLOGENY OF SEX AND ASEX

In addition to its role in adaptation and microevolution, sex also shows undeniable links with macroevolutionary processes. The most obvious link is that speciation itself only occurs in sexual lineages (including the origin of asexual or hermaphroditic species from sexual species). Some of the consequences of sex are also believed to play a role in speciation: sexual selection in particular is interpreted as a factor driving population divergence in various ways (West-Eberhard, 1983). Using a hypothetical example of a bird species, natural selection may favour different levels of male brightness in two environments (this might occur if camouflage were more important in one environment than in the other). In this case, females from the two localities attempting to read male fitness would diverge in their preference for male brightness; eventually, that may lead to females from one population refusing to mate with males from the other. At that point, reproductive isolation and speciation may occur as a result of sexual selection. Other models establish alternative links between sexual selection and speciation (Coyne and Orr, 2004; Ritchie, 2007).

In this context, the question is whether sexual selection can succeed where natural selection failed – or whether it can vindicate the hypothesis of reinforcement or adaptive speciation. Some authors have argued that sexual selection is strong enough to cause speciation even in sympatry or without physical isolation between populations (Turner and Burrows, 1995). However, empirical evidence has not fully demonstrated the point. On the contrary, it seems that species where sexual selection involves female choice tend to diverge, like all the others, via physical isolation or niche specialisation; later, divergence in 'recognition mechanisms' between the sexes (or the match between female preference and male traits) are likely to follow as a consequence rather than cause of population differentiation, and to act at best as an additional factor increasing the likelihood of accidental reproductive isolation (Panhuis *et al.*, 2001; Seehausen *et al.*, 2008). In particular, divergent female choice should contribute to the evolution of pre-zygotic isolating mechanisms between already differentiated populations. Thus, assortative mating is more likely to assist allopatric speciation than to cause adaptive speciation by itself.

Nonetheless, sexual selection does play an important role in speciation: if adaptive evolution is faster in sexual species, and if mate recognition mechanisms may accelerate accidental reproductive isolation, then sexually reproducing lineages should be more diverse and abundant than asexual ones (Williams, 1975). Sexual species should be more abundant both because they appear more quickly, and because they die or undergo extinction more slowly. The switch to asexuality should be a result of short-run advantages of eliminating the cost of males; but in the long run, sexual lineages should present more diversification, respond more quickly to changing conditions and pathogens and occupy more adaptive niches than asexual ones. For this reason, most asexual species are recent offshoots from sexual groups, and few of them last for long. The distribution of sexual and asexual species seems to confirm the conclusion, with asexual lineages being as a rule scattered across the animal phylogeny (White, 1978; Maynard Smith, 1978; Rice, 2002b; Barraclough *et al.*, 2003).

The existence of asexual species may therefore be mostly a consequence of the diversification of sexual species, and their occasional exposure to ecological conditions under which sexual reproduction is too costly. In conclusion, asexuality should not be seen as the evolutionary ancestor of sex: at least among animals, asexual reproduction as a rule derives from the costly consequences of sex.

SEX AND BIOLOGICAL COMPLEXITY

Many conclusions follow from the understanding that sex has to be differentiated from its various consequences. Maynard Smith's two-fold cost of sex offers an example: the cost is in fact a result of other adaptations that evolved in sexual species, such as the existence of males and balanced sex ratios, which under certain circumstances may be maladaptive in comparison with hypothetical asexual competitors; the cost does not derive from sex or genetic exchange itself.

Although sex has been undeniably a crucial player in the history of life, it can be argued that it was not a major transition in evolution as argued by Maynard Smith and Szathmáry (1995). Their argument was that fertilisation or the formation of diploid zygotes exemplified the origin of a minimal super-unit derived from two haploid gametes, whereas meiotic division and the fusion of haploid gametes would represent a new form of transmission of genetic information to offspring. However, sex as genetic exchange *did not* count as a key stage in the evolution of biological complexity. The first weakness in Maynard Smith and Szathmáry's argument is the failure to distinguish between sex and one of its consequences: in their model, the transition from asex to sex was defined as the origin of obligatory sexual reproduction, meiosis and genetic recombination – late consequences evolving billions of years after the origin of sex and genetic recombination in ancestors of bacteria, archaea and viruses (Forterre, 2006).

This misunderstanding is responsible for another weakness of their hypothesis, namely that sex represented a new form of transmission of biological information. Neither sex nor sexual reproduction (its incorrect *proxy*) is 'new' to evolution in the same way that genetic or developmental information were. Sex is by definition a way of exploring the combinatorial potentialities of the intrinsically modular system of *genetic* information, whether in its purest (the transfer of genes between bacteria) or most sophisticated forms (through sexual reproduction that makes genetic recombination compulsory); it may also involve transmission of *developmental* (or epigenetic) information in the form of mechanisms such as genomic imprinting (Reik and Walter, 2001).

Genetic and developmental information were responsible for new types of phenotypic organisation or biological order, namely disposable proteins and disposable somatic cells. The most intuitive demonstration that sex did not engender the origin of a new level of biological organisation is that asexual animal species evolving from sexual ones do not seem to 'lose' information and descend to a lower level of biological organisation; there is no reason to believe that existing asexual salamanders are less complex than the sexual species from which they derived (Robertson *et al.*, 2006). In contrast, we should certainly argue for a decrease in complexity in the case of the evolution of a unicellular species from a multicellular one (for a possible example, see Leroi *et al.*, 2003).

If sex and its consequences are not a new form of biological organisation, why are they important in evolution? Sex has contributed to microevolution as a facilitator of adaptation: operating on modular inheritance, it allows for individual deleterious mutations to be discarded, and for advantageous mutations to be transferred into the same offspring even when they originate in different lineages. Regarding macroevolution, sex engendered various consequences including speciation itself. Genetic exchange magnifies the problem of compatibility between genes present in the same individual; and in sexually reproducing individuals the convergence of paternal and maternal genotypic lineages becomes a necessity. Speciation in those cases emerged as a result of negative epistasis, or the impossibility of certain genetic or genotypic combinations to generate viable organisms (Wade, 2002). Genetic exchange and faster rates of adaptation on the one hand and negative epistasis underlying speciation on the other produced biological diversity at levels that would not have been attained had evolution depended exclusively on mutation and natural selection.

If we wanted to point to the main contribution of sex to the origin of a new biological code and phenotypic organisation, we should focus our attention not on obligatory sexual reproduction but on another consequence of sex, namely sexual selection. The conflict between sexes over reproductive strategies has led to the evolution of various forms of symbolic interaction: many ornaments in males evolve as symbols of fitness chosen by females. Animal signals (Maynard Smith and Harper, 2003) in the form of singing, colourful structures, display behaviours and others may have evolved mostly in the context of sexual selection, and contributed to new forms of transmission and exchange of information between organisms – i.e. to the evolution of information stored not in genes but in brains. As such, behaviour is undoubtedly a new form of biological information distinct from the genetic and developmental codes of life (Jablonka and Lamb, 2005). In the next chapter, the relation between brains, behaviour and social interactions is discussed in detail.

6

Animal societies: the case of incomplete evolutionary transitions

The study of animal societies, now deeply engrained in evolutionary theory, was first undertaken by philosophers dreaming of the foundation of ideal human societies. Published in 1651, Thomas Hobbes' *Leviathan* is one of many treatises grieving about the chasm between the real world of human suffering and the perfect society that we could have built together. According to Hobbes, humans were naturally in an eternal state of war against each other, as expressed by the classic aphorism *homo homini lupus est* (man is a wolf to man); the essence of human sociability is generalised conflict. In contrast to human societies, Hobbes believed that living organisms were examples of collective harmony in which individual organs or parts serve the higher purpose of survival of the whole. For this reason he proposed that the solution to human social misery should be organic: humans should willingly oppose individualism, constrain self-interest and define themselves as separate organs of a higher-level whole, the State or social Leviathan. The voluntary creation of a higher-level social organism based on co-operation and division of labour would be the ultimate antidote to social conflict, selfishness and war.

Soon it was discovered that the dream of a Leviathan, and the analogy between ideal co-operative societies and real living organisms, ran much deeper than Hobbes could have ever imagined. With his *Micrographia* published in 1665, Robert Hooke communicated the discovery both of the living cell and of multicellularity; this finding, later developed into the modern cell theory by Schleiden and Schwann, meant that all macroscopic organisms are in fact living societies of cells, divided by structure and function, and serving the purpose of the survival of multicellular wholes. Thus, multicellular organisms exemplified what for Hobbes was the ultimate human dream: the creation of a higher-order entity based on co-operation.

The advent of evolutionary theory has strengthened the case for a deep analogy between multicellular organisms and animal societies. The foundation of evolutionary social theory (Hamilton, 1964; Trivers, 1971; Axelrod, 1984; Frank, 1998; Hölldobler and Wilson, 2008) is the belief that natural selection, which we commonly associate with widespread competition among selfish individuals, may also produce co-operative group life. For example, certain ecological or social contexts might favour the evolution of division of labour, represented by the origin of castes (workers, soldiers and queens) in eusocial species, the social equivalent to specialised somatic lines. In addition, genetic relatedness may reduce conflict and increase co-operation and altruism among individuals; this is the central tenet of Hamilton's (1964) kin selection theory. It is now known that somatic and germline cells are as a rule genetically identical, whereas it was reassuring for evolutionary biologists to discover that many eusocial species are characterised by very high levels of relatedness among castes.

For the reasons above, various attempts were made at modelling the evolution of collective super-units through social co-operation. This includes the theory of aggregation formulated by Haldane and Huxley (1927), the social super-organism proposed by Wilson (1975), and the origin of super-units resulting from major transitions in evolution (Maynard Smith and Szathmáry, 1995). Maynard Smith and Szathmáry attempted to fit social evolution into the scheme of major transitions by pointing to the aggregational nature of animal societies, and by interpreting the origin of human societies as the culmination of macroevolution and the last evolutionary transition. By generalising the view of co-operation and aggregation as the key to increases in complexity, by consolidating the view of animal societies as a further step towards the evolution of organic super-units, and by placing humans at the top of a scale of complexity, the macroevolutionary theory of Maynard Smith and Szathmáry seems to have resurrected the human Leviathan – no longer as a historical and political body resulting from a social contract, but as a biological entity evolving by natural selection.

Unfortunately, their conclusions were too optimistic. Despite some common selective pressures and adaptive solutions, multicellular organisms and animal societies remain fundamentally different types of biological entities. This is true for a simple reason: whereas multicellular organisms are finished articles or proper super-units evolved by aggregation, all known animal societies are (at best) examples of *incomplete* transitions in evolution. Although they differ in how far they have evolved towards a true social super-unit or biological Leviathan, it remains true that no animal society has yet evolved into a true super-organism as defined by Maynard Smith and Szathmáry themselves. This does not mean that animal societies are just 'mobs of selfish individuals' (Williams, 1996), as many display remarkably high levels of interdependency, co-operation and genetic similarity. Insect and mammalian societies in particular are certainly more than a sum of individual and selfish parts, forming impressive social wholes that share many characteristics with multicellularity, such as division of labour and even reproductive withdrawal (Wilson, 1975; Clutton-Brock, 1991).

However, dissimilarities between societies and multicellular wholes are also obvious. First, it is now recognised that division of labour in animal societies is not necessarily associated with altruism and a common social good: sentinels, reproductive helpers and other 'altruists' are often selfish individuals maximising their own fitness (Clutton-Brock *et al.*, 2001); in other words, what could be apparently interpreted as a harmonious division of labour may be in fact just a result of different selfish strategies.

Second, complete genetic identity, an almost universal feature of multicellular organisms (in which all cells are derived by clonal division or mitosis from a zygote and therefore carry the same genes), has not been observed in any social species, including eusocial insects, termites and mammals. The reason is that without exception all examples of animal societies displaying high levels of co-operation are sexually reproducing species, which necessarily implies some level of outbreeding, heterozygosity and genetic variation. Disappointingly, known asexual species that produce clonal offspring (and therefore resemble the clonal production of genetically identical somatic cells) fail to display highly co-operative social behaviour (and are not even expected to do so; see Dawkins, 1979); thus, we are yet to identify a true 'social soma' in animal societies.

Third, differently from reproductive withdrawal exemplified by disposable somatic cells whose function is to support the perpetuation of germline cells across generations, sterility in animal societies has often been shown to result from selfish reproductive strategies rather than co-operation. In some cases what seemed to be altruistic reproductive withdrawal aimed at favouring the reproduction of other group members is just the sacrifice of current reproduction by some individuals with the aim of maximising their own future reproduction (Komdeur *et al.*, 1997). In other cases, sterility of certain individuals is the result of coercion of subordinate females by dominant members rather than altruism (O'Riain *et al.*, 2000). In summary, animal societies certainly involve some level of co-operation among individuals; but contrary to multicellular organisms in which cells are nothing more than component parts of a whole, co-operative individuals in animal societies (including sterile ones) are still competing against other group members over (direct or indirect) reproduction.

The failure of animal societies to have so far achieved the evolutionary status of super-organisms has a direct consequence to current theories of biological complexity: it reveals inconsistencies in both Maynard Smith and Szathmáry's theory of major transitions and in the rationale behind multilevel selection (Nowak, 2006). But this failure is, at the same time, what makes animal societies so important to macroevolutionary theory: being super-units in the making, they may offer the best model for understanding the selective forces that were behind the origin of multicellularity – a true case of evolutionary increase in biological complexity. In the following, two types of selective forces frequently seen as able to bind individuals together in societies are analysed: kin selection, the principle behind the evolution of true altruism; and reciprocation, the mechanism explaining the origin of co-operative (but still selfish) behaviour.

Recently, Nowak (2006) proposed a unification of all forces of social aggregation under a single scheme and described the conditions under which known forms of social co-operation may have evolved. Due to its multiple manifestations and widespread occurrence, Nowak argued that 'natural co-operation' should be accepted as a third fundamental evolutionary principle alongside variation and natural selection. Nowak's point is probably true, but the principle carries with it a macroevolutionary consequence: as much as variation and natural selection, natural co-operation does not necessarily produce increases in biological complexity. Thus, the study of animal societies will lead us to an important conclusion: levels of selection are not the same as levels of biological or phenotypic organisation. This mistake was caused by the unique case of multicellular organisms, those super-units that represent at the same time a level of selection and a level of phenotypic organisation. In contrast, the key to the understanding of the evolution of social groups is that although they are legitimate levels of selection, they are not a level of organisation: as discussed below, the social Leviathan remains a human dream.

THE PROBLEM OF CO-OPERATION

The fundamental drama of social life is summarised by the question: to compete or to co-operate? Given the ubiquitous presence of both competitive and co-operative behaviours in most animal societies, and even the alternation of those behaviours in the same individual, we can readily conclude that there is no absolute or universal solution to the problem. On the one hand, competition and selfishness are easy to implement, as they are individualist strategies that avoid unnecessary dependency on other group members; but selfishness may be costly by creating a state of generalised war, and by failing to explore the advantages of group work such as division of labour. On the other hand, by joining forces, co-operative individuals may be able to achieve what isolated individuals cannot; but co-operation creates dependency on others, increased costs of helping unrelated and sometimes even unknown individuals, and the risk of fitness losses due to cheating whenever co-operation is not reciprocated, among others. In summary, the conflict between individual versus group interest is as present in humans as in other animal species, and co-operation is for this reason a phenomenon hard to explain.

The presence of apparently co-operative and altruistic behaviours in animals has been explained by some evolutionary hypotheses. Two theories in particular dominated early phases of the debate: group selectionism and universal individualism. Darwin himself had no doubt about the existence of truly co-operative behaviour in animal species; he believed that heroes and martyrs had a selective reason to exist, and that altruistic or heroic behaviours were a feature of social life. Using the report of a fellow naturalist, this is how Darwin described in the *Descent of Man* the response of baboons to an attack by a group of wild dogs in the Ethiopian savannah:

> [the dogs] were again encouraged to the attack; but by this time all the baboons had reascended the heights, excepting a young one, about six months old, who, loudly calling for aid, climbed on a block of rock and was surrounded. Now one of the largest males, a true hero, came down again from the mountain, slowly went to the young one, coaxed him, and triumphantly led him away – the dogs being too much astonished to make an attack (Darwin, 1871: 76).

According to Darwin, one face of heroism exhibited by the adult male was the potential individual sacrifice: the baboon hero placed himself at risk in order to save another group member, a behaviour that could not apparently derive from selfish motivation. The second aspect is the idea of admiration by other group members: even the attacking dogs seemed to have been impressed by the hero's bravery. Darwin believed that admiration or reputation was a key aspect in the evolution of co-operative behaviours; as seen later, this theme has become central in current theories of social evolution (Nowak and Sigmund, 2005; Suzuki and Akiyama, 2005; Nowak, 2006; Sommerfeld *et al.*, 2008).

Darwin's view implies that factors such as the higher survivorship of weaker group members and the high praise awarded to co-operative individuals should suffice to explain why heroism has evolved. This view is known as 'naïve group selection' (Wilson and Sober, 1994); it is the idea that heroism and co-operative behaviour evolved because survivorship and fitness are higher in groups hosting heroes and other altruistic members. Another example is given by insect societies, where most individuals do not reproduce but dedicate their existence as soldiers, workers or foragers to the reproductive success of a royal family or queen. It seems natural to believe that soldiers evolved in ants, bees and wasps because they protect their societies; that workers evolved because they keep the colony functioning; that foragers find food for all; and that the queen reproduces and keeps the colony alive. In isolation, those entities are meaningless; together, they would work as a single super-organism (Wilson, 1975; Wilson and Hölldobler, 2005).

Although intuitively appealing, group selectionism has been thoroughly criticised and rejected by most evolutionary biologists (Williams, 1966; Dawkins, 1976). According to Williams, the evolution of traits such as heroism can be better understood if we ask the question: is heroism adaptive *to the hero*? Although heroes are clearly advantageous to their groups, reproduction is performed by individuals; the question is therefore whether heroes and their genes have any advantage in the struggle for survival. That is a fundamental problem with naïve group selectionism: heroism does not seem to be advantageous for heroes themselves. The reason is that those who display heroic behaviour put themselves at a higher risk of death; in the long run, the higher mortality rates expected among heroes in comparison with non-heroes (consisting of the selfish, cowardly or merely weak individuals) must lead to the prevalence of the latter. In summary, since survival and reproduction are more relevant at the individual than at the group level (Fisher, 1930), natural selection implies that individual selection for selfishness prevails over group selection for heroism. The argument applies not only to heroism but to altruistic and co-operative behaviour in general.

Due to the failure of naïve group selectionism, a second popular answer to the enigma of co-operation was its outright denial (Williams, 1966, 1996). From this perspective, any apparent case of heroism or altruism observed in nature is reinterpreted as an illusion (Alexander, 1987); as graphically expressed by Ghiselin (1974), 'scratch an altruist and watch a hypocrite bleed'. The behaviour exhibited by Darwin's baboon hero must be explained as some form of self-interested strategy; rescuing the endangered juvenile must have been an attempt at obtaining some gain (higher social status, reputation, additional females, helping his own offspring). If this view is true in general, it should be concluded that there is no true altruism, and societies do not exist as co-operative super-entities; despite the appearances, they are nothing more than mobs of selfish individuals.

Current evolutionary theories of social evolution consider Williams' views to be equally wrong. There are various examples of altruism shown to reduce individual fitness of actors and to increase fitness of recipients, such as sentinel behaviour and parental care when directed towards offspring or related individuals (Hamilton, 1964); besides, there are undeniable examples of true co-operation in animal societies involving both costs and benefits to participants (Trivers, 1971). As seen below, it is generally agreed that true co-operation can and did evolve by natural selection, and for this reason many animal societies are certainly more than mobs.

Two main ideas came to replace the unsatisfactory views of group selectionism and strict individualism. The first view, originally outlined by Darwin and others but given a definitive formulation by Hamilton (1964), states that individuals should act altruistically towards their kin; true altruism may evolve under the condition of genetic relatedness. The second idea is that altruism and co-operation are compatible with selfish interest, *if* there is reciprocity; in other words, co-operation may evolve if co-operation is advantageous for actors and recipients, and if all individuals can be (simultaneously or not) actors and recipients (Trivers, 1971). The main consequences of the two theories, kin selection and reciprocal altruism, are discussed in the following.

RELATEDNESS AS THE ORIGIN OF TRUE ALTRUISM

For over a century, evolutionary biologists including Darwin believed in a link between kinship and the occurrence of altruistic behaviour. Darwin (1859) had already noticed that the sterility of soldiers and workers in insect societies was somewhat paradoxical, since it apparently prevents genes from soldiers and workers to propagate across generations, and together with genes, the altruistic traits themselves. Darwin guessed that the solution to the paradox was that soldiers and workers were all members of the same family or kin group, if they descend from the same queen mother; for this reason, soldiers and workers in fact help their own littermates (including future queens and reproductive males), and those propagate their genes. Haldane (1932) developed the argument further and argued that he would happily sacrifice his life for two brothers or four cousins. By doing so, Haldane proposed a continuous or quantitative relationship between levels of relatedness and levels of altruism between individuals: the more closely related to an individual, the more likely you are to be altruistic towards him or her. The link was also almost literally formulated in a footnote from a classic article by Medawar on the evolution of senescence:

> Grandparents, though not fertile, may yet promote (or impede) the welfare of their grandchildren, and so influence the mode of propagation of their genes. A gene for grandmotherly indulgence should therefore prevail over one for callous indifference, in spite of the fact that the gene is propagated *per procurationem* and not by the organism in which its developmental effect appears. Selection for grandmotherly indulgence I should describe as 'indirect', and the indirect action of selection becomes important whenever there is any high degree of social organization. The genes that make for efficient and industrious worker bees, for example, are of vital importance to the bee community, though not propagated by the worker bees themselves (Medawar, 1952: 45).

Interestingly, this quote contains not only the essence of kin selection theory, but also the basis for the grandmother hypothesis later proposed by Hawkes and collaborators (1998) to explain the evolution of human menopause. However, it was Hamilton (1964) who presented the theory linking relatedness and altruism in mathematical format. Let us assume that an allele a occurs in a population and commands a given altruistic behaviour by its carriers. Hamilton's rule states that truly altruistic behaviours may evolve if

$$br - c > 0.$$

The rule implies that if the benefit (b) to the recipient of an altruistic act is higher than the cost (c) of the behaviour to the altruistic actor, then the allele a and the altruistic act may be favoured by natural selection – provided that the level of relatedness r between them (when r is the likelihood that both actor and recipient inherited a from a common ancestor) is large enough. In other words, altruism may evolve at a cost to the actor (and to the copy of the allele a it carries) if the benefit to the recipient is higher (provided that there is a large enough likelihood that a is also carried by the recipient); under those conditions, the allele a can be indirectly replicated. This rationale explained why altruistic acts such as the protective behaviour displayed by Darwin's baboon hero could have evolved; if one assumes that the hero was in fact the father or a close relative of the juvenile baboon, he was in fact saving the life of a carrier of his own genes. It has been recently shown that baboon males actively support their male offspring (Buchan *et al.*, 2003).

Kin selection also establishes a distinction between two levels of analysis: individual and genetic. From the point of view of the altruistic actor, there is only a cost: the actor loses direct reproduction by supporting another individual. This is not true from the point of view of the allele a, which may experience both a direct cost (in the actor) and an indirect benefit (in the recipient) if present in both. Therefore, although individuals may be truly altruistic, the genes underlying altruistic actions are selfish. Kin selection is therefore the theoretical source of the concept of the selfish gene (Dawkins, 1976). In summary, individuals may behave altruistically only if selfish genes for altruism spread and are maintained by selection.

Despite some similarities, it is clear that kin selection theory does not justify a reinstatement of Williams' strict individualism: although genes are truly selfish, individuals are truly altruistic vehicles, regarding both the motivation of behaviours and the effect of their actions. In concrete terms, this means that actors operate so as to increase fitness of related individuals without expecting or receiving any type of reciprocation; for example, the case of mothers dispensing parental care, or workers helping queens in insect societies.

Another consequence of kin selection is the concept of kin group as an intermediate level of selection between the individual and the group. At the same time, it predicts the evolution of behaviours that cannot be described as either selfish or heroic; they are altruistic, but exclusively directed towards related individuals. It should be remembered that we are all related to each other (all living organisms share a common ancestor); what differs is the level of relatedness between any two individuals. For this reason, each organism is the centre of its own relatedness circle, and the theory of kin selection predicts that each organism will be more co-operative towards more closely related individuals, with selfishness increasing towards less related ones. Kin selection means that the same individuals may exhibit extremely altruistic and extremely selfish behaviours: no hero is an absolute hero, and no mother is an absolute good mother. For all those reasons, kin selection goes beyond the dichotomy between individual and group, and is a successful alternative to both extreme individualism and naïve group selection.

The logic of kin selection has been extensively applied and tested in its various predictions. If true altruism is a consequence of relatedness or shared genes between organisms, societies exhibiting high average relatedness should exhibit higher levels of co-operation. Conveniently, the classic example of co-operative societies, the hymenopteran eusocial insects (bees, wasps and ants), present a special form of genetic system (haplodiploidy) that contributes to higher group relatedness. The haplodiploid system can be more easily described as a combination of sexual and parthenogenetic reproduction. When eggs are fertilised, diploid females are obtained, whereas unfertilised eggs give rise to haploid males. Males do not perform any function in insect colonies except reproduction. Despite some exceptions, as a rule female castes differ among themselves due to nurture rather than nature: individuals develop into queens, soldiers and workers as a function of food allocation, which is under the control of workers (Hölldobler and Wilson, 2008).

In one particular case, the haplodiploid system produces a particularly important consequence. When queens mate with a single male, relatedness between different members of an insect colony shows asymmetries. The relatedness r of an individual A to an individual B can be broadly estimated as the proportion of genes in A expected to be present in B. For example, whereas sisters in diploid species share half their genes ($r = 0.5$), in the case of haplodiploids they share three quarters (i.e. all the genes from the haploid fathers that have only one copy of each gene to pass on to descendants, and half the genes from the diploid mother). This means that female offspring are more closely related to their sisters than to their own putative offspring. This is why Hamilton (1964) proposed that haplodiploidy causes a predisposition towards eusociality: due to the high relatedness between sisters, females were more likely to evolve into sterile workers assisting a queen that specialises in reproduction; workers thereby maximise their indirect fitness at the expense of direct or personal reproduction.

Kin selection also predicts selfishness between more distantly related individuals, as equally exemplified by sisters and brothers in hymenopteran societies. Whereas females are related by $r = 0.75$ to their sisters, they are related to brothers by $r = 0.25$ (under the assumption of a single father). This means that sisters should be more interested in the birth of females than of males – more precisely, three times more interested, as a sister carries three times as many shared genes as a brother (Trivers and Hare, 1976). However, the queen should not agree with workers in relation to preference for female offspring, since she is equally related to their sons and daughters ($r = 0.5$). Since queens control the sex of offspring at birth, whereas workers determine which offspring is fed and reaches adulthood, conflict over sex ratios is expected to occur. Some studies have confirmed the prediction in some species, with males being selectively killed by workers and queens fighting back by producing more males than females; the final outcome is a fraction of males typically ranging between one third and one half, or a balance between queen and workers (Sundström *et al.*, 1996). In summary, kin selection and conflict over sex ratios mean that queens and workers are not necessarily doing what is best for the species, but rather what is good for their genes; the latter may command workers to nurture their sisters on the one hand and to kill their own brothers on the other (Strassmann and Queller, 2007).

Instances of reproductive assistance or co-operative breeding are not limited to social insects, and 'helpers' are observed in some species of birds and mammals including humans (Clutton-Brock, 1991; Hrdy, 2009). In Seychelles warblers, for example, female helpers stay in the nest and assist reproductive females feeding young offspring, instead of creating their own nest (Komdeur *et al.*, 1997). This behaviour was also explained by the logic of direct versus indirect reproduction: as predicted by kin selection, the helpers in this species were found to be daughters assisting their mothers in raising their own siblings.

Another example of altruistic behaviour in animal societies is the case of sentinels found in various social species (Hamilton, 1964). The classic example are the Belding ground squirrels, a species characterised by female kin bonding (i.e. females remain in the group in which they are born) and by a higher degree of relatedness between females than between males (which migrate between groups). Many predictions from kin selection theory were observed in this species (Sherman, 1977). As in the case of the altruistic behaviour of workers and soldiers in insect societies, sentinel behaviour is performed almost exclusively by females; sentinel behaviour is proportional to relatedness, meaning that females are more likely to alarm call to their daughters than to their nieces.

Kin selection interprets co-operation as a result of truly altruistic motivations, controlled by selfish genes that command actions favouring their replication at the expense of altruistic actors; this is why true sentinels or reproductive helpers do not demand reciprocation from the related individuals that they benefit. Kin selection theory, which postulates that relatedness causes or at least predisposes individuals to co-operation, can be questioned on a few main grounds. Does relatedness really precede co-operation, or is it the contrary? As seen above, hymenopteran insects are seen as a classic example of kin selection; however, ants, wasps and bees are not the only eusocial species exhibiting non-reproductive castes: termites, for example, are equally well known for the existence of a royal (reproductive) family, sterile soldiers and workers, colonies and co-operative breeding practices. But termites are mostly diploid (with some parthenogenetic exceptions; Matsuura *et al.*, 2009), and so are other eusocial species of shrimp, spiders – and even a mammalian species.

The discovery of eusociality in African naked mole rats was important and surprising (Jarvis, 1981). In this species there is a royal family consisting of a single reproductive female, a few reproductive males, and a few other females reproductively suppressed (physically or chemically) by the queen; some occasional workers; a few migrants that prevent total inbreeding in groups were also observed (O'Riain *et al.*, 1996); finally, there are sterile workers (males and females) that perform all the work in the colony. Kin selection seems to explain co-operative behaviour and reproductive withdrawal in this species too: the average relatedness in colonies is high, being reported as $r = 0.81$ in one study (Reeve *et al.*, 1990), and a more modest $r = 0.46$ in another (Burland *et al.*, 2002). As in termites, high relatedness in naked mole rats is not caused by haplodiploidy, but by higher levels of inbreeding and a small founding population. Thus, the genetic predisposition offered by haplodiploidy may be a far less fundamental factor to eusociality than some ecological challenges shared by eusocial species, such as the processing of cellulose and colonisation of large, underground environments; those factors may have predisposed species to social division of labour and group integration, and as a consequence of higher group success, to higher inbreeding too. In summary, high relatedness may be a consequence of co-operative societies, rather than their cause (Wilson and Hölldobler, 2005).

Another criticism is that genetic relatedness may not be the explanation for some examples of heroic behaviour because they may not be heroic at all. Sentinel behaviour, for example, may be more self-ish and its association with kin bonding less universal than expected. A well-studied social species with familiar sentinels are meerkats, and careful studies have shown that sentinel behaviour in meerkat groups can be strictly explained by selfish reasons – that is, by interest in individual survival (Clutton-Brock et al., 2001). There seems to be no evidence for a co-operative or concerted effort of meerkat sentinels to offer vigilance to other group members. Meerkats perform two regular activities to maximise survival: one is foraging, and the other is sentinel behaviour. One expects a cycle or alternation between the two activities. When an individual is hungry, the main risk to survival is starvation, and at that point it is expected to switch to foraging. When foraging is finished, the risk of death by starvation is reduced, and the risk to survival posed by predation becomes temporarily higher. This rationale implies that a switch from foraging to sentinel behaviour can be expected from purely selfish or individualistic reasons. The selfish nature of sentinel behaviour in meerkats was demonstrated in various ways: sentinels are momentarily well-fed organisms, they are observed at short distance to burrows where they can hide, and they do not display preference for signalling the presence of predators to related individuals. Thus, a sentinel group seems to emerge not from division of labour or co-operation, but as a by-product of the constant alternation of selfish individuals in the role of selfish sentinels.

There is still a mystery to be explained. If sentinel behaviour in meerkats is self-interested rather than altruistic or co-operative, why do sentinels bother emitting alarm calls that are perceived by other group members and useful to them? Based on the scenario above, after spotting a predator the selfish sentinels should simply escape to the closest burrow in silence. There are at least two possible explanations for why they produce alarm calls. First, alarm calling may be directed to the *predators* rather than other meerkats: alarm calls would be a way of showing the predator that the sentinel is the most alert member in the group, and therefore the most likely to escape; the sentinel is signalling the message that the predator would do better by chasing another meerkat. Second, each sentinel may be alerting other group members to the presence of predators, but they do it for a selfish reason: by making all group members aware of the presence of a predator, sentinels may reduce the likelihood that the attack is successful; this might reduce further attacks to that particular group. However, this scenario would involve group selection (between groups with and without sentinels), which as seen is questionable on many grounds; the difference is that the motivation of alarm calling in this case would be selfish (the survival of the sentinel) rather than altruistic (the survival of the group or other group members).

In addition to the problem with genetic relatedness as a cause of social co-operation, a further question regarding kin selection is whether co-operation must necessarily be selfless; in other words, is altruism the main form of co-operation in animal societies? The answer is clearly negative; various forms of co-operation only exist under the condition of a reward to co-operative individuals – or as universally known by humans, co-operation may be a matter of an eye for an eye. In such cases, if the return to the actors is higher than that cost, co-operation may evolve simply because it is advantageous for all co-operators.

The social wasp *Polistes dominulus* provides a good example of what is meant by selfish co-operation (Queller *et al.*, 2000). These wasps also present a social structure that includes fertile queen and related infertile female workers; but colonies also exhibit subordinate females, which remain in the colony, restrain themselves from reproduction and maximise overall colony success; but contrary to helpers in Seychelles warblers, those females are unrelated to the queen. Why do those females help in the reproduction of their competitor? Subordinate females are faced with a choice: to remain in the nest, or to found a new one. However, their positive effect on colony size and survival indicates that nests with a single founding female are much less likely to succeed. For this reason, rather than starting a new colony, it is advantageous for subordinate females to wait for the current queen to die and then inherit her multi-female colony. This suggests that subordinate females help the current queen not for altruistic or selfless reasons, but because playing the waiting game (i.e. trading early for later reproduction) is the best possible reproductive strategy.

In summary, two of the main difficulties with the theory of kin selection are first that genetic relatedness may not necessarily precede altruism, and second that co-operation is not necessarily altruistic and can in principle be guided by selfish interests. Both problems point to the same conclusion: theories of co-operation in animal societies should also address cases involving unrelated individuals.

SELFISH CO-OPERATION: AN EYE FOR AN EYE, A HELPING HAND
FOR A HELPING HAND

The most obvious alternative to genetic relatedness as an explanation
for co-operative behaviour is selfish interest. The reason is simple: co-
operating with another group member (not necessarily a family member) may be the best way of increasing individual fitness, even if that
implies the success of one or a few of many unrelated competitors.
This is in essence the theory of reciprocal altruism proposed by Trivers
(1971). Despite its somewhat misleading name, the theory proposes
that co-operative behaviour is not exclusively altruistic; instead of
reciprocal altruism, it would be more appropriate to call it the theory
of 'selfish co-operation' (Stevens and Hauser, 2004). While kin selection proposes that true altruistic behaviour evolves towards kin at the
expense of a cost to the selfless actor, the theory of reciprocal altruism
argues that self-interested co-operation may evolve if participants are
both actors and recipients, and if benefits are greater than costs irrespective of relatedness.

If co-operation may be advantageous for all, why is it rather rare
in comparison with more frequent competitive interactions that are
costly and many times end up in general loss (Williams, 1996)? To answer
this question, game theory has been extensively utilised in evolutionary studies to model conditions and outcomes of social interactions
(Axelrod and Hamilton, 1981; Maynard Smith, 1982). A particular
game, named 'Prisoner's Dilemma' or alternatively the 'sculling game'
(Maynard Smith and Szathmáry, 1995), is commonly used to explain
why co-operation may not evolve even when it is the most beneficial
solution to a given adaptive problem. As an example, let us assume two
humans living in a mainland village next to the sea; also assume that
on a near island there grows a food item to which we associate an arbitrary fitness value of +4 units. The island can only be reached by boat,
with the physical cost of paddling to the island being higher than the
benefit from the food that can be brought back home by one person;
for example, let us say that the cost of paddling to the island is −6 fitness units. Under these conditions, no sea travel is expected to evolve,
since it engenders a net fitness loss (benefit − cost = −2).

This conclusion changes when we propose that the two men
decide to share the boat and travel together. In this case, the physical
cost of sculling (−6) is shared and reduced to −3 per individual. The
new calculation shows that there is a net gain of +1 unit available,
as benefits (+4) are greater than the cost (−3). This is a clear example

of how group effort may make resources available that are unattainable by selfish players: large-game hunting and nest building, among others, would be examples of the real opportunities of gain by all co-operative individuals. Thus, it seems that in many cases general co-operation may be a better strategy than general competition.

However, the main use of the sculling game is to show why the social Leviathan has *not* evolved. Imagine the two seafarers now on their second trip together. During the journey, the sculler sitting at the back of the boat may have a tempting thought: to stop paddling. It should be remembered that the reason for their co-operation was selfish interest in the first place, or a gain of individual fitness units. After the start of their co-operative effort, a new way of maximising individual fitness emerges: the change from co-operator (which includes costs and benefits) to the more comfortable role of passenger (which only involves benefits of travelling). Whereas co-operation engenders a net gain of +1 in our example, if one of the travellers stops paddling there is a gain of +4 units (the benefits from travelling without costs); the exploited co-operator will incur a cost of −2 (the benefit of +4 units, and the original cost of −6 units from doing all the work). Thus, cheating is advantageous and compatible with self-interest.

If selfish interest guides behaviour, asymmetrical arrangements are not expected to last. From the point of view of the co-operative sculler that paid a fitness price in the second trip, there is an option: to defect as soon as possible so as to avoid further losses. Defecting would represent a relative gain (from the loss of −2 units per travel to no gain), but also the end of their short-lived co-operative enterprise. As a result, the two players waste a good opportunity to maximise their individual fitness, and food will rot on the near island. The sculling game explains why co-operation is not universal, despite the obvious advantages of teamwork: the reason is that in many cases motivation behind co-operation may be selfish (the well-being of the co-operative actor) rather than altruistic (the well-being of a related or unrelated recipient). Thus, despite the fact that living in an ideal co-operative Leviathan would be better than in selfish isolation, it would be even more advantageous to be part of the Leviathan without co-operating with it. As expressed by Williams (1996), in social interactions the best strategy is always to defect. For this reason, even if co-operative animal groups were constantly created, the problem is the difficulty of preventing the spread of selfish individuals; in summary, social Leviathans are unlikely to be 'evolutionary stable strategies' (Maynard Smith, 1982).

A possible criticism of this argument is that the advantages or disadvantages of co-operation should always be analysed in the long run. In the example above, cheating may bring a short-term benefit after one single trip; however, cheating causes a much greater loss because it interrupts co-operation; in other words, the benefit of extra +3 units resulting from cheating in the second trip would cause a loss of +10 units corresponding to 10 future trips that were cancelled due to double defection. Thus, co-operation may serve individual interest – if actors are patient enough. However, the fact remains that selfishness and defection have not been eliminated in most animal societies. Evolutionary theory has relied on the concept of 'temporal discounting' (Rachlin and Green, 1972; Ainslie, 1974) to explain the tendency of individuals to favour short-run over long-run interests. Temporal discounting seems to occur because the present is more certain (or real) than the future, and animal behaviour evolved to take risk and uncertainty into account.

As an example, assume that individuals are faced with a choice between receiving a given resource affecting fitness now or in the future; let us use the anthropocentric example of money. Given a choice between £10,000 now and £10,000 in ten years time, the best choice is to accept the money now as there is no gain in waiting. But what if the choice is between the same £10,000 now, and a future gain of £1,000,000: in this case, the result would probably be different. Due to the significantly higher value of the future gain, most individuals would rather wait for ten years and then enjoy the advantage of a much larger amount of money. From this, we infer the existence of a value between £10,000 and £1,000,000 at which individuals switch to choosing the future gain; let us say that this value is £20,000. If offers are under £20,000, individuals are likely to choose the immediate gain; offers over this value would mostly be accepted; finally, people would be indifferent to £10,000 now or £20,000 in ten years time, or alternatively, half the subjects would choose £10,000 now, and half the £20,000 in the future.

From that, a rate of temporal discounting can be calculated: if £10,000 now is valued the same as £20,000 in ten years, the future gain is losing half its value in ten years in the mind of choosing subjects, or 5% per year. A value close to 5% per year was in fact found in some experiments involving humans (Weitzman, 2001). Temporal discounting occurs in other species too. Blue jays were trained to adopt co-operative behaviours (sharing of food) in a setting that favoured reciprocation (Stephens et al., 2002). Co-operation decreased after a few rounds of interactions at an estimated rate of 50% per second, possibly reflecting the higher level of uncertainty regarding reciprocation by other group members faced by blue jays in their natural environment.

Risk of non-reciprocation by a partner is a main reason for why self-interested individuals may prefer smaller but immediate gains to larger but more uncertain future gains, as the latter are dependent on the existence and behaviour of self-interested partners. If animals could just make sure that reciprocation by partners occurs, co-operation levels would be higher.

THE CONDITIONS FOR SELFISH CO-OPERATION

Another contribution of the theory of reciprocal altruism was the analysis of possible conditions preventing cheating and discounting, a requirement for selfish co-operation to be a strategy resilient to selfish individualism. One condition would be the occurrence of multiple interactions between individuals (Trivers, 1971); the perspective of only a single or a few interactions means by definition the impossibility of future reciprocation. Thus, stable co-operation should be more likely to evolve in species characterised by long lifespans (including social mammals). Smaller groups, where individuals (that have or have not reciprocated co-operation in the past) are more easily recognisable, should be more favourable to direct reciprocation than large groups where interactions are more likely to be anonymous; in larger groups, indirect reciprocation might be possible (Alexander, 1987). Reciprocation will also be favoured by ecological factors such as foraging habits that involve potentially high returns to collective action: whereas folivory is compatible with solitary foraging, hunting large game is more likely to involve co-operation in the long run. Finally, the cognitive ability to recognise previous reciprocators and discriminate against defectors (in the form of non-reciprocation or punishment) would also favour long-term co-operation. Axelrod and Hamilton (1981) and Nowak and Sigmund (1993) have proposed strategies such as the 'Tit-for Tat' and 'Win Stay, Lose Shift' that demonstrate that co-operative behaviour may outperform selfishness in the long run under the conditions of repeated interactions, ecological gains from co-operation, recognition of partners and possible punishment of defectors.

The argument implies that animal taxa exhibiting long lives, more stable groups, higher cognitive abilities and higher encephalisation, such as primates (Dunbar, 1998), passeriform birds (Cnotka *et al.*,

2008) and cetaceans (Marino, 2002), are expected to exemplify co-operative arrangements among unrelated individuals. An interesting case is the red-winged blackbird, an American species of long-lived, monogamous, highly encephalised and colonial birds that evolved a sophisticated system of nest defence. This system is operated by adult males, and the main predators are corvids that feed on eggs.

Olendorf et al. (2004) tested three hypotheses for the existence of this co-operative policing. The first is kin selection, which predicts that males should only police nests hosting eggs that will generate related offspring or occupied by related adult males. The second possibility is 'by-product mutualism', similar to that observed in meerkat sentinels; each male should act only in his own interest and guard his own nest. Large numbers of males in a colony would imply the accidental origin of a 'police' from a mob of selfish guarding males. In this case, selfish males should only guard their own nests or nests containing their extra-pair offspring (known to occur in the species). The final alternative is reciprocal altruism, predicting both self-interested co-operation among policing males irrespective of relatedness, and retaliation against non-co-operative males that fail to play their share in policing the colony nests.

A series of experiments revealed the correct answer. First, kin selection was rejected due to the lack of association between helping behaviour and relatedness. Second, there was a negative association between extra-pair offspring and nest guarding, contrary to the positive association predicted by the hypothesis of by-product mutualism. Finally, reciprocal altruism was corroborated by the observation of co-operation among unrelated males and by the existence of retaliation against defectors. This was demonstrated by an experiment consisting of the simulation of a predator attack and the removal of some adult males, which were prevented from defending nests and therefore forced by the experimenter to defect. The result was that in subsequent attacks males selectively refused to help the individuals forced into non-co-operation.

Another example was given by Australian bottlenose dolphins, also known for their large brains and advanced cognitive abilities. Dolphins have long lifespans, live in large groups, and were the most encephalised mammals until the emergence of the genus *Homo* (Marino, 1996). A well-studied population of bottlenose dolphins was found in the Australian Shark Bay and consisted of about 400 individual males (Connor et al., 1999). Major contests over territory control and two distinct types of co-operative alliances among males were observed. One type of coalition consisted of very stable and small pairs or triads that sometimes included juveniles. The authors observed a second type of grouping, a 'super-alliance' that included a total of 14 members. Intriguingly, those 14 males were not commonly seen together; when territorial disputes occurred against one of the stable group of 2–3 males, different combinations of the 14 super-alliance members were recruited, and those combinations always outnumbered the stable pairs and were often successful in contests.

It was later shown (Krützen *et al.*, 2003) that this population of Australian bottlenose dolphins exemplified a contrast between two forms of social co-operation. DNA analysis showed that dolphins in the small groups were related as brothers or as father and offspring, explaining the presence of subadults and the long-term associations. On the other hand, the super-alliance included only unrelated individuals. This shows that reciprocal altruism managed to produce co-operation of a more sophisticated and broad nature in bottlenose dolphins; using a human analogy, the super-alliance is in fact a dolphin mafia in which brotherhood is defined not by blood but by reciprocal co-operation. Needless to say, the principle of co-operation behind the super-alliance is the strict self-interest of each one of its members.

A final example is offered by a study of defence alliances between Diana monkeys and red colobus monkeys in an Ivory Coast forest (Noë and Bshary, 1997; Dunbar, 1997). Both species are targeted by chimpanzees during the hunting season, with the cost of predation to monkeys corresponding to an average of one death for every two chimpanzee attacks. It was also shown that the formation of large parties of Diana and red colobus monkeys is effective in reducing fatalities, and that most defence parties are initiated by the red colobus (the main target of chimpanzees); in this case, co-operation occurs between members of two species.

All the examples show that co-operation in animal species is not necessarily altruistic or kin-based: the principle of selfish co-operation may even extend across different species facing a common ecological challenge.

THE BIRTH OF THE SELFLESS APE

The theory of reciprocal altruism seems to be the perfect framework for understanding the extreme sociality of humans. Since the origin of the genus *Homo*, ancestral humans have been characterised by co-operative hunting of large game and foraging of various foodstuffs, increased sociability and higher encephalisation (Kaplan *et al.*, 2000, Lewin and Foley, 2004). Extant traditional societies depend upon strictly collective practices such as agriculture, hunting, war, and above all language and other cultural practices (Diamond, 1997). However, in historical times (and especially in post-industrial societies) co-operative behaviour was transformed and now extends well beyond the boundaries of kin or local groups, and includes honourable acts such as blood donation and charity work besides more trivial ones such as paying taxes and obeying laws. Those facts suggest that the special nature of human sociality could be explained by two factors: reciprocal altruism moulding human behaviour from the origins of our species, and relatively recent historical and cultural features transforming social organisation and creating new forms of human co-operation.

Despite its apparent theoretical promise, the account outlined above has recently faced fierce opposition from the theory of 'strong reciprocity' (Bowles and Gintis, 2002; Gintis, 2003; Engelen, 2008), which rejects reciprocal altruism as an explanation for human behaviour. This rejection is based on one underlying assumption: the denial of selfishness as the explanation for human social co-operation. The theory of strong reciprocity proposes that unique co-operative behaviours displayed by humans both in traditional and post-industrial societies cannot be explained by current evolutionary theories of co-operation, which would only work for other animal societies (Boyd and Richerson, 2005). For example, true altruism in eusocial insects and some social mammals is explained by genetic relatedness as proposed by kin selection theory; but in human societies, some altruistic actions such as blood giving are explicitly intended to assist anonymous recipients. Self-interested co-operation as proposed by reciprocal altruism would also fail to explain behaviours such as animal rights activism or charity work, whose subjective return (a moral sense of doing what is right or fair) cannot be translated into an apparent fitness benefit to actors. Thus, although it is common sense that our species differs from others due to our sophisticated culture and high cognitive skills, the theory of strong reciprocity suggests that human behaviour is unique for an additional reason: only humans are truly altruistic and co-operative, independently from the conditions of genetic relatedness and individual fitness returns (Fehr and Fischbacher, 2003).

What is the evidence for their claim? Almost invariably, the argument for the uniqueness of human behaviour and our strong tendency to co-operate starts with an experiment known as the 'ultimatum game' (Güth *et al.*, 1982). This economic game consists of a single, anonymous interaction between two players A and B, whose task is to reach an agreement regarding the division of a resource. Player A is offered a given resource, let us say 10 monetary units (MU). The role of player A in the game is to offer a fraction of that amount (usually between a minimum of 1 MU and a maximum of 10 MU). The role of player B is to make a decision: to accept or reject the offer from player A. The game ends in one of two possible outcomes. For example, Player B may accept and keep an offer of 2 MU, in which case player A keeps the remaining fraction of the resource (8 MU). Player B may also reject the offer, and in this case neither A nor B receives anything (i.e. the 10 MU are lost). Thus, both players A and B win, provided they can agree on the distribution of the resource.

The problem is that players may disagree on the distribution of resources, on the value of the offer (player A) and on the decision to accept or reject it (player B). If we assume, as postulated by the theory of reciprocal altruism, that individuals are selfish and constantly trying to maximise their fitness in social interactions, what would be the expected behaviour of players A and B? Since the interaction is anonymous and non-repeated, reciprocation and punishment are not possible or effective. For this reason, the behaviour that maximises the gain of player B is to accept *any* offer, including the minimum one (of 1 MU). The reason is simple: any accepted offer including the minimum is better than rejecting it and receiving no money. Thus, the behaviour that maximises the fitness of player A is to offer the minimum amount; any offer higher than that would be unnecessarily generous.

Surprisingly, experiments originally performed with university students in Europe and the USA using real money showed that the predictions from reciprocal altruism were wrong. The most common offer from players A corresponds to *half* the money, even when substantial amounts were at stake (Sanfey *et al.* 2003). In addition, offers below 20% of the total are frequently rejected, showing that players B consistently choose to receive nothing over agreeing to a non-egalitarian division of money. Thus, despite being instructed to play the ultimatum game with the aim of defeating an opponent and maximising individual gain, players prefer to co-operate apparently to achieve the 'common good'. Fehr and Fishbacher (2003) argue that human behaviour as revealed in the ultimatum game is a clear refutation of the postulate of selfishness; accordingly, instead of self-interested reciprocation, they propose that human behaviour is dictated by the principle of strong reciprocity, which is unique to humans for being directed towards unrelated and even anonymous individuals.

> The evolutionary success of our species and the moral sentiments that have led people to value freedom, equality, and representative government are predicated upon strong reciprocity and related motivations that go beyond inclusive fitness and reciprocal altruism (Fehr and Fishbacher, 2003).

The reference to the 'evolutionary success of our species' suggests that strong reciprocity is a characteristic that appeared in humans well before historical times, and therefore refers to a feature of human biology. The ultimatum game also reveals what we already knew from the examples of blood giving and similar activities: 'moral sentiments' such as fairness guide human action (Camerer, 1997). In the ultimatum game, fairness is exemplified both by equitable offers and by the costly rejection of unfair or selfish ones; this indicates that humans are willing to sacrifice their own personal interests in order to enforce the general principle of fairness. For this reason, costly punishment observed in humans would differ from some forms of punishment observed in other species. As seen earlier in the example of red-winged blackbirds, the theory of reciprocal altruism with repeated interactions predicts that the main form of punishment for non-co-operation or defection in animal societies may be non-co-operation with defectors, although active self-interested punishment in the form of coercion has also been found in vertebrate and insect societies (Clutton-Brock and Parker, 1995; Frank, 1995; Ratnieks and Wenseelers, 2005; Rankin et al., 2007). In contrast, the costly and fairness-driven form of punishment unique to humans was named 'altruistic punishment' (Fehr and Gächter, 2002) and interpreted as a key element binding human societies together.

> Rejections in the ultimatum game can be viewed as altruistic acts because most people view the equal split as the fair outcome (Fehr and Fischbacher, 2003).

The tendency to punish violations of fair co-operation even at an individual cost was also discussed by Fehr and Fischbacher (2003) in a different experiment: the 'dictator game' with a third party. In the classic dictator game (Hoffman et al., 1994), player A dictates the division of the available resource, with player B having no power to reject the offer as in the ultimatum game. The modified version of the game includes a third party or player C who needs to make a choice: to spend a monetary endowment on punishing player A for unfair offers, or to selfishly keep the money. Fehr and Fishbacher argued that the selfishness postulate or reciprocal altruism predicts that player C should never punish unfair dictators at a cost. Contrary to the predictions, experiments using college students consistently showed players C offering up to a third of their money endowment to punish unfair offers.

If strong reciprocity and altruistic punishment represent features of human nature rather than recent cultural phenomena, the familiar puzzle of social evolution is posed: how could those traits evolve by natural selection, if at least apparently they are not fitness-maximising behaviours? The proposed answer is a third unique component of human social behaviour: extensive 'gene-culture co-evolution' (Fehr and Fischbacher, 2003), or the evolution of human behaviour as an adaptation to human culture, seen as our niche and environment. As mentioned earlier, Darwin was a pioneer in proposing in *The Descent of Man* that the moral values and norms exhibited in human societies must have evolved by natural selection:

> There can be no doubt that a tribe including many members who, from possessing in a high degree the spirit of patriotism, fidelity, obedience, courage, and sympathy, were always ready to give aid to each other and to sacrifice themselves for the common good, would be victorious over most other tribes; and this would be natural selection (Darwin, 1871: 166).

Darwin's explanation was already shown to be problematic: although selection between groups would in principle favour the spread of groups containing heroes and other co-operative members, individual selection favours the relatively faster spread of selfish individuals within those groups and of genes commanding selfish behaviours. The point made by proponents of strong reciprocation is that the argument against group selection does not work in the case of human social evolution for a special reason: human culture (Richerson and Boyd, 2001). Cultural norms, including those that command social co-operation and punish defection, can spread even faster than genes; the reason is that whereas genes can only spread vertically across generations, cultural norms can spread horizontally across populations and groups.

Since human groups may be defined by cultural rather than genetic identity, they are able to expand and multiply through the unique mechanism of cultural group selection. The major events in the recent evolution and geographic expansion of modern humans seem to derive less from biological or genetic differences among populations, and more from cultural and technological advantages enjoyed by some human groups. This includes the modern European expansion following the great navigations that imposed languages, religions and laws upon native groups in America, Africa, Asia and Oceania; demographic events in pre-history such as the spread of agriculturalists at the expense of hunter-gatherers (Lewin and Foley, 2004); and even earlier processes prior to the Holocene.

> First, a long period of evolution in the Pleistocene shaped the innate 'social instincts' that underpin modern human behavior. During this period, much genetic change occurred as a result of humans living in groups with social institutions heavily influenced by culture, including cultural group selection. On this timescale, genes and culture *coevolve*, and cultural evolution is plausibly a leading rather than lagging partner in this process. We sometimes refer to the process as 'culture–gene coevolution'... Evidence suggests that genetic changes in the social instincts over the last 10,000 years are insignificant (Richerson *et al.*, 2003: 367).

The argument for gene-culture co-evolution also implies that if the main factor behind individual success in the struggle for survival is the adherence to social norms responsible for group success, then individuals who obey group rules and punish defectors should be favoured by natural selection.

> Those individuals best able to avoid punishment and acquire the locally relevant norms were more likely to survive... Genetic changes, leading to moral emotions like shame and a capacity to learn and internalize local practices, would allow the cultural evolution of more sophisticated institutions that in turn enlarged the scale of cooperation. These successive rounds of coevolutionary change continued until eventually people were equipped with capacities for cooperation with distantly related people, emotional attachments to symbolically marked groups, and a willingness to punish others for transgression of group rules (Richerson *et al.*, 2003: 371).

Thus, rounds of selection for co-operative behaviour, operating for thousands of years in human societies until about the start of the Holocene, eventually produced the unique behavioural patterns of strong reciprocity and altruistic punishment. Humans maintain social cohesion by defending the culture to which they belong, by attacking their enemies, and by fighting to convert members of other groups. Members of our species evolved to be obedient and norm abiding due to a long-lasting selective process that began with the origin of human culture itself. In summary, the image of humans that emerges from the theory proposed by Fehr, Gintis, Boyd and collaborators is that of a moral soldier. The human hero takes immense pleasure in being a part of a larger social Leviathan; this pleasure resulting from co-operating and punishing defectors (recently shown to be physical; de Quervain *et al.*, 2004; Zak *et al.*, 2007; Israel *et al.*, 2009) is ultimately the result of humans acting in the name of fairness rather than genetic relatedness or selfish interest.

We are thus left with the impression that past theoreticians have completely misinterpreted the nature of humans in society; rather than a wolf to other men as portrayed by Hobbes, man is a moral and selfless ape.

SCRATCHING THE STRONG RECIPROCATOR

Despite the popularity that the selfless ape theory has recently enjoyed, there are flaws in all its three postulates of strong reciprocity, altruistic punishment and gene-culture co-evolution. First, are humans really non-selfish reciprocators? As seen above, the evidence for this claim is invariably based on economic experiments, especially the ultimatum game performed on college students. Although the predominance or egalitarian division of resources are interpreted as evidence that humans have a natural tendency to be fair, the results may without exception be interpreted as expressions of self-interest.

We may start by asking whether there is an alternative explanation for the typically egalitarian offers by player A in the ultimatum game. A first hint is given by the results – often under-reported by proponents of strong reciprocity – of another game, the classic dictator game (in its original version that excludes a third party), in which player A imposes an offer that player B cannot reject. Since the dictator game is played under similar conditions to the ultimatum game (a one-shot, anonymous interaction) and was also performed almost exclusively on samples of college students, the theory of strong reciprocity would predict that subjects in the role of player A should still make fair offers of around half the available money; but disappointingly, the result in this case is that subjects typically make the minimum offer (Forsythe *et al.*, 1994). In other words, humans do not display 'advantageous inequity aversion', or rejection of inequality when they are able to secure a more than fair share of resources. For some reason, humans seem to be less interested in fairness and equality when they dictate rather than negotiate the distribution of resources with an equally self-interested opponent.

If human subjects are selfish in the role of dictators, a possibility is that egalitarian offers in the ultimatum game may be equally (although not apparently) selfish. In my own informal simulations of the ultimatum game with students, subjects in the role of player A have consistently reported a second reason (besides 'fairness') for egalitarian offers: the fear that player B will retaliate a low offer with a rejection (this is the same point made by Kravitz and Gunto, 1992). Players A consistently admit that egalitarian offers are made not because they are fair and satisfy the interests of both players: they are simply more likely to secure acceptance of the offer. Interestingly, many players name both fairness and the fear of having the offer rejected as simultaneous motivations. Proponents of the selfless ape perspective have not been able to account for strictly selfish offers in the dictator game; faced with the challenge, they prefer to argue (somehow contradictorily) that despite being strong reciprocators, humans may still be partially selfish (Fehr and Fischbacher, 2003).

The same comment applies to altruistic punishment, which was proposed as an explanation for behaviours such as rejection of low offers by players B in the ultimatum game, or the punishment of selfishness by players C in the dictator game with a third party. There is an equally convincing explanation for the apparently non-selfish behaviour of punishers: the somewhat confusing nature of the two discussed economic games. To understand this point, notice that ball, card or table games establish competition between players, which must result in winners and losers. Professional sports such as football, tennis and others add a second dimension to games: winning means both defeating opponents (wining a match or race) *and* winning a prize that can be spent in real life. Professional games work by linking the two outcomes: players must normally defeat opponents in order to be awarded a higher prize (exceptions can almost always be explained by situations in which losing a match contributes to winning a championship; in those cases, teams or players must win the championship in order to win the prize).

Contrary to the straightforward logic of professional games, the ultimatum and dictator games sometimes introduce an unusual circumstance: the uncoupling between winning the game (defeating the other player) and winning the award (maximising the prize money). A concrete example clarifies the point. In an ultimatum game with an endowment of 10 MU, let us imagine a player B who has been made the minimum offer of 1 MU. The two options are to reject the offer, resulting in a 0–0 result (or nil–nil draw with player A and no prize money); and to accept the offer, resulting in a 9–1 defeat to player A and prize money of 1 MU. The ultimatum game thus involves the circumstance that, given the choice between a defeat (9–1) and a draw (0–0), it is the *defeat* in the game that awards the higher prize in real life. It is reasonable to argue that the decoupling between the game result and the prize may introduce uncertainty and doubt among players, who are instructed to play for a prize.

The rejection of low offers in the ultimatum game may therefore have an alternative explanation: subjects may simply play the game to win as instructed by the experimenter, refusing to lose to player A and opting for the draw as the best match result, disregarding the prize value involved. The refusal to accept a lower award than a second player (or to lose the game to the other player), even at the cost of winning no prize, is known as 'disadvantageous inequity aversion' (Fehr and Schmidt, 1999). This behaviour was described in humans and other primate species such as capuchin monkeys (Brosnan and de Waal, 2003) and chimpanzees (Brosnan *et al.*, 2005). For being observed in other species, disadvantageous inequity aversion is an explanation for rejections of low offers that does not require the assumption of altruistic punishment as a uniquely human behaviour: rejections are selfish in the sense that they simply avoid defeat to a competitor.

An indirect attempt at showing the uniqueness of human social behaviour was presented by Silk and collaborators (2005). They performed experiments similar to the dictator game in chimpanzees, our closest evolutionary relatives, and concluded that contrary to humans they exhibit no 'pro-social' tendencies; chimpanzees behaved as selfish dictators only interested in maximising their returns (i.e. in securing provision of food) but indifferent to the well-being of other group members (by showing no preference for the costless choice of securing the same provision of food to other chimpanzees). However, the experiments can hardly be accepted as evidence for the uniqueness of human behaviour; as seen, humans are as selfish as chimpanzees when placed in the role of player A in the dictator game, whereas chimpanzees, like humans, were shown to reject low offers in experiments equivalent to the ultimatum game. In summary, humans and chimpanzees seem to manifest similar behavioural patterns: both species exhibit disadvantageous inequity aversion in the ultimatum game, and no advantageous inequity aversion in the dictator game.

It is important to notice that the apparent 'irrationality' of human behaviour in economic games (i.e. the failure to act as *Homo economicus* and maximise the individual prize) may be modified by learning. When the ultimatum experiment was performed on Economics students, results were very different: almost all offers are at the minimum level, and almost all of them are accepted (Kahneman *et al.*, 1986; Carter and Irons, 1991). This means that *Homo economicus* may not be a natural state, but a learned pattern exhibited by individuals trained for profit maximisation, typically in anonymous interactions that constitute the 'market'. In summary, although self-interested behaviour (including selfish co-operation predicted by reciprocal altruism) evolved in humans by natural selection and predates *Homo sapiens* itself, specific cultural expressions of self-interested social behaviour such as the *Homo economicus* have probably developed only in historical times in particular societies such as the pioneering capitalist countries of Europe.

This leads to the third postulate of the selfless ape theory, namely the biological transformation of human social behaviour by gene-culture co-evolution. Henrich *et al.* (2005, 2006) were aware of the drawbacks of trying to infer universal patterns of human behaviour from exclusively Westernised, university-educated samples. For this reason, they performed a worldwide round of the ultimatum game on 15 small-scale, pre-industrial societies covering four continents and various economic bases (horticulturalism, hunter-gathering, pastoralism, farming, whale hunting). The results showed a high level of inter-population variation in the behaviour of subjects both in the role of player A (with average offers ranging from 15% to over 50% of the total prize) and player B in the ultimatum game (with average rejection of low offers ranging from zero to 100%), and in administering costly punishment in a third party punishment game.

Henrich and collaborators concluded that the results indicated a clear violation of the selfishness axiom, since no society conformed to a universal rule of a minimum offer by player A, and acceptance of the minimum offer by player B. However, this interpretation is clearly biased; for some reason, the authors did not mention that the results also show a violation by most societies of the postulates of strong reciprocity and altruistic punishment (namely a universal predominance of fair offers of 50% and rejection of unfair offers). Overall, what the experiments indicate is that neither *Homo economicus* nor the selfless ape is a universal description of human nature. It is easy to see why: patterns of co-operation in human societies are highly dependent upon cultural and economic factors such as economic basis, market integration and others as shown by Henrich and collaborators themselves. Societies such as the Lamalera whale-hunters that depend on co-operation among large numbers of unrelated individuals tended to be highly generous and egalitarian in their offers; but in societies in which subsistence does not require co-operation beyond relatively independent family units, such as the Machiguengua and Tsimane slash-and-burn horticulturalists, average offers were significantly below 50%.

In summary, the idea that life in co-operative groups since the Pleistocene has shaped our 'social instincts' in the form of universal 'co-operation with distantly related people, emotional attachments to symbolically marked groups, and a willingness to punish others for transgression of group rules' is simply not confirmed by evidence. This does not deny that culture has transformed human adaptation, or that genes and culture have not co-evolved; it simply rejects the idea that the process of gene-culture co-evolution has transformed human nature from the selfish beast exemplified by chimpanzees as portrayed by Silk and collaborators (2005) into a selfless ape characterised by strong reciprocation and altruistic punishment.

CONCLUSION: ANIMAL SOCIETIES AND BIOLOGICAL COMPLEXITY

Some animal societies are impressive examples of advanced co-operation, altruism and division of labour. Eusocial animals and hymenopteran insects in particular exemplify the power of relatedness and inclusive fitness as a source of social cohesion, and represent hard evidence for the theory of kin selection. Highly encephalised mammals such as primates and dolphins add a second dimension to social theory by exemplifying the extent to which selfish co-operation among unrelated individuals may also evolve, be it in the form of super-alliances in dolphins or multispecies parties in primates, among other examples. Humans extended the boundaries of social co-operation due to the role played by cultural innovation and language. We must therefore conclude that the animal societies inspiring the development of evolutionary social theory are certainly more than mobs of selfish individuals.

A more specific question is whether animal societies are examples of a major transition in evolution. Is any known animal society an example of evolutionary aggregation giving rise to a new superunit or social Leviathan, as originally proposed by Haldane and Huxley (1927)? Do they also involve a new form of transmission of biological information as proposed by Maynard Smith and Szathmáry (1995)? On closer examination, this does not seem the case. Even the extreme cases of social integration singled out by evolutionary biologists, such as humans, eusocial animals and encephalised selfish co-operators such as dolphins, still live in groups of competing individuals; contrary to genetically identical somatic cells, those individuals cannot be characterised as disposable phenotypes. This was exemplified by the widespread occurrence of conflict and divergent interests even among eusocial castes (workers and the queen), and of self-interest as the foundation of co-operation among unrelated individuals both in natural alliances and in simulations of economic games in humans.

Natural co-operation (Nowak, 2006) in all its forms, including kin selection and reciprocal altruism, has certainly bound individuals together in animal societies; but although it may have led to the origin of multicellularity, it has not yet led to the formation of an equivalent animal super-unit. There is a possibility that animal societies may eventually evolve into social super-units; after all, multicellular animals are evolutionarily more recent than cells, and may need extra time to aggregate into a Leviathan. At present, all known eusocial animals and selfish co-operators are more similar to social unicellular organisms such as certain bacteria (Galperin, 2008) and slime moulds (Eichinger et al., 2005; Bonner, 2008) than to true multicellular species.

Despite not representing a major transition as defined by Maynard Smith and Szathmáry, animal societies do relate in a crucial way to the origin of higher levels of biological complexity. The reason is that social life, like sexual selection, has certainly contributed to the evolution of behavioural traits that require information unable to be stored and transmitted by genes; in other words, sociality has contributed to the evolution of the brain into an information carrier and processor. Despite offering different explanations for social evolution, the theories of kin selection and reciprocal altruism have at a least one common feature: they only work under the condition of individual discrimination or recognition (Tibbetts and Dale, 2007). According to kin selection, altruism evolves as a form of co-operation linking members of the same kin group, which implies discrimination against unrelated or less-related individuals, exemplified by the preference of ant, bee and wasp workers for their sisters at the expense of their brothers, or by the disregard of female Belding ground squirrels for the safety of non-kin.

Reciprocal altruism or selfish co-operation between unrelated organisms on the other hand requires each individual to classify others into two fundamental categories: co-operators and defectors. Due to the requirement of individual discrimination, social animals had to evolve into calculating machines (Nowak and Sigmund, 2005); however, information on the identity and quality of interacting individuals cannot be directly or at least not exclusively coded in DNA. Animal brains allowed for individual discrimination on the basis of different types of sensorial input, so as to dictate choices and strategies regarding co-operation or competition (i.e. when and how much to co-operate), and to regulate communication and signalling between individuals.

From this perspective, what makes humans unique is not a new form of aggregation, but the fact that the human brain controls a species-specific mechanism of information storage and signalling. Contrary to the theory of strong reciprocity and its idea of an egalitarian or selfless human social mind not found even in our closest evolutionary relative, the feature that places humans on a unique and higher level on the natural scale of biological complexity is language. Humans alternate between defection and co-operation as much as any other social animals, but language opened the way to the expansion of extended phenotypes and material culture to a degree not observed in other species. As argued in the following pages, language also allowed humans to evolve past evolution by inspiring the creation of the first inorganic phenotypic entities able to store fitness-related information.

7

The new 'Chain of Being': hierarchical evolution and biological complexity

Selective and historical factors contribute to produce Darwin's ill-defined sentiment that living organisms are more complex now than at earlier stages of the evolution of life. A few theoretical solutions to the problem of complexity in macroevolution have been proposed and have enjoyed some success, the most popular of which being the model of major transitions and the corresponding logic of levels of selection. As seen in previous chapters, multilevel selection and major transitions are incomplete accounts of complexity for a simple reason: they rest upon the idea of aggregation and the part-to-whole argument as the main marker of biological complexity, and for this reason they fail to successfully include processes such as the origin of information-carrying brains and human language into a scheme of evolutionary increases in complexity.

The limitations of the aggregation model do not imply that the idea of evolutionary increases in complexity should be abandoned. A solution presented in this chapter is a change in perspective from an aggregational to a hierarchical view of evolution: instead of using the part-to-whole criterion of complexity, biological complexity could be defined on the basis of a hierarchy of mechanisms of information. This change of perspective reveals the existence of more than one Principle of Order from Order in living organisms and the reasons for the evolution of new inheritance modes from the original genetic code.

The existence of different biological codes has been identified and analysed (Maynard Smith and Szathmáry, 1995; Barbieri, 2003; Jablonka and Lamb, 2005), but those studies have not fully explored the interaction between new systems of inheritance and new forms of phenotypes, or how those interactions have affected levels of biological organisation. Some of those difficulties vanish when the evolution of complexity is reinterpreted as the historical transformation of Schrödinger's Principle of Order from Order. By classifying life forms according to a hierarchy of biological organisation, the idea of a new 'Great Chain of Being' (Lovejoy, 1936) in the organic world is re-established – this time, not as a static and anthropocentric chain, but as an evolving chain. To understand why and how evolution has resulted in a hierarchy of complexity, we must first discard a factor that, contrary to widespread belief, *cannot* explain trends in macroevolution: the thermodynamical background to organic evolution.

THERMODYNAMICS VERSUS BIOLOGICAL INFORMATION

For some physicists entropy and information are two sides of the same coin and as inseparable as life and death. A thermodynamical approach to biological complexity has been developed under the assumption formulated by Lewis (1930) that 'gain in entropy always means loss of information, and nothing more'. This view implies that if increase in the entropy of a system implies loss of information, any factor potentially *reducing* entropy should at least in theory favour increases in information content.

If this is true, then a possible reversal of the Second Law of Thermodynamics (which dictates increases in entropy in closed systems) and the apparent evolutionary increase in biological complexity on Earth might actually represent two opposite sides of the same coin. As claimed by Schneider and Sagan (2005), the entropy-reducing factor operating on the Earth and the ultimate explanation for the origin and evolution of life is the constant influx of solar energy to the biosphere. Whereas entropy must necessarily increase in a closed system or in the universe as a whole according to the Second Law, in a non-equilibrium, non-isolated system such as the biosphere we may observe local decreases in entropy (Nicolis and Prigogine, 1977), and therefore a local increase in 'order' and 'information'. In essence, evolution would consist in selection for more efficient ways of harvesting solar energy, leading to more ordered and information-rich living entities. The formula was summarised by Avery (2003: 90):

> A flood of information-containing free energy reaches the earth's biosphere in the form of sunlight... much of it is degraded into heat, but part is converted into cybernetic information and preserved in the intricate structures which are characteristic of life. The principle of natural selection ensures that as this happens, the configurations

> of matter in living organisms constantly increase in complexity,
> refinement and statistical improbability. This is the process which we
> call evolution, or in the case of human society, progress.

According to the argument, for as long as the Sun bathes our planet with
a gigantic supply of 'information-containing' free energy, increases in
biological and even social complexity are inevitable. Unfortunately the
reasons for such optimism are unjustified. Avery's statement neglects
the fact that life is just one of many possible outcomes of introducing
free energy into a system. As summarised by Doyne Farmer (2005),
'life is inherently an out-of-equilibrium phenomenon, but then so is
an explosion. Something other than nonequilibrium thermodynamics is needed to explain why these are fundamentally different'. The
'something other' than thermodynamics is the condition behind 'the
ability of matter to store information and to implement functional
relationships', namely the mechanisms of DNA replication and protein synthesis; it is biological information itself.

Avery's mistake, shared with most of the literature on thermodynamics and evolution, is to neglect Schrödinger's distinction between
physical and biological order. Entropy and information are two sides
of the same thermodynamical coin only in the world of statistical composition: that is, in the world ruled by the Principle of Order from
Disorder. Biological organisation in contrast derives from the ability of
DNA to store information, with thermodynamical factors being only a
constraint. For this reason, evolutionary trends in complexity are compatible with (but not a necessary consequence of) the Second Law of
Thermodynamics; increased complexity must be understood as transformations in such 'ability of matter to store information', or more
precisely, in changes in the way biological information is coded.

SCHRÖDINGER'S PRINCIPLE AND THE EVOLUTION OF ORDER

Instead of thermodynamics, Schrödinger (1944) relied on the foundations of quantum mechanics to show how order may oppose the tendency towards entropy-induced disorder and emerge in the biological
world. Schrödinger's Principle of Order from Order postulated that
living organisms cannot result from statistical composition alone and
must derive from some form of organisation at the microscopic level;
in other words, it predicted the existence of molecules responsible for
storing biological information. By proposing that information-bearing
molecules should resemble linear aperiodical crystals, it directly
inspired Crick and collaborators in their discoveries of the molecular

basis of inheritance: in all known organisms, genetic information is stored in DNA (or RNA) and translated into a second type of order (amino acid sequence), a view that somehow mirrored the previously established distinction between genotype and phenotype (Johannsen, 1911).

Despite capturing the essence of life, namely the feedback between DNA coding for functional molecules and proteins assisting in DNA replication, the Principle of Order from Order has a weakness: its formulation was not set in an evolutionary context. Contrary to the static view implied by Schrödinger, there are many reasons to believe that the principle *has* evolved. Although the pair DNA–protein is present in the life cycle of all known organisms (including retroviruses), biological organisation went beyond 'DNA order' and 'protein order'. On the one hand, biological information may adopt forms other than genetic information stored in DNA sequences, such as information stored in animal brains. On the other hand, phenotypes and their functional units are expressed in forms other than protein sequences, as exemplified by somatic cells (containing both proteins and DNA itself) or 'extended phenotypes' such as human and chimpanzee tools, beaver dams and bowerbird nests.

Schrödinger's Principle of Order from Order might eliminate most of the difficulties in the schemes of major transitions and levels of selection, provided it is analysed as an evolving principle. The evolutionary version of Schrödinger's Principle of Order from Order (ESP) is here formulated as:

> Entities that originally evolved as phenotypic units may gradually adopt a role of information carriers themselves. This has on a few occasions led to the origin of a new type of biological information coding for a new form of phenotypic organisation.

This view implies that changes in levels of biological complexity correspond to the evolution of new biological codes, or new pairs of carriers of biological information (DNA molecules, transcription factors, animal brains, human language) and disposable phenotypic units (amino acid sequences, somatic cells, learned or cultural behaviours, and human cultural phenotypes). This view resembles in various aspects the models proposed by Buss (1987), Maynard Smith and Szathmáry (1995), Barbieri (2003) and Jablonka and Lamb (2005). However, the ESP differs from those views by proposing that the origin of new biological codes is *gradual* and based on the evolutionary process of *modularity transfer* outlined below.

RNA: the source of the genetic code and organic modularity

Schrödinger's postulation of a source of biological order at the microscopic level inspired the discovery of the genetic code. For being the earliest and more universal code of biological information in extant organisms, the origin of the genetic code presents a special problem similar to the origin of the first species or living organism; the origin of the first code requires special models such as the RNA World, the genetic tag hypothesis and others. What we know is that the modularity of DNA and of encoded proteins derives directly from the pre-existence of ribozymes in the RNA World. The original modularity of RNA is also the reason why it can perform functions of mediation (messenger, transfer RNAs) and regulation (RNA interference) of genetic information in our DNA World; with the evolution of the genetic code, RNA transferred its modular organisation into DNA and protein modularity.

Protein modularity and the origin of the developmental code

Assuming the modular nature of genetic information as a starting point, the ESP may clarify the evolution of additional systems of biological information. As emphasised by Maynard Smith and Szathmáry (1995), the central feature of DNA-based inheritance is modularity: DNA stores messages as sequences of nucleotides, which are converted into proteins or modular sequences of amino acids. DNA-based information is distributed over genes and genomes that are equally modular. It is easy to see how this has facilitated the adaptive diversification of proteins and phenotypes: whereas modular DNA allows for point mutations, deletions and additions of single nucleotides, modular genes allow for the mutation, deletion and addition of *cis*-regulatory units and coding units (or exons), and modular genomes (subdivided into genes or Mendelian particles of inheritance) allow for the removal, addition or multiplication of genes leaving other units untouched. A related consequence of the modular organisation of genetic information is alternative splicing that generates different proteins, including transcription factors, from the same coding sequence (Kondrashov and Koonin, 2003).

The genetic code works by translating modularity from information (nucleotide) sequence into functional (amino acid) sequence. Since proteins inherit the property that makes DNA a suitable performer of an information-bearing role, an evolutionary option is created: one of the functions that proteins may evolve in their gradual process of adaptive diversification is the function of *modular information carrier* itself. This possibility was eventually explored with the origin of transcription factors regulating gene expression: instead of performing the original and more common structural or enzymatic role of proteins, they became part of the flow of genetic information in unicellular and later in multicellular organisms. The result is that, in addition to the genetic code establishing a primary correspondence between DNA triplets and specific amino acids, gene regulation implies a new form of correspondence between information-carrying protein sequences and the *cis*-regulatory regions to which they specifically bind.

Transcription factors may have originally evolved in unicellular organisms as gene regulators; however, the system of matched pairs of transcription factors and *cis*-regulatory regions only became the basis for a new and more complex form of phenotypic organisation in multicellular organisms. The new type of disposable phenotypic entity based on derived informational proteins (and previously existing RNA molecules) was the disposable somatic cell. Whereas the system of information involving information-carrying proteins and *cis*-regulatory regions in unicellular organisms evolved to modulate genetic information, in multicellular organisms the system became the developmental code defining a new form of Order from Order: a new functional, disposable entity (the somatic cell) specified by the operation of information-carrying proteins interacting with *cis*-regulated genes.

It should be noticed that this developmental code still requires the existence and operation of the genetic code, which in its turn depended on the survival of RNA; the reason is that transcription factors need to be coded and transmitted across generations by genes. The unique role of the developmental code is expressed by the paradox posed by Huxley and de Beer (1934): genes alone cannot explain the organisation and development of multicellular organisms (since as a rule the same genes are present in differentiated somatic cells). Furthermore, somatic cells are a phenotypic entity containing DNA molecules in a new function: that of a disposable molecule that stores information not meant to be directly transmitted across generations, but to provide a subset of genes that, under the control of transcription factors and non-coding RNAs, specify the features of a given disposable cell type.

Not by accident, the key concept in evo-devo studies addressing the origin and diversity of multicellular organisation is developmental modularity (Wagner *et al.*, 2007). From the perspective of the ESP, the modular nature of multicellular organisms evolved as one of the consequences of adaptive evolution operating on organisms characterised by the modular organisation of DNA, genes and genomes.

The modular build of multicellular organisms has been central both to their origin and adaptive diversification, as it allows in principle for the mechanism of variation and selection to affect a given developmental territory without affecting the development of other regions. For this reason, modularity has been interpreted as the developmental basis for microevolution (Stern, 2000). Specialised functional modules in the form of new appendages, organs or body segments are to a large extent the features behind adaptive specialisation of animal species (Carroll *et al.*, 2001). In summary, natural selection has produced functionally diversified modules of somatic cell types through a process analogous to the adaptive diversification of proteins.

Neural cells and brain modularity

The evolution of animal body plans produced one particularly far-reaching consequence: the origin of the neuron or neural cell and the later evolution of animal brains. The animal brain centralises a series of functions that already existed in unicellular organisms and even in some plants, such as responsiveness to light or chemical environment, control of movement and regulation of metabolism (Striedter, 2005; Greenspan, 2007). The neuron and brain activity led to the evolution and diversification of animal behaviour (Jablonka and Lamb, 2006). Like proteins and somatic cells, behaviours such as particular episodes of display, movement, mating and others can be interpreted as disposable and modular phenotypic entities (Heisenberg, 2009) that need a neural hard copy from which they can be generated multiple times.

Brains and behaviour represent new phenotypic features unique to certain animal taxa that only evolved due to the pre-existence of the developmental code and multicellular modularity. However, they do not define a new and higher level of organisation by themselves. In various or possibly all organisms, brains control forms of 'innate' behaviour (i.e. behaviours undergoing strict vertical transmission from parent to offspring; Lehmann *et al.*, 2008); in some species they may even correspond to all observed behaviour. However, not all animal behaviours are innate and various studies have revealed the extent to which they can be learned and culturally transmitted among individuals (Laland and Janik, 2006). Culture and the 'inheritance of acquired behaviour' has been observed in primates and cetaceans, including chimpanzees (Whiten *et al.*, 1999), orangutans (van Schaik *et al.*, 2003), capuchin monkeys (Perry *et al.*, 2003), whales (Rendell and Whitehead, 2001) and dolphins (Krützen *et al.*, 2005). Active teaching of prey-handling skills (with adults supervising pups practising with live prey) has been recently reported in wild meerkats (Thornton and McAuliffe, 2006). Among many true songbirds (oscine Passeriformes) songs must be learned from other individuals and are not present as an instinct at birth (Marler and Slabbekoorn, 2004; Moore, 2004). Brains have therefore evolved into information carriers at some point (or points) in the animal phylogeny. In the taxa where it is an information carrier, the brain became a repository for ecological information (registering features of the environment), social information (on relatedness and co-operativeness of other group members) and individual history (as a register of trials and errors regarding reproductive and foraging efforts). The theories of co-operation summarised earlier exemplify why the possession of those types of information contributes to individual fitness in many social species.

Information stored in animal brains corresponds to a specific form of biological information coding for learned or cultural behaviour, and is consistent with the hypothesis of modular transfer. 'Memes' (Dawkins, 1976) are after all units of information transferred between animal brains and able to produce certain phenotypic effects. It is clear that extending the argument for 'modularity transfer' to neural information faces challenges: the relative lack of knowledge of both brain structure and of the neural foundations of processes such as memory, learning and thinking (Crick, 1994; Simmons and Young, 1999), and the absence of a clear evolutionary and phylogenetic account of when and on which taxa learning, culture and information-carrying brains have evolved. However, the current (and quickly growing) evidence does not contradict the hypothesis that brain modularity is a source of behavioural modularity, with the idea that cognition and animal minds are modular being championed by various authors (Fodor, 1983; Mithen, 1996; Reader, 2006; for criticisms, see Panksepp and Panksepp, 2000; Wagner and Wagner, 2003).

Brain modularity and its subdivision into interacting functional regions has led to discoveries of specific links between a module and a given behaviour, as expressed in the concept of 'dedicated systems' or neural systems largely responsible for a single behavioural function

(Simmons and Young, 1999). In humans, although links between brain regions and behaviours are less commonly exclusive and unidimensional, regions associated with pleasure in co-operation and punishment (the dorsal striatum; de Quervain *et al.*, 2004), decision making (amygdala, orbital and medial prefrontal cortex; de Martino *et al.*, 2006), and other cognitive aspects such as new memory formation (the hippocampus; Squire, 1987) have also been identified. Species interpreted as exhibiting 'higher' cognition and more sophisticated cultural features seem to evolve brains both with more specialised functional regions and with more intricate connectivity patterns among them; in humans, for example, language has been primarily associated with two cortical areas (Broca's area or the 'seat of grammar', and Wernicke's area or the 'seat of meaning and sound structure') which are part of a larger network possibly including the striatum, thalamus and other regions (Fisher and Marcus, 2006).

Thus, the modularity of brain function and structure, a consequence of developmental modularity, has been the foundation for the evolutionary diversification of animal behaviour and of cognitive functions. Accordingly, not only function but also the evolution of brains has often been characterised by some degree of 'mosaicism' in mammals (Barton and Harvey, 2000) and birds (Iwaniuk *et al.*, 2004), with the size of a given brain module correlating across species more strongly or exclusively with modules to which they are functionally and neuronally linked.

Language: the code for human culture and technology

A derived behaviour in animals is inter-individual signalling, or as a behaviour or structure that evolved to effectively modify the behaviour of another organism (Maynard Smith and Harper, 2003). Animal signals are exemplified both by structural features such as aposematic colours and by behaviours such as vocalisations. As exemplified by alarm calls that contribute to individual fitness or fitness of related individuals, vocalisations evolved as repeatable (and in this sense disposable) phenotypic entities that mediate interactions between individuals.

It is easy to see that vocalisations, for being modular and observed in animals capable of acquiring information through social learning, had the potential to evolve into information carriers themselves. The occurrence of vocalisations carrying meaning has been observed in various species; 'vocal cultures' have been identified in bottlenose dolphins and hunchback whales (Janik and Slater, 1997), with all males in a population learning a common song from each other, with the song in some cases being gradually transformed over time (Noad *et al.*, 2000); and vervet monkeys are known to use three different alarm calls indicating the presence of snakes, eagles or leopards to other group members (Seyfarth and Chenay, 1992). If those vocalisations carrying a specific meaning are learned rather than innate (which is normally demonstrated through comparisons between calls in different populations, i.e. the ethnographic method; Wrangham *et al.*, 1994), they could be interpreted as simple memes (Reader and Laland, 1999). Grammar, at least in its simplest forms, may not be a privilege of humans either (Gentner *et al.*, 2006): European starlings are songbirds able to recognise and distinguish between correct and incorrect examples of recursive grammar, defined as the use of sentences ('I like birds') as parts of other sentences ('she knows that I like birds'). This result refutes at least partially the claim that recursion forms are an element of a strictly human faculty for language (Hauser *et al.*, 2002). However, recursive norms in European starlings have not been observed in the wild and only occurred after a long learning process involving tens of thousands of trials; thus, although the cognitive potential for grammar seems to be present, European starlings are not language users in the sense that humans are.

Despite the continuity with other forms of animal communication based on vocalisations, human language is unique due to the larger scale of our word system and the emergence of a generational grammar (possibly as a consequence of larger number of vocal signals; Nowak *et al.*, 2000) that can produce infinite numbers of sentences and meanings from a set of vocal modules or words (Hauser *et al.*, 2002). The point at which language evolved in the hominin lineage is a controversial topic. Although it is generally assumed that language evolved at some point after the origin of the genus *Homo* about 1.8 million years ago, some authors claim that no species prior to modern humans were able to speak (Mithen, 2007). Whatever the specific phylogenetic case, the vocalisations or words employed in human language are both phenotypic, disposable animal signals and modular information carriers, or 'discrete components that have their own meaning' (Nowak *et al.*, 2000) and organised via a linguistic code or grammar.

Language is responsible for a significant share of what is known as human culture, both in its social and technological aspects. The general presence of 'oral traditions' in traditional societies (as a body of knowledge built and preserved by many individuals and potentially surviving their death) conveys the idea that language helps conferring universality to social norms and knowledge of the external world. Not by accident, theories of the origin of language tend to fall into three categories: some believe that language evolved as a mediator of social relations, with learning meaning mostly the gradual mastering of social rules (Power, 1998; Dunbar, 1998); others point to sexual selection favouring the evolution of language as a display mechanism (Miller, 2000); whereas others propose that language transmits information about the environment, with learning being mostly 'technical' (Greenfield, 1991). Those hypotheses are not mutually exclusive; together, they show how language has led to a unique diversification of culture in humans both in its technological and social aspects.

Understanding how language became the code for a new and exclusively human form of phenotype requires an analysis of extended phenotypes (Dawkins, 1982). They were defined by Dawkins as all the effects of genes, including those manifested beyond the bodies carrying them. A limitation of the original definition is that not all extended phenotypes are encoded in genes; for example, some may depend on information stored and transmitted by animal brains (i.e. they may be coded by memes rather than genes). Nest building in birds or dam building in beavers do seem to be effects of genes, as those are innate actions involving no learning or teaching from other individuals. However, dam building in humans is clearly a learned process, and such extended phenotypes that need to be learned only evolved due to the existence of the animal brain as an extended carrier of information. The concept of 'niche construction' (Oddling-Smee et al., 2003), or adaptation through the transformation of the environment occupied by a species, somehow generalises the concept of extended phenotypes.

For the current argument, we should notice that learning was the condition for the existence of both animal culture in general and of *material* culture in particular. Whereas chimpanzees are known to exhibit cultural variation in certain learned behaviours (hand clasps are an example; McGrew et al., 2001), they also present cultural variation in extended phenotypes, such as variable use among populations of tools including spears and termite-fishing sticks (Haslam et al., 2009). Whereas material culture has been observed in chimpanzees and other spices, human language led to an expansion of material culture to much higher usage levels; all human societies depend on material culture, and various aspects of social organisation gravitate around the production of learned or cultural extended phenotypes, including tools and other supplements to human biology such as clothing, besides the techniques required for food production through hunting, agriculture and other foraging strategies (Pagel and Mace, 2004). Due to language, culturally extended phenotypes change more quickly than human biological phenotypes, as technical information or memes can be transferred between individuals (both horizontally and vertically) more quickly than genes are transferred across generations. It is the universal dependence of human survival on learned extended phenotypes, unknown in any other species, that defines human material culture as a unique form of phenotypic organisation.

THE HISTORICAL TRANSFORMATION OF SELECTION

The evolutionary version of Schrödinger's Principle of Order clarifies many of the phenomena described by the theories of major transitions and levels of selection. In addition, the ESP does not exhibit their main drawback: it does not necessarily interpret the evolution of complexity as the result of aggregation of previously independent individuals. Increases in biological complexity occur due to the origin of new forms of biological organisation, but only rarely do the latter consist of super-units formed by previously existing individuals. Multicellular organisms are the most important exception and did evolve due to the deployment of cells as a new form of disposable entity; but proteins or extended cultural phenotypes were not derived from biological entities previously capable of independent replication, but from amino acids and raw materials used in making stone tools.

The rejection of the aggregation model has another consequence: it implies that natural selection itself has a history. The aggregation models do not seem to imply a fundamental change in the operation of natural selection due to an implicit association between levels of organisation and levels of selection (Keller, 1999). If aggregation held as a general principle, the evolution of higher complexity could be described as a series of progressively more inclusive super-units or biological Leviathans; those would result from the successive predominance of group selection over individual selection. The predominance of groups would occur whenever generalised co-operation was more advantageous than generalised competition. This view was summarised by Nowak (2006):

> Co-operation is needed for evolution to construct new levels of organization. Genomes, cells, multicellular organisms, social insects,

and human society are all based on co-operation. Co-operation means
that selfish replicators forgo some of their reproductive potential
to help one another. But natural selection implies competition and
therefore opposes co-operation unless a specific mechanism is at work.
Here I discuss five mechanisms for the evolution of co-operation: kin
selection, direct reciprocity, indirect reciprocity, network reciprocity,
and group selection.

Nowak's formulation reproduces the misunderstanding behind the
theory of major transitions: new levels of organisation are based on co-
operation among individuals that eventually become components of a
larger whole. Individuals may live in groups; those groups may become
levels of selection due to the advantages of co-operation; groups may
then eventually evolve into a level of organisation or new super-unit.
Nowak generalises the link between major transitions and levels of
selection by postulating five possible aggregating forces, contrary to
Maynard Smith and Szathmáry (1995) who showed a clear preference
for kin selection as the mechanism behind aggregation. It is easy to
understand their preference: kin selection is an example of an invari-
ant force potentially acting at the level of genes, individuals, societies
and even beyond societies; all that changes at each level is what is
'individual' and what is the 'group'.

We have already discussed why levels of selection are not the
same as levels of organisation: new levels of organisation result from
modularity transfer, or the origin of new forms of modular phenotypic
organisation from modular information systems and vice versa. Thus,
humans represent more complex organisation not for forgoing some
of their reproductive potential (which is a feature observed in many
other co-operative breeders) and becoming a super-unit, but because
of a new system of information: modular language and the features of
culture depending on it – traits that simply do not fit into Nowak's list
of levels of organisation.

If levels of organisation – genetic, developmental, behavioural
and linguistic – differ not as parts to a whole but as progressively
derived forms of modular organisation, natural selection would be
expected to change due to the new information carriers (or how
variation is manifested) and disposable units (or how differential
fitness is produced). Evolutionary theory has already discovered
principles describing selection at different levels of organisation;
the ESP reinterprets those independently formulated 'laws' as consequences of the historical transformation of the Principle of Order
from Order.

Fisher's fundamental principle of natural selection

A general formulation of natural selection was proposed by Fisher (1930) with his fundamental principle stating that the rate of adaptive evolution of a population is proportional to its additive genetic variance. Fisher's principle is a consequence of the genetic code, and its appeal to additive genetic variation only requires the existence of the gene as a unit of inheritance. His theory of micromutations in contrast is strongly dependent upon the modularity of DNA and the possibility of modular changes in DNA sequence; however, if applied to multicellular organisms, it cannot be demonstrated exclusively at the genetic level. As discussed in Chapter 2, the tempo of adaptive evolution seems to be determined by the balance between the structural independence of genes described by Mendelian laws and the levels of interdependence of gene effects on phenotypic traits (i.e. levels of pleiotropy). The special problem of gradualism in metazoan evolution thus depends on developmental modularity, which determines the balance between genes and pleiotropy. However, Fisher's principle would hold in a world consisting only of genes and coded proteins; it derives from the genetic code present in all organisms, and is for this reason the most universal manifestation of natural selection.

The principle of disposable soma

The possibility of renewing phenotypes, exemplified by the disposability of proteins, is amplified in multicellular organisms due to the functional distinction between somatic cells and germ cells. More importantly, the disposability of the soma is the reason for a nearly universal trait of life: the nearly universal existence of life cycles in multicellular organisms. The disposability of somas is responsible for a key property affecting adaptation in multicellular organisms and metazoans especially: the power of natural selection acting on them decreases with somatic age. Thus, Weismann's principle is the specific manifestation of natural selection that only appeared with the origin of multicellular organisation.

The memetic principle

Kin selection and reciprocal altruism, the two most successful solutions to the problem of social life in animals, explain cases of social interaction in which an individual acts in the interest of another and acts so as to increase its fitness. Those ideas were generalised by Nowak with his five rules of social co-operation. However, co-operation is not a sufficient road to the evolution of higher complexity. It was not sociability and co-operation themselves (as they are observed even in bacteria or entities such as lichens) that made animal societies special, but the evolution of behaviour (innate and learned) as a form of phenotype affecting interactions with other individuals. In multicellular species (in which modular bodies, organs and cell types already existed) social behaviour evolved through the mediation of animal brains.

The principle of natural co-operation as an aggregator of selfish individuals was already present in the unicellular world, but social evolution was transformed after the evolution of animal brains, organs that store information in the forms of memes or units of information transmitted between individuals. Natural selection operating on memes has transformed sexual selection and mating strategies in some species and social evolution in others by leading to new ways of discrimination between co-operative and defecting group members, kin and non-kin, and calculation of relative costs and benefits of co-operation.

The cultural group selection principle

Memes undeniably acquired a unique character in *Homo sapiens*, where in association with language they led to a revolution in the use of culturally extended phenotypes. The proponents of the strong reciprocity model have relied on the abundant evidence for inter-group conflict and on cultural group selection. Competition among human groups is, to a large measure, external to human biology and relies on features (extended phenotypes such as weapons and armours) beyond the organic worlds. Both the technical information and social organisation required for the production of those extended phenotypes is carried by language, or more precisely, by oral traditions created by human groups and whose information content spreads across individuals and is unlikely to be stored in any individual brain. In summary, cultural group selection and the creation of a unique niche mostly based on culturally transmitted extended phenotypes are elements of human evolution.

The selective mechanisms above are consequences of the evolutionary transformation of Schrödinger's Principle of Order from Order and represent new contexts in which natural selection was expressed. Although they were originally formulated as 'laws' of microevolution, they are historical products resulting from the evolution of a new level of organisation. For this reason, they represent the joint product of contingency (the raw materials that evolved into new phenotypic entities, such as amino acids or vocalisations) and a background of necessity given by selection. In summary, different levels of biological organisation define a hierarchy in evolution, whereas the principles of microevolution (or forms of competition among individuals) present their own historical transformation. Together, those two factors confer macroevolution with a strong Darwinian flavour.

THE HIERARCHICAL NATURE OF MACROEVOLUTION

If new systems of information have successively appeared and led to the origin of new forms of phenotypic organisation, macroevolution must be interpreted as a hierarchical process. A first argument for the existence of hierarchies in macroevolution is that new biological codes do not imply the elimination of their ancestors; on the contrary, they rely on the existence of previously existing codes both for their evolution and operation.

New forms of biological information must depend on previous biological codes according to the concept of modularity transfer. Barbieri (2003) has pointed out that new organic codes do not replace or eliminate existing ones, but the ESP implies an even stronger postulate: from the point of view of their operation, a previously existing code *cannot* disappear with the origin of a new one. The reason is that although new codes derive from the origin of new information carriers, the latter are still produced as phenotypic entities. For example, the developmental code was built upon transcription factors and other signalling proteins; however, transcription factors are still proteins, which therefore require the existence of protein synthesis and the genetic code (and also of RNA itself, which predates the genetic code itself). The same is true for behavioural phenotypes: they rely on information carried by neural cells, which cannot exist without the developmental code that specifies neural cells and modularly organised brains. Human language codes for a range of cultural phenotypes that could not be possibly stored in genes; but human language is dependent on the existence of organisms carrying genes, transcription factors and brains. Thus, macroevolution reveals a functional and evolutionary hierarchy of information carriers.

The hierarchy of codes can alternatively be expressed through their phenotypes. Proteins, somatic cells, learned animal behaviours (including social behaviour and culturally determined extended phenotypes), and culturally extended human phenotypes are disposable phenotypic entities evolving in chronological succession. Those entities are the units of organisation pointing to increasing biological complexity and to a hierarchy of types of organisms. However, those phenotypes are not necessarily super-units formed from previously existing ones, and the ESP therefore provides a more satisfactory criterion of complexity than super-unit formation. It implies that a taxon is more complex than another if its phenotypic set, or the sum of all phenotypic levels, includes a more derived level in the hierarchy of biological codes: linguistic humans are more complex than other behavioural organisms; the latter are more complex than developmental phenotypes; and those are more complex than phenotypes that depend exclusively on proteins coded by genes. This conclusion is in general agreement with the classification suggested by Jablonka and Lamb (2006) and diverges from the scheme derived from the theory of major transitions (in which sex or the origin of chromosomes, for example, corresponded to increases in complexity).

It is also clear that the hierarchical view derived from the ESP does not imply linearity or inevitability in macroevolution: although the developmental code requires the existence of the genetic code, the former has not necessarily evolved in all evolutionary lineages; although multicellularity has evolved multiple times as a consequence of a developmental code that required proteins, DNA and RNA, protein genes do not necessarily evolve into transcription factors or information carriers in all species.

Finally, contrary to the claims by Jablonka and Lamb (2005) that the contrast between genetic versus non-genetic mechanisms of inheritance implies a conflict between Darwinian and Lamarckian views of evolution, the hierarchical view derived from the ESP indicates that systems of biological information depend upon each other, and that they were products of Darwinian evolution. For those reasons, the impression shared by Darwin, Haldane, Mayr and others that evolutionary increases in complexity have in fact occurred is neither an anthropocentric illusion nor a macroevolutionary accident: it is a historical product of the operation of selection. Historical changes in levels of organisation are fundamental changes in the character of life that have occurred because the nature of carriers of information, phenotypic entities, and the way biological codes convert information into organisation can be historically transformed.

HISTORICAL HUMANS: THE TECHNOLOGICAL CODE AND
THE END OF EVOLUTION

Although the logic of transformations of Schrödinger's Principle is not
based on anthropocentric criteria, it places humans at the top of the
hierarchy of biological complexity – as did the theory of major transitions and the scenario of four biological codes proposed by Jablonka
and Lamb. Although the two latter models ascribe a special place to
humans in evolution due to language, the position of *historical* humans
is less clear in their formulation.

As seen earlier, animal culture depends on information-storing
brains and the behavioural code, and is observed in species other than
humans; furthermore, information required for the maintenance
of some extended phenotypes, or material culture, is also present
in other species. Thus, neither cultural transmission nor material
culture distinguishes humans from other species. Language in contrast is a uniquely human trait and has accelerated both accumulation
and transmission of cultural traditions and the creation of culturally
extended phenotypes. Since language is a universal feature present in
all known populations, the argument above applies to *Homo sapiens* as
a whole. However, historic humans did witness a further transition
in order – this time, a form of transition extending beyond biological
evolution itself. If the origin of new levels of complexity involves the
origin of new information carriers from existing phenotypic entities,
written language must distinguish historical humans from traditional
societies where culture can be only orally transmitted and stored.

Maynard Smith and Szathmáry's two books on major transitions
(1995, 1999) conclude with paragraphs pointing to two new transitions
occurring *after* the origin of language in humans, namely the origin of
writing and the more recent creation of digital storing means such as
computers. This distinction is lost in Jablonka and Lamb's characterisation of all humans as the 'symbolic species' (an argument based on
Deacon, 1997). In the light of the ESP, Maynard Smith and Szathmáry's
view seems to be the more justified. The co-existence of language and
language-dependent cultural phenotypes created the possibility that
items of material culture might evolve into information bearers themselves. Written language originated as a variation on extended phenotypes; not by accident, it was originally engraved in clay tablets or
stones as an extension of stone-tool technology; more recently it was
transformed by paper and then by metallurgy with the introduction
of metal movable-type printing in Korea and China in the thirteenth

century and two centuries later in Europe, where large-scale book printing started (Crystal, 1987). Thus, *non-biological* records of language such as clay tablets or books correspond to a new category of entity: an 'extended information carrier' derived not from a biological phenotypic entity, but from a culturally acquired and modified extended phenotype. Computers are a new type of non-biological information carrier resulting from advances in electronics and other special branches of contemporary material culture. The use of extended information carriers is the foundation of what some authors have named the human 'extended mind' (Clark, 2008).

The evolution of non-biological information carriers has a special place in the debate on biological complexity. Although the origin of a new information carrier would suggest a distinction between historical (i.e. written language users) and traditional societies, the ESP differs from old schemes that classified historical societies at a higher level on a scale of biological 'progress'. The ESP explicitly attributes the demographic supremacy of historical over traditional societies (for example, of Europeans over native Americans, Africans and Australians after the great navigations in the modern era) not to biological differences, but to differences in material culture (in this case, mostly warfare technology). The reason for the frequent technological superiority of historical societies is non-biological itself – namely, the use of extended information carriers and written language.

Another question is whether historical societies, which depend both upon non-biological information carriers and upon non-biological extended phenotypes, should still be interpreted as part of the evolutionary process; or whether the origin of extended information carriers represented a last stage in the transformation of the Principle of Order from Order. The answer seems to be negative: whereas previous transformations represented a transformation of Schrödinger's Principle, the recent cultural revolution represented a step beyond evolution and Schrödinger's definition of Order from Order. The origin of a 'technological code' that extends beyond Schrödinger's Principle is the reason why historical changes in social, cultural and economic organisation present similarities with the evolutionary process, but is not part of it. This similarity between evolution and historical change has inspired views such as 'social Darwinism' that have unsuccessfully tried to translate the mechanisms of selection into social processes. This criticism also applies to recent and incorrect applications of Darwinian selection to purely historical processes; for example, Mesoudi *et al.* (2004) have argued that industrial patents could be compared to random mutations in natural populations as units of cultural innovation, neglecting the fact that patents are essentially 'Lamarckian' and goal-directed features of historical societies, rather than randomly produced variants.

Finally, it is impossible to ignore an apparent analogy between the transition to human history and the origin of life itself. As seen earlier, life can be equated with the origin of the DNA World, which established a distinction between the first exclusive information carrier (DNA) and the first exclusively functional entities (protein). Similarly to the autocatalytic ribozymes that transferred its information roles to DNA and functional roles to proteins in the DNA World, thus becoming the mediator and regulator between the two new molecular types, historical humans seem to have evolved into mediators between cultural information predominantly stored in extended information carriers on the one hand, and the production of cultural extended phenotypes on the other; those two processes could be seen as 'education' and 'work' respectively. Biological evolution and natural selection in historical societies are for this reason much less relevant to the rise and fall of genes, populations or civilisations than the fate of material culture itself. It is known that culture has transformed human biology in traditional societies (a classic example being the recent and convergent evolution of adult tolerance to lactose in pastoralist societies; Tishkoff et al., 2007). A possibility is that technology may eventually transform human biology even in historical societies so as to adapt the human phenotype to the function of regulator and mediator between non-biological information carriers and cultural phenotypes; that process would be analogous to the evolution of mediating and regulating functions of RNA after the origin of the DNA World.

HIERARCHICAL EVOLUTION AND THE ROOTS OF DARWINISM

The special status of historical humans has played a confounding role in analyses of biological complexity in the recent past, not least by inspiring the formulation of anthropocentric views of evolution. The distinction between biological and historical change can bring some clarification to the problem: although cultural change in historical humans evolved as a product of a hierarchy of biological organisation, human culture developed into a process beyond biological evolution and biological organisation. For this reason, if we exclude historical humans from the picture of macroevolution and remove any possible anthropocentric prejudices, it is reasonable to assume that increases in complexity do represent a real phenomenon in macroevolution.

The concept of a hierarchy of biological order potentially re-establishes the idea of a 'Great Chain of Being' (Lovejoy, 1936). The difference is that whereas the old Chain originally represented a static and linear picture of creation in which species differed by degrees of perfection, the hierarchy of complexity defined by the ESP implies a dynamical chain in which phenotypic entities are transformed into information carriers and vice versa, and to which new terminal links or levels of phenotypic organisation can be added. This perspective, characterised by hierarchy and dynamism, is fully compatible with the view of organic evolution favoured by Darwin himself. Darwin was a firm believer in the existence of levels of complexity or even 'perfection' in the living world, as revealed in one of his most cited writings: the final paragraph in the *Origin of Species*.

> It is interesting to contemplate an entangled bank, clothed with many plants of many kinds, with birds singing on the bushes, with various insects flitting about, and with worms crawling through the damp earth, and to reflect that these elaborately constructed forms, so different from each other, and dependent on each other in so complex a manner, have all been produced by laws acting around us. These laws, taken in the largest sense, being Growth with Reproduction; Inheritance which is almost implied by reproduction; Variability from the indirect and direct action of the external conditions of life, and from use and disuse; a Ratio of Increase so high as to lead to a Struggle for Life, and as a consequence to Natural Selection, entailing Divergence of Character and the Extinction of less-improved forms.

Darwin's conclusion is frequently interpreted as an almost poetical rendering of the creative power ascribed to natural selection, or as an example of his belief in natural selection as a principle creating endless and most beautiful life forms. It is less commonly acknowledged that the paragraph also refers to an implicit hierarchy of life: although laws such as natural selection have produced a large variety of living forms, some of those forms should be more 'exalted' than others; those superior forms are the 'higher animals' that include humans.

> Thus, from the war of nature, from famine and death, the most exalted object which we are capable of conceiving, namely, the production of the higher animals, directly follows. There is grandeur in this view of life, with its several powers, having been originally breathed into a few forms or into one; and that, whilst this planet has gone cycling

on according to the fixed law of gravity, from so simple a beginning endless forms most beautiful and most wonderful have been, and are being, evolved.

There is certainly more grandeur in a view of evolution that attributes living diversity to natural selection than to a view centred on contingency. According to Darwin, there is even more grandeur in a view that interprets life forms as tiers of an evolutionary hierarchy. If we interpret the transformations of life at the macroevolutionary level as an extraordinary product of natural selection, namely the transformation of Order itself, then instead of being criticised for allegedly anthropocentric prejudice we would be able to enjoy both the grandeur of the biological world resulting from natural selection and of the cultural world created by historical *Homo sapiens*.

References

Abraham, R. G. and van den Bergh, S. (2001). Astrophysics – the morphological evolution of galaxies. *Science*, **293**, 1273–8.

Adami, C. (2002). What is complexity? *BioEssays*, **24**, 1085–94.

Aiello, L. C., Bates, N. and Joffe, T. (2001). In defense of the expensive tissue hypothesis. In *Evolutionary Anatomy of the Primate Cerebral Cortex*, ed. D. Falk and K. R. Gibson. Cambridge: Cambridge University Press, pp. 57–78.

Ainslie, G. W. (1974). Impulse control in pigeons. *Journal of Experimental Analysis of Behavior*, **21**, 485–9.

Akam, M. (1998). Hox genes in arthropod development and evolution. *Biological Bulletin*, **195**, 373–4.

Alexander, R. D. (1987). *The Biology of Moral Systems*. New York: Aldine de Gruyter.

Andersson, M. and Iwasa, Y. (1996). Sexual selection. *Trends in Ecology and Evolution*, **11**, A53–8.

Andersson, M. and Simmons, L. W. (2006). Sexual selection and mate choice. *Trends in Ecology and Evolution*, **21**, 296–302.

Angus, R. A. and Schultz, R. J. (1983). Meristic variation in homozygous and heterozygous fish. *Copeia*, 287–99.

Arnold, J. R. and Libby, W. F. (1949). Age determinations by radiocarbon content – checks with samples of known age. *Science*, **110**, 678–80.

Arthur, W. and Kettle, C. (2001). Geographic patterning of variation in segment number in geophilomorph centipedes: clines and speciation. *Evolution and Development*, **3**, 34–40.

Austad, S. N. (1993). Retarded senescence in an insular population of Virginia opossums (*Didelphis virginiana*). *Journal of Zoology*, **229**, 695–708.

Averof, M. and Akam, M. (1995). Hox genes and the diversification of insect and crustacean body plans. *Nature*, **376**, 420–3.

Averof, M. and Cohen, S. M. (1997). Evolutionary origin of insect wings from ancestral gills. *Nature*, **385**, 627–30.

Avery, J. (2003). *Information Theory and Evolution*. Singapore: World Scientific.

Axelrod, R. (1984). *The Evolution of Cooperation*. New York: Basic Books.

Axelrod, R. and Hamilton, W. D. (1981). The evolution of cooperation. *Science*, **211**, 1390–6.

Azevedo, R. B. R., Lohaus, R., Braun, V., *et al.* (2005). The simplicity of metazoan cell lineages. *Nature*, **433**, 152–6.

Barbash, D. A. and Ashburner, M. (2003). A novel system of fertility rescue in *Drosophila* hybrids reveals a link between hybrid lethality and female sterility. *Genetics*, **163**, 217–26.

Barbieri, M. (2003). *The Organic Codes.* Cambridge: Cambridge University Press.

Barnes, A. I. and Partridge, L. (2003). Costing reproduction. *Animal Behaviour*, **66**, 199–204.

Barraclough, T. G., Birky, C. W. and Burt, A. (2003). Diversification in sexual and asexual organisms. *Evolution*, **57**, 2166–72.

Barrett, R. D. H. and Schluter, D. (2008). Adaptation from standing genetic variation. *Trends in Ecology and Evolution*, **23**, 38–44.

Barton, R. A. and Harvey, P. H. (2000). Mosaic evolution of brain structure in mammals. *Nature*, **405**, 1055–8.

Bateson, W. (1894). *Materials for the Study of Variation.* London: McMillan.

Becerra, A., Delaye, L., Islas, S. and Lazcano, A. (2007). The very early stages of biological evolution and the nature of the last common ancestor of the three major cell domains. *Annual Review of Ecology Evolution and Systematics*, **38**, 361–79.

Bender, W., Akam, M., Karch, F. A., *et al.* (1983). Molecular genetics of the Bithorax Complex in *Drosophila melanogaster*. *Science*, **221**, 23–9.

Bennett, J. H. (1999). Foreword to R. A. Fisher (1930). In *The Genetical Theory of Natural Selection: A Complete Variorum Edition.* Oxford: Oxford University Press, pp. vi–xxii.

Berry, A. (2000). Blessed with more than avoirdupois. *Nature*, **406**, 561–2.

Bjork, A. and Pitnick, S. (2006). Intensity of sexual selection along the anisogamy–isogamy continuum. *Nature*, **441**, 742–5.

Blasco, M. A. (2005). Telomeres and human disease: ageing, cancer and beyond. *Nature Reviews Genetics*, **6**, 611–22.

Bonner, J. T. (1998). The origins of multicellularity. *Integrative Biology*, **1**, 27–36.

Bonner, J. T. (2006). *Why Size Matters.* Princeton, NJ: Princeton University Press.

Bonner, J. T. (2008). *The Social Amoebae: The Biology of Cellular Slime Molds.* Princeton, NJ: Princeton University Press.

Bowles, S. and Gintis, H. (2002). *Homo reciprocans. Nature*, **415**, 125–8.

Bowman, S. (1990). *Interpreting the Past: Radiocarbon Dating.* Berkeley, CA: University of California Press.

Boyd, R. and Richerson, P. J. (2005). Solving the puzzle of human cooperation. In *Evolution and Culture*, ed. S. Levinson. Cambridge, MA: MIT Press, pp. 105–32.

Braendle, C. and Felix, M. A. (2006). Sex determination: ways to evolve a hermaphrodite. *Current Biology*, **16**, R468–71.

Brakefield, P. M., Gates, J., Keys, D., *et al.*, (1996). Development, plasticity and evolution of butterfly eyespot patterns. *Nature*, **384**, 236–42.

Brideau, N. J., Flores, H. A., Wang, J., Maheshwari, S., Wang, X. and Barbash, D. A. (2006). Two Dobzhansky-Muller genes interact to cause hybrid lethality in Drosophila. *Science*, **314**, 1292–5.

Brooks, R. (2000). Negative genetic correlation between male sexual attractiveness and survival. *Nature*, **406**, 67–70.

Brosnan, S. F. and de Waal, F. B. M. (2003). Monkeys reject unequal pay. *Nature*, **425**, 297–9.

Brosnan, S. F., Schiff, H. C. and de Waal, F. B. M. (2005). Chimpanzees' (*Pan troglodytes*) reactions to inequity during experimental exchange. *Proceedings of the Royal Society Series B*, **1560**, 253–8.

Brown, P., Sutikna, T., Morwood, M. J., *et al.* (2004). A new small-bodied hominin from the late Pleistocene of Flores, Indonesia. *Nature*, **431**, 1055–61.

Buchan, J. C., Alberts, S. C., Silk, J. B. and Altmann, J. (2003). True paternal care in a multi-male primate society. *Nature*, **425**, 179–81.

Budd, G. E. (1999). Does evolution in body patterning genes drive morphological change – or vice versa? *BioEssays*, **21**, 326–32.

Bulmer, M. G. and Parker, G. A. (2002). The evolution of anisogamy: a game-theoretic approach. *Proceedings of the Royal Society Series B,* **269**, 2381–8.

Bunge, M. A. (2003). *Emergence and Convergence*. Toronto, Canada: Toronto University Press.

Burke, A. C., Nelson, C. E., Morgan, B. A. and Tabin, C. (1995). Hox genes and the evolution of vertebrate axial morphology. *Development*, **121**, 333–46.

Burland, T. M., Bennett, N. C., Jarvis, J. U. M. and Faulkes, C. G. (2002). Eusociality in african mole-rats: new insights from patterns of genetic relatedness in the Damaraland mole-rat (*Cryptomys damarensis*). *Proceedings of the Royal Society Series B*, **269**, 1025–30.

Burnet, F. M. (1945). *Virus as Organism*. Cambridge, MA: Harvard University Press.

Burton-Chellew, M. N., Koevoets, T., Grillenberger, B. K., *et al.* (2008). Facultative sex ratio adjustment in natural populations of wasps: cues of local mate competition and the precision of adaptation. *American Naturalist*, **172**, 393–404.

Buss, L. W. (1987). *The Evolution of Individuality*. Princeton, NJ: Princeton University Press.

Cabana, T., Jolicoeur, P. and Michaud, J. (1993). Prenatal and postnatal-growth and allometry, head circumference, and brain-weight in Quebec children. *American Journal of Human Biology*, **5**, 93–9.

Camerer, C. F. (1997). Progress in behavioral game theory. *Journal of Economic Perspectives*, **11**, 167–88.

Cant, M. A. and Johnstone, R. A. (2008). Reproductive conflict and the separation of reproductive generations in humans. *Proceedings of the National Academy of Sciences of the USA*, **105**, 5332–6.

Canzian, F., McKay, J. D., Cleveland, R. J., *et al.* (2006). Polymorphisms of genes coding for insulin-like growth factor I and its major binding proteins, circulating levels of IGF-1 and IGFBP-3 and breast cancer risk: results from the EPIC study. *British Journal of Cancer*, **94**, 299–307.

Carey, J. R. and Judge, D. S. (2002). *Longevity Records: Life Spans of Mammals, Birds, Amphibians, Reptiles, and Fish*. Monographs on Population Aging, 8. Odense: Odense University Press

Carninci, P. (2009). The long and short of RNAs. *Nature*, **457**, 974–5.

Carpenter, W. B. (1839). *Principles of General and Comparative Physiology*. London: John Churchill.

Carroll, S. B. (2003). Genetics and the making of *Homo sapiens*. *Nature*, **422**, 849–57.

Carroll, S. B. (2006). *Endless Forms Most Beautiful*. London: Weidenfeld & Nicolson.

Carroll, S. B. (2008). Evo-devo and an expanding evolutionary synthesis: a genetic theory of morphological evolution. *Cell*, **134**, 25–36.

Carroll, S. B., Weatherbee, S. D. and Langeland, J. A. (1995). Homeotic genes and the regulation and evolution of insect wing number. *Nature*, **375**, 58–61.

Carroll, S. B., Grenier, J. K. and Weatherbee, S. D. (2001). *From DNA to Diversity: Molecular Genetics and the Evolution of Animal Design*. Malden, MA: Blackwell Scientific.

Carter, J. and Irons, M. (1991). Are economists different, and if so, why? *Journal of Economic Perspectives*, **5**, 171–7.

Cech, T. R. (2002). Ribozymes, the first twenty years. *Biochemical Society Transactions*, **30**, 1162–6.

Cerit, H. and Avanus, K. (2007). Sex identification in avian species using DNA typing methods. *World's Poultry Science Journal*, **63**, 91–9.

Charlesworth, B., Lande, R. and Slatkin, M. (1982). A neo-Darwinian commentary on macroevolution. *Evolution*, **36**, 474–98.

Charnov, E. L. (1993). *Life History Invariants*. Oxford: Oxford University Press.

Charnov, E. L. and Ernest, S. K. M. (2006). The offspring-size/clutch-size trade-off in mammals. *American Naturalist*, **167**, 578–82.

Charnov, E. L., Smith, J. M. and Bull, J. J. (1976). Why be an hermaphrodite. *Nature*, **263**, 125–6.

Cheverud, J. (1996). Developmental integration and the evolution of pleiotropy. *American Zoologist*, **36**, 44–50.

Chipman, A. D., Arthur, W. and Akam, M. (2004). A double segment periodicity underlies segment generation in centipede development. *Current Biology*, **14**, 1250–5.

Clark, A. (2008). *Supersizing the Mind: Embodiment, Action, and Cognitive Extension*. Oxford: Oxford University Press.

Clutton-Brock, T. H. (1991). *The Evolution of Parental Care*. Princeton, NJ: Princeton University Press.

Clutton-Brock, T. H. and Parker, G. A. (1995). Punishment in animal societies. *Nature*, **373**, 209–16.

Clutton-Brock, T. H., Brotherton, P. N. M., Russell, A. F., *et al.* (2001). Cooperation, control, and concession in meerkat groups. *Science*, **291**, 478–81.

Cnotka, J., Güntürkün, O., Rehkämper, G., Gray, R. D. and Hunt, G. R. (2008). Extraordinary large brains in tool-using New Caledonian crows (*Corvus moneduloides*). *Neuroscience Letters*, **433**, 241–5.

Cohen, A. A. (2004). Female post-reproductive lifespan: a general mammalian trait. *Biological Reviews*, **79**, 733–50.

Cohen, I. B. (1987). *The Birth of a New Physics*. Harmondsworth, UK: Penguin Books.

Cohn, M. J. and Tickle, C. (1999). Developmental basis of limblessness and axial patterning in snakes. *Nature*, **399**, 474–9.

Collins, S. A. and Luddem, S. T. (2002). Degree of male ornamentation affects female preference for conspecific versus heterospecific males. *Proceedings of the Royal Society Series B*, **269**, 111–17.

Connor, R. C., Heithaus, M. R. and Barre, L. M. (1999). Superalliance of bottlenose dolphins. *Nature*, **397**, 571–2.

Conway Morris, S. (2001). We were meant to be. *New Scientist*, **176**, 26–9.

Conway Morris, S. (2003). *Life's Solution*. Cambridge: Cambridge University Press.

Conway Morris, S. (2006). Darwin's dilemma: the realities of the Cambrian 'explosion'. *Philosophical Transactions of the Royal Society Series B*, **361**, 1069–83.

Coyne, J. A. (2005). Endless forms most beautiful: the new science of evo devo. *Nature*, **435**, 1029–30.

Coyne, J. A. and Orr, H. A. (1998). The evolutionary genetics of speciation. *Philosophical Transactions of the Royal Society of London, Series B*, **353**: 287–305.

Coyne, J. A. and Orr, H. A. (2004). *Speciation*. Sunderland, MA: Sinauer.

Coyne, J. A., Barton, N. H. and Turelli, M. (1997). Perspective: a critique of Sewall Wright's shifting balance theory of evolution. *Evolution*, **51**, 643–71.

Crampton, H. E. (1928). The differentiation of species. *Science*, **67**, 615–19.

Crick, F. (1970). Central dogma of molecular biology. *Nature*, **227**, 561–3.

Crick, F. H. C. (1981). *Life Itself: Its Origin and Nature*. New York: Simon and Schuster.

Crick, F. H. C. (1994). *The Astonishing Hypothesis: The Scientific Search for the Soul*. London: Simon and Schuster.

Crick, F. H. C., Barnett, L., Brenner, S. and Watts-Tobin, R. J. (1961). General nature of genetic code for proteins. *Nature*, **192**, 1227–32.

Cromie, G. A, Connelly, J. C. and Leach, D. R. (2001). Recombination at double-strand breaks and DNA ends: conserved mechanisms from phage to humans. *Molecular Cell*, **8**, 1163–74.

Crystal, D. (1987). *The Cambridge Encyclopedia of Language*. Cambridge: Cambridge University Press.

Darwin, C. (1859). *On the Origin of Species*. Cambridge, MA: Harvard University Press.

Darwin, C. (1868). *The Variation of Animals and Plants under Domestication*. London: John Murray.

Darwin, C. (1871). *The Descent of Man, and Evolution in Relation to Sex*. Princeton, NJ: Princeton University Press.

Davidson, E. H. and Erwin, D. H. (2006). Gene regulatory networks and the evolution of animal body plans. *Science*, **311**, 796–800.

Davidson, E. H. and Levine, M. (2008). Properties of developmental gene regulatory networks. *Proceedings of the National Academy of Sciences of the USA*, **105**, 20063–6.

Davis, A.W., Roote, J., Morley, T., Sawamura, K., Herrmann, S. and Ashburner, M. (1996). Rescue of hybrid sterility in crosses between *D. melanogaster and D. simulans*. *Nature*, **380**, 157–9.

Dawkins, R. (1976). *The Selfish Gene*. Oxford: Oxford University Press.

Dawkins, R. (1979). Twelve misunderstandings of kin selection. *Zeitschrift für Tierpsychologie*, **51**, 184–200.

Dawkins, R. (1982). *The Extended Phenotype*. Oxford: Oxford University Press.

Deacon, T. W. (1997). *The Symbolic Species: The Co-Evolution of Language and the Brain*. London: W. W. Norton.

de Martino, B., Kumaran, D., Seymour, B. and Dolan, R. J. (2006). Frames, biases, and rational decision-making in the human brain. *Science*, **313**, 684–7.

de Quervain, D. J.-F., Fischbacher, U., Treyer, V., *et al.* (2004). The neural basis of altrusitic punishment. *Science*, **305**, 1254–8.

de Robertis, E. M. and Sasai, Y. (1996). A common plan for dorsoventral patterning in Bilateria. *Nature*, **380**, 37–40.

de Vries, H. (1906). *Species and Varieties, their Origin by Mutation*. Chicago, IL: Open Book.

Denver, D. R., Morris, K., Lynch, M. and Thomas, W. K. (2004). High mutation rate and predominance of insertions in the *Caenorhabditis elegans* nuclear genome. *Nature*, **430**, 679–82.

Desmond, A. and Moore, J. (1991). *Darwin*. London: Penguin.

Diamond, J. M. (1991). Why are pygmies small? *Nature*, **354**, 111–12.

Diamond, J. M. (1997). *Guns, Germs and Steel: The Fates of Human Societies*. New York: W. W. Norton.

Dobzhansky, T. (1934). Studies on hybrid sterility. I. Spermatogenesis in pure and hybrid *Drosophila pseudoobscura*. *Zeitschrift fur Zellforschung und Mikroskopische Anatomie*, **21**, 169–21.

Dobzhansky, T. (1937). *Genetics and the Origin of Species*. New York: Columbia University Press.

Dobzhansky, T. (1955). *Evolution, Genetics, and Man*. New York: Wiley & Sons.

Dobzhansky, T. (1967). *The Biology of Ultimate Concern*. New York: New American Library.

Doebeli, M. (1996). A quantitative genetic competition model for sympatric speciation. *Journal of Evolutionary Biology*, **9**, 893–909.

Doebeli, M., Dieckmann, U., Metz, J. A. and Tautz, D. (2005). What we have also learned: adaptive speciation is theoretically plausible. *Evolution*, **59**, 691–5.

Doolittle, W. F. and Sapienza, C. (1980). Selfish genes, the phenotype paradigm and genome evolution. *Nature*, **284**, 601–3.

Doyne Farmer, J. (2005). Cool is not enough. *Nature*, **436**, 627–8.

Duffy, J. E. (1996). Eusociality in a coral-reef shrimp. *Nature*, **381**, 512–14.

Dunbar, R. I. M. (1997). The monkeys' defence alliance. *Nature*, **386**, 555–7.

Dunbar, R. I. M. (1998). The social brain hypothesis. *Evolutionary Anthropology*, **6**, 178–90.

Dunbar, R. I. M. and Shultz, S. (2007). Evolution in the social brain. *Science*, **317**, 1344–7.

Eichinger, L., Pachebat, J. A., Glockner, G., *et al.* (2005). The genome of the social amoeba *Dictyostelium discoideum*. *Nature*, **435**, 43–57.

Eigen, M. (1971). Selforganization of matter and evolution of biological macromolecules. *Naturwissenschaften*, **58**, 465–523.

Einstein, A. and Infeld, L. (1938). *The Evolution of Physics: From Early Concept to Relativity and Quanta*. Cambridge: Cambridge University Press.

Enard, W., Khaitovich, P., Klose, J., *et al.* (2002). Intra- and interspecific variation in primate gene expression patterns. *Science*, **296**, 340–3.

Engelen, B. (2008). The sources of cooperation – on strong reciprocity and its theoretical implications. *Theory and Psychology*, **18**, 527–44.

Eppley, S. M. and Jesson, L. K. (2008). Moving to mate: the evolution of separate and combined sexes in multicellular organisms. *Journal of Evolutionary Biology*, **21**, 727–36.

Evans, J. D. and Wheeler, D. E. (1999). Differential gene expression between developing queens and workers in the honey bee, *Apis mellifera*. *Proceedings of the National Academy of Sciences of the USA*, **96**, 5575–80.

Fehr, E. and Fischbacher, U. (2003). The nature of human altruism. *Nature*, **425**, 785–91.

Fehr, E. and Gächter, S. (2002). Altruistic punishment in humans. *Nature*, **415**, 137–40.

Fehr, E. and Schmidt, K. M. (1999). A theory of fairness, competition, and cooperation. *Quarterly Journal of Economics*, **114**, 817–68.

Fernando, P., Vidya, T. N. C., Payne, J., *et al.* (2003). DNA analysis indicates that Asian elephants are native to Borneo and are therefore a high priority for conservation. *Plos Biology*, **1**, 110–15.

Feynman, R. P. (1965). *The Character of Physical Law*. London: Penguin.

Feynman, R. P. (1985). *QED: The Strange Theory of Light and Matter*. Princeton, NJ: Princeton University Press.

Fisher, R. A. (1930). *The Genetical Theory of Natural Selection: A Complete Variorum Edition*. Oxford: Oxford University Press.

Fisher, S. E. and Marcus, G. F. (2006). The eloquent ape: genes, brains and the evolution of language. *Nature Reviews Genetics*, **7**, 9–20.

Fitzpatrick, B. M., Fordyce, J. A. and Gavrilets, S. (2008). What, if anything, is sympatric speciation? *Journal of Evolutionary Biology*, **21**, 1452–9.

Fodor, J. A. (1983). *The Modularity of Mind*. Cambridge, MA: MIT Press.

Foerster, K., Delhey, K., Johnsen, A., Lifjeld, J. T., and Kempenaers, B. (2003). Females increase offspring heterozygosity and fitness through extra-pair matings. *Nature*, **425**, 714–17.

Foley, R. A. and Lee, P. C. (1991). Ecology and energetics of encephalization in hominid evolution. *Philosophical Transactions of the Royal Society Series B*, **334**, 223–32.

Fontaneto, D., Herniou, E. A., Boschetti, C., *et al.* (2007). Independently evolving species in asexual bdelloid rotifers. *Plos Biology*, **5**, 914–21.

Forbes, L. S. (1997). The evolutionary biology of spontaneous abortion in humans. *Trends in Ecology and Evolution*, **12**, 446–50.

Forbes, S., Thornton, S., Glassey, B., Forbes, M. and Buckley, N. J. (1997). Why parent birds play favourites. *Nature*, **390**, 351–2.

Forsythe, R., Horowitz, J. L., Savin, N. E. and Sefton, M. (1994). Fairness in simple bargaining experiments. *Game and Economic Behavior*, **6**, 347–69.

Forterre, P. (2006). The origin of viruses and their possible roles in major evolutionary transitions. *Virus Research*, **117**, 5–16.

Franceschi, C., Bonafè, M., Valensin, S., *et al.* (2000). Inflamm-aging: an evolutionary perspective of immunosenescence. *Annals of the New York Academy of Sciences*, **908**, 244–54.

Frank, S. A. (1995). Mutual policing and repression of competition in the evolution of cooperative groups. *Nature*, **377**, 520–2.

Frank, S. A. (1998). *Foundations of Social Evolution*. Princeton, NJ: Princeton University Press.

Fraser, C., Hanage, W. P. and Spratt, B. G. (2007). Recombination and the nature of bacterial speciation. *Science*, **315**, 476–80.

Galis, F. (1999). Why do almost all mammals have seven cervical vertebrae? Developmental constraints, Hox genes, and cancer. *Journal of Experimental Zoology*, **285**, 19–26.

Galis, F., Van Dooren, T. J. M., Feuth, J. D., *et al.* (2006). Extreme selection in humans against homeotic transformations of cervical vertebrae. *Evolution*, **60**, 2643–54.

Galperin, M. Y. (2008). Social bacteria and asocial eukaryotes. *Environmental Microbiology*, **10**, 281–8.

Garcia-Fernández, J. and Holland, P. W. (1994). Archetypal organization of the amphioxus Hox gene cluster. *Nature*, **370**, 563–6.

Garvin, J. C., Dunn, P. O., Whittingham, L. A., Steeber, D. A. and Hasselquist, D. (2008). Do male ornaments signal immunity in the common yellowthroat? *Behavioral Ecology*, **19**, 54–60.

Gavrilets, S. (1997). Hybrid zones with Dobzhansky-type epistatic selection. *Evolution*, **51**, 1027–35.

Gavrilets, S. (2005). "Adaptive speciation" – it is not that easy: a reply to Doebeli *et al. Evolution*, **59**, 696–9.

Gavrilets, S. and Waxman, D. (2002). Sympatric speciation by sexual conflict. *Proceedings of the National Academy of Sciences of the USA*, **99**, 10533–8.

Gehring, W. J. (1998). *Master Control Genes in Development and Evolution*. New Haven, CT: Yale University Press.

Gellon, G. and McGinnis, W. (1998). Shaping animal body plans in development and evolution by modulation of Hox expression patterns. *BioEssays*, **20**, 116–25.

Gell-Mann, M. (1994). *The Quark and the Jaguar*. London: Abacus.

Gentner, T. Q., Fenn, K. M., Margoliash, D. and Nusbaum, H. C. (2006). Recursive syntactic pattern learning by songbirds. *Nature*, **440**, 1204–7.

Gerhart, J. (2000). Inversion of the chordate body axis: Are there alternatives? *Proceedings of the National Academy of Sciences of the USA*, **97**, 4445–8.

Gerhart, J. and Kirschner, M. (1997). *Cells, Embryos, and Evolution*. Oxford: Blackwell Science.

Ghiselin, M. T. (1969). Evolution of hermaphroditism among animals. *Quarterly Review of Biology*, **44**, 189–208.

Ghiselin, M. T. (1974). *The Economy of Nature and the Evolution of Sex*. Berkeley, CA: University of California Press.

Gilbert, S. F., Opitz, J. M. and Raff, R. A. (1996). Resynthesizing evolutionary and developmental biology. *Developmental Biology*, **173**, 357–72.

Gilbert, W. (1986). The RNA world. *Nature*, **319**, 618.

Gillespie, D. O. S., Russell, A. F. and Lummaa, V. (2008). When fecundity does not equal fitness: evidence of a quantity–quality trade-off in pre-industrial humans. *Proceedings of the Royal Society Series B*, **275**, 713–22.

Gilson, E. and Géli, V. (2007). How telomeres are replicated. *Nature Reviews Molecular Cell Biology*, **8**, 825–38.

Ginaldi, L., Loreto, M. F., Corsi, M. P., Modesti, M. and De Martinis, M. (2001). Immunosenescence and infectious diseases. *Microbes and Infection*, **3**, 851–7.

Gintis, H. (2003). The hitchhiker's guide to altruism: gene-culture coevolution, and the internalization of norms. *Journal of Theoretical Biology*, **220**, 407–18.

Gintis, H., Smith, E. A. and Bowles, S. (2001). Costly signaling and cooperation. *Journal of Theoretical Biology*, **213**, 103–19.

Goddard, M. R., Charles, H., Godfray, J. and Burt, A. (2005). Sex increases the efficacy of natural selection in experimental yeast populations. *Nature*, **434**, 636–40.

Goldschmidt, R. (1940). *The Material Basis of Evolution*. New Haven, CT: Yale University Press.

Goldsmith, T. H. and Zimmerman, W. F. (2001). *Biology, Evolution, and Human Nature*. New York: Wiley & Sons.

Goodwin, B. (1994). *How the Leopard Changed its Spots*. New York: Simon & Schuster.

Gordon, A. D., Green, D. J. and Richmond, B. G. (2008). Strong postcranial size dimorphism in Australopithecus afarensis: results from two new resampling methods for multivariate data sets with missing data. *American Journal of Physical Anthropology*, **135**, 311–28.

Gould, S. J. (1977). *Ontogeny and Phylogeny*. Cambridge, MA: Harvard University Press.

Gould, S. J. (1980). *The Panda's Thumb*. New York: W. W. Norton.

Gould, S. J. (1989). *Wonderful Life*. London: Penguin.

Gould, S. J. (2002). *The Structure of Evolutionary Theory*. Cambridge, MA: Harvard University Press.

Gould, S. J. and Lewontin, R. C. (1979). Spandrels of San Marco and the Panglossian paradigm: a critique of the adaptionist program. *Proceedings of the Royal Society Series B*, **205**, 581–98.

Greenfield, P. M. (1991). Language, tools, and brain: the ontogeny and phylogeny of hierarchically organized sequential behavior. *Behavioral and Brain Sciences*, **14**, 531–50.

Greenman, C., Stephens, P., Smith, R., *et al*. (2007). Patterns of somatic mutation in human cancer genomes. *Nature*, **446**, 153–8.

Greenspan, R. J. (2007). *An Introduction to Nervous Systems*. Cold Spring Harbor, NY: Cold Spring Harbor Laboratory Press.

Gregory, J. (1931). *A Short History of Atomism from Democritus to Bohr*. London: A. & C. Black.

Grober, M. S. and Rodgers, E. W. (2008). The evolution of hermaphroditism. *Journal of Theoretical Biology*, **251**, 190–2.

Guerrier-Takada, C., Vanbelkum, A., Pleij, C. W. A. and Altman, S. (1988). Novel reactions of RNAse P with a transfer-RNA-like structure in turnip yellow mosaic-virus RNA. *Cell*, **53**, 267–72.

Güth, W., Schmittberger, R. and Schwarze, B. (1982). An experimental analysis of ultimatum bargaining. *Journal of Economic Behavior and Organization*, **3**, 367–88.

Hadany, L. and Beker, T. (2007). Sexual selection and the evolution of obligatory sex. *BMC Evolutionary Biology*, **7**, 245–52.

Haeckel, E. (1896). *The Evolution of Man*. New York: Appleton.

Haldane, J. B. S. (1932). *The Causes of Evolution*. London: Longmans Green.

Haldane, J. B. S. and Huxley, J. (1927). *Animal Biology*. Oxford: Oxford University Press.

Hamilton, W. D. (1964). The genetical evolution of social behaviour. *Journal of Theoretical Biology*, **7**, 1–52.

Hamilton, W. D. (1966). The moulding of senescence by natural selection. *Journal of Theoretical Biology*, **12**, 12–45.

Hamilton, W. D. (1967). Extraordinary sex ratios. *Science*, **156**, 477–88.

Hamilton, W. D. (1980). Sex versus non-sex parasite. *Oikos*, **35**, 282–90.

Hamilton, W. D. (1996). *Narrow Roads of Gene Land. Volume 1: Evolution of Social Behaviour*. Oxford: W. H. Freeman.

Hamilton, W. D. and Zuk, M. (1982). Heritable true fitness and bright birds: a role for parasites. *Science*, **218**, 384–7.

Hamilton, W. D., Axelrod, R. and Tanese, R. (1990). Sexual reproduction as an adaptation to resist parasites (a review). *Proceedings of the National Academy of Sciences of the USA*, **87**, 3566–73.

Harman, D. (1956). Aging: a theory based on free-radical and radiation-chemistry. *Journal of Gerontology*, **11**, 298–300.

Harmon, L. J., Matthews, B., Des Roches, S., *et al.* (2009). Evolutionary diversification in stickleback affects ecosystem functioning. *Nature*, **458**, 1167–70.

Harvey, P. H. and Nee, S. (1991). How to live like a mammal. *Nature*, **350**, 23–4.

Harvey, P. H. and Purvis, A. (1999). Understanding the ecological and evolutionary reasons for life history variation: mammals as a case study. In *Advanced Ecological Theory*, ed. J. McGlade. Oxford: Blackwell, pp. 232–48.

Haslam, M., Hernandez-Aguilar, A., Ling, V., *et al.* (2009). Primate archaeology. *Nature*, **460**, 339–44.

Hauser, M. D., Chomsky, N. and Tecumseh Fitch, W. (2002). The faculty of language: what is it, who has it, and how did it evolve? *Science*, **298**, 1569–79.

Hawkes, K., O'Connell, J. F., Blurton Jones, N. G., Alvarez, H., and Charnov, E. L. (1998). Grandmothering, menopause, and the evolution of human life histories. *Proceedings of the National Academy of Sciences of the USA*, **95**, 1336–9.

Hawkes, K. and Paine, R. R., eds. (2006). *The Evolution of Human Life History*. Santa Fe, CA: SAR Press.

Hayakawa, T., Angata, T., Lewis, A. L., Mikkelsen, T. S., Varki, N. M. and Varki, A. (2005). A human-specific gene in microglia. *Science*, **309**, 1693.

Hazen, R. M. (2005). *Genesis: The Scientific Quest for Life's Origin*. Washington, DC: Joseph Henry Press.

Heisenberg, M. (2009). Is free will an illusion? *Nature*, **459**, 164–5.

Hempel, C. G. (1966). *Philosophy of Natural Science*. Upper Saddle River, NJ: Prentice Hall.

Henig, R. M. (2000). *A Monk and Two Peas: The Story of Gregor Mendel and the Discovery of Genetics*. London: Weidenfeld & Nicolson.

Henrich, J., Boyd, R., Bowles, S., *et al.* (2005). "Economic man" in cross-cultural perspective: behavioural experiments in 15 small-scale societies. *Behavioural and Brain Sciences*, **28**, 795–855.

Henrich, J., McElreath, R., Barr, A., *et al.* (2006). Costly punishment across human societies. *Science*, **312**, 1767–70.

Herbig, U., Ferreira, M., Condel, L., Carey, D. and Sedivy, J. M. (2006). Cellular senescence in aging primates. *Science*, **311**, 1257.

Hill, K. and Hurtado, M. (1996). *Ache Life History*. New York: Aldine de Gruyter.

Hill, R. S. and Walsh, C. A. (2005). Molecular insights into human brain evolution. *Nature*, **437**, 64–7.

Hirt, R. P., Healy, B., Vossbrinck, C. R., *et al.* (1997). A mitochondrial hsp70 orthologue in Vairimorpha necatrix: molecular evidence that microsporidia once contained mitochondria. *Current Biology*, **7**, 995–8.

Hoekstra, H. E. and Coyne, J. A. (2007). The locus of evolution: evo devo and the genetics of adaptation. *Evolution*, **61**, 995–1016.

Hoffman, E., McCabe, K., Shachat, K. and Smith, V. (1994). Preferences, property rights, and anonymity in bargaining games. *Game and Economic Behavior*, **7**, 346–80.

Holbert, O. (2008). Gene regulation by transcription factors and microRNAs. *Science*, **319**, 1785–6.

Holland, P. W. H., Holland, L. Z., Williams, N. A. and Holland, N. D. (1992). An amphioxus homeobox gene: sequence conservation, spatial expression during development and insights into vertebrate evolution. *Development*, **116**, 653–62.

Hölldobler, B. and Wilson, E. O. (2008). *The Superorganism: The Beauty, Elegance, and Strangeness of Insect Societies*. London: W. W. Norton.

Hostert, E. E. (1997). Reinforcement: a new perspective on an old controversy. *Evolution*, **51**, 697–702.

Hrdy, S. B. (2009). *Mothers and Others: The Evolutionary Origins of Mutual Understanding*. Cambridge, MA: Harvard University Press.

Hughes, K. A. and Reynolds, R. M. (2005). Evolutionary and mechanistic theories of aging. *Annual Review of Entomology*, **50**, 421–45.

Hughes, K. A., Alipaz, J. A., Drnevich, J. M. and Reynolds, R. M. (2002). A test of evolutionary theories of aging. *Proceedings of the National Academy of Sciences of the USA*, **99**, 14286–91.

Hutter, P. (1997). Genetics of hybrid inviability in *Drosophila*. *Advances in Genetics*, **36**, 157–85.

Huxley, J. (1932). *Problems of Relative Growth*. Baltimore, MD: Johns Hopkins University.

Huxley J. and de Beer, G. (1934). *The Elements of Experimental Embryology*. Cambridge: Cambridge University Press.

Imai, K. S., Hino, K., Yagi, K., Satoh, N. and Satou, Y. (2004). Gene expression profiles of transcription factors and signaling molecules in the ascidian embryo: towards a comprehensive understanding of gene networks. *Development*, **131**, 4047–58.

Israel, S., Lerer, E., Shalev, I., *et al.* (2009). The oxytocin receptor (OXTR) contributes to prosocial fund allocations in the dictator game and the social value orientations task. *PLoS One*, **4**, e5535.

Istrail, S. and Davidson, E. H. (2005). Logic functions of the genomic cis-regulatory code. *Proceedings of the National Academy of Sciences of the USA*, **102**, 4954–9.

Iwaniuk, A. N., Dean, K. M. and Nelson, J. E. (2004). A mosaic pattern character-izes the evolution of the avian brain. *Proceedings of the Royal Society Series B*, **271**, Supplement 4, S148–51.

Jablonka, E. and Lamb, M. (2005). *Evolution in Four Dimensions*. Cambridge, MA: MIT Press.

Jablonka, E. and Lamb, M. J. (2006). The evolution of information in the major transitions. *Journal of Theoretical Biology*, **239**, 236–46.

Jacob, F. and Monod, F. (1961). Genetic regulatory mechanisms in the synthesis of proteins. *Journal of Molecular Biology*, **3**, 318–56.

Janik, V. M. and Slater, P. J. B. (1997). Vocal learning in mammals. *Advances in the Study of Behavior*, **26**, 59–99.

Jarne, P. and Auld, J. R. (2006). Animals mix it up too: the distribution of self-fertilization among hermaphroditic animals. *Evolution*, **60**, 1816–24.

Jarvis, J. U. M. (1981). Eusociality in mammals: cooperative breeding in naked mole-rats colonies. *Science*, **212**, 571–3.

Jerison, H. J. (1973). *Evolution of the Brain and Intelligence*. New York: Academic Press.

Johannsen, W. (1911). The genotype conception of heredity. *American Naturalist*, **45**, 129–59.

Johnson, P. A. and Gullberg, U. (1998). Theory and models of sympatric speciation. In *Endless Forms: Species and Speciation*, ed. D. H. Howard and S. H. Berlocher. New York: Oxford University Press, pp. 79–89.

Kahneman, D., Knetsch, J. and Thaler, R. H. (1986). Fairness as a constraint on profit sharing: entitlements in the market. *American Economic Review*, **76**, 728–41.

Kaplan, H., Hill, K., Lancaster, J. and Hurtado, A. M. (2000). A theory of human life history evolution: diet, intelligence, and longevity. *Evolutionary Anthropology*, **9**, 156–85.

Kaplan, H. S. and Robson, A. J. (2009). We age because we grow. *Proceedings of the Royal Society Series B*, **276**, 1837–44.

Kappeler, P . and Pereira, M. E., eds. (2003). *Primate Life Histories and Socioecology*. Chicago, IL: University of Chicago Press.

Katinka, M. D., Duprat, S., Cornillot, E., *et al.* (2001). Genome sequence and gene compaction of the eukaryote parasite encephalitozoon cuniculi. *Nature*, **414**, 450–3.

Keeling, P. J. (2001). Parasites go the full monty. *Nature*, **414**, 401–2.

Keightley, P. D. and Otto, S. P. (2006). Interference among deleterious mutations favours sex and recombination in finite populations. *Nature*, **443**, 89–92.

Keller, L., ed. (1999). *Levels of Selection in Evolution*. Princeton, NJ; Princeton University Press.

Keller, L. F., Reid, J. M. and Arcese, P. (2008). Testing evolutionary models of senescence in a natural population: age and inbreeding effects on fitness components in song sparrows. *Proceedings of the Royal Society Series B*, **275**, 597–604.

Kellis, M., Patterson, N., Endrizzi, M., Birren, B. and Lander, E. S. (2003). Sequencing and comparison of yeast species to identify genes and regula-tory elements. *Nature*, **423**, 241–54.

Kettle, C., Arthur, W., Jowett, T. and Minelli, A. (1999). Homeotic transforma-tion in a centipede. *Trends in Genetics*, **15**, 393.

Keys, D. N., Lewis, D. L., Selegue, J. E., *et al.* (1999). Recruitment of a hedgehog regulatory circuit in butterfly eyespot evolution. *Science*, **283**, 532–4.

Khaitovich, P., Hellmann, I., Enard, W., *et al.* (2005). Parallel patterns of evolution in the genomes and transcriptomes of humans and chimpanzees. *Science*, **309**, 1850–4.

Kimura, M. (1961). Natural selection as process of accumulating genetic information in adaptive evolution. *Genetical Research*, **2**, 127–40.

Kimura, M. (1983). *The Neutral Theory of Molecular Evolution*. Cambridge: Cambridge University Press.

King, M. C. and Wilson, A. C. (1975). Evolution at two levels in humans and chimpanzees. *Science*, **188**, 107–16.

Kirkpatrick, M. (1987). Sexual selection by female choice in polygynous animals. *Annual Review of Ecology and Systematics*, **18**, 43–70.

Kirkwood, T. B. L. (1977). Evolution of aging. *Nature*, **270**, 301–4.

Kirkwood, T. B. L. and Rose, M. R. (1991). Evolution of senescence: late survival sacrificed for reproduction. *Philosophical Transactions of the Royal Society Series B*, **332**, 15–24.

Kirschner, M. C. and Gerhart, J. C. (2005). *The Plausibility of Life*. New Haven, CT: Yale University Press.

Klein, R. G. (2000). Archeology and the evolution of human behavior. *Evolutionary Anthropology*, **9**, 17–36.

Kodric-Brown, A. and Brown, J. H. (1984). Truth in advertising: the kinds of traits favored by sexual selection. *American Naturalist*, **124**, 309–23.

Kokko, H. and Jennions, M. (2003). It takes two to tango. *Trends in Ecology and Evolution*, **18**, 103–4.

Kokko, H., Jennions, M. D. and Brooks, R. (2006). Unifying and testing models of sexual selection. *Annual Review of Ecology Evolution and Systematics*, **37**, 43–66.

Komdeur, J., Daan, S., Tinbergen, J. and Mateman, C. (1997). Extreme adaptive modification in sex ratio of the Seychelles warbler's eggs. *Nature*, **385**, 522–5.

Kondrashov, A. S. (1984). Deleterious mutations as an evolutionary factor. 1. The advantage of recombination. *Genetical Research*, **44**, 199–217.

Kondrashov, A. S. (1998). Measuring spontaneous deleterious mutation process. *Genetica*, **102–3**, 183–97.

Kondrashov, A. S. and Kondrashov, F. A. (1999). Interactions among quantitative traits in the course of sympatric speciation. *Nature*, **400**, 351–4.

Kondrashov, F. A. and Koonin, E. V. (2003). Evolution of alternative splicing: deletions, insertions and origin of functional parts of proteins from intron sequences. *Trends in Genetics*, **19**, 115–19.

Korpelainen, H. (2000). Variation in the heritability and evolvability of human lifespan. *Naturwissenschaften*, **87**, 566–8.

Kravitz, D. A. and Gunto, S. (1992). Decisions and perceptions of recipients in ultimatum bargaining games. *Journal of Socio-Economics*, **21**, 65–84.

Krebs, J. R. and Davies, N. B. (1987). *An Introduction to Behavioural Ecology*, 2nd edn. Oxford: Blackwell Scientific.

Krützen, M., Sherwin, W. B., Connor, R. C., *et al.* (2003). Contrasting relatedness patterns in bottlenose dolphins (Tursiops sp.) with different alliance strategies. *Proceedings of the Royal Society Series B*, **270**, 497–502.

Krützen, M., Mann, J., Heithaus, M. R., *et al.* (2005). Cultural transmission of tool use in bottlenose dolphins. *Proceedings of the National Academy of Sciences of the USA*, **102**, 8939–43.

Kruuk, L. E. B., Slate, J., Pemberton, J. M., *et al.* (2002). Antler size in red deer: heritability and selection but no evolution. *Evolution*, **56**, 1683–95.

Kukalová-Peck, J. (1983). Origin of the insect wing and wing articulation from the arthropodan leg. *Canadian Journal of Zoology*, **61**, 1618–69.

Lahdenperä, M., Lummaa, V., Helle, S., Tremblay, M. and Russell, A. F. (2004). Fitness benefits of prolonged post-reproductive lifespan in women. *Nature*, **428**, 178–81.

Lahr, M. M. (1996). *The Evolution of Modern Human Diversity*. Cambridge: Cambridge University Press.

Lahr, M. M. and Foley, R. (2004). Palaeoanthropology: human evolution writ small. *Nature*, **431**, 1043–4.

Laland, K. N. and Janik, V. M. (2006). The animal cultures debate. *Trends in Ecology and Evolution*, **21**, 542–7.

Lande, R. (1981). The minimum number of genes contributing to quantitative variation between and within populations. *Genetics*, **99**, 541–53.

Laplace, P. S. (1774). Memoire sur la probabilité des causes par les événements. In *Oeuvres Complètes* (1891), Volume 8. Paris: Gauthier-Villars, pp. 27–65.

Lawrence, P. (1992). *The Making of a Fly: The Genetics of Animal Design*. Oxford: Blackwell Scientific.

Lee, R. (2003). Rethinking the evolutionary theory of aging: transfers, not births, shape senescence in social species. *Proceedings of the National Academy of Sciences of the USA*, **100**, 9637–42.

Lee, R. B. and Daly, R., eds. (1999). *The Cambridge Encyclopedia of Hunters and Gatherers*. Cambridge: Cambridge University Press.

Lehmann, L., Foster, K. R., Borenstein, E. and Feldman, M. W. (2008). Social and individual learning of helping in humans and other species. *Trends in Ecology and Evolution*, **23**, 664–71.

Lemaire, P. (2006). How many ways to make a chordate? *Science*, **312**, 1145–6.

Leroi, A. M., Koufopanou, V. and Burt, A. (2003). Cancer selection. *Nature Reviews Cancer*, **3**, 226–31.

Levine, M. and Tjian, R. (2003). Transcription regulation and animal diversity. *Nature*, **424**, 147–51.

Lewin, B. (2007). *Genes IX*. Sudbury, MA: Jones & Bartlett Publishers.

Lewin, R. and Foley, R. A. (2004). *Principles of Human Evolution*. Oxford: Blackwells Publishing.

Lewis, E. B. (1978). Gene complex controlling segmentation in Drosophila. *Nature*, **276**, 565–70.

Lewis, G. N. (1930). The symmetry of time in physics. *Science*, **71**, 569–76.

Lewontin, R. C. (1970). The units of selection. *Annual Review of Ecology and Systematics*, **1**, 1–18.

Lewontin, R. C. (1979). Sociobiology as an adaptationist program. *Behavioral Science*, **24**, 5–14.

Li, M. and Vitanyi, P. (1997). *An Introduction to Kolmogorov Complexity and its Applications*, 2nd edn. New York: Springer-Verlag.

Li, X. M., Quigg, R. J., Zhou, J., *et al.* (2008). Clinical utility of microarrays: current status, existing challenges and future outlook. *Current Genomics*, **9**, 466–74.

Libby, W. F. (1955). *Radiocarbon Dating*, 2nd edn. Chicago, IL: University of Chicago Press.

Lindsay, R. S., Hanson, R. L., Wiedrich, C., *et al.* (2003). The insulin gene variable number tandem repeat class i/iii polymorphism is in linkage disequilibrium with birth weight but not type 2 diabetes in the Pima population. *Diabetes*, **52**, 187–93.

Lockwood, C. A., Menter, C. G., Moggi-Cecchi, J. and Keyser, A. W. (2007). Extended male growth in a fossil hominin species. *Science*, **318**, 1443–6.

Lovejoy, A. O. (1936). *The Great Chain of Being*. Cambridge, MA: Harvard University Press.

Lowe, C. J. and Wray, G. A. (1997). Radical alterations in the roles of homeobox genes during echinoderm evolution. *Nature*, **389**, 718–21.

Ludwig, M. Z., Palsson, A., Alekseeva, E., *et al.* (2005). Functional evolution of a cis-regulatory module. *PLoS Biology*, **3**, e93.

Lynch, V. J. and Wagner, G. P. (2008). Resurrecting the role of transcription factor change in developmental evolution. *Evolution*, **62**, 2131–54.

Mallet, J. (2001). The speciation revolution: commentary. *Journal of Evolutionary Biology*, **14**, 887–8.

Mangelsdorf, P. C. (1967). Preface. In *Experiments in Plant Hybridisation*, ed. G. Mendel. Cambridge, MA: Harvard University Press, pp. v–vii.

Margulis, L. (1970). *Origin of Eukaryotic Cells*. New Haven, CT: Yale University Press.

Margulis, L. and Sagan, D. (2000). *What is Life? The Eternal Enigma*. Berkeley, CA: California University Press.

Marino, L. (1996). What can dolphins tell us about primate evolution? *Evolutionary Anthropology*, **5**, 81–5.

Marino, L. (2002). Convergence of complex cognitive abilities in cetaceans and primates. *Brain, Behavior and Evolution*, **59**, 21–32.

Marler, P. R. and Slabbekoorn, H. (2004). *Nature's Music: The Science of Birdsong*. London: Academic Press.

Marshall, C. R. (2006). Explaining the Cambrian "explosion" of animals. *Annual Review of Earth and Planetary Sciences*, **34**, 355–84.

Martinez, P., Rast, J. P., Arenas-Mena, C. and Davidson, E. H. (1999). Organization of an echinoderm Hox gene cluster. *Proceedings of the National Academy of Sciences of the USA*, **96**, 1469–74.

Matsuura, K., Vargo, E. L., Kawatsu, K., *et al.* (2009). Queen succession through asexual reproduction in termites. *Science*, **323**, 1687.

Matus, D. Q., Pang, K., Marlow, H., *et al.* (2006). Molecular evidence for deep evolutionary roots of bilaterality in animal development. *Proceedings of the National Academy of Sciences of the USA*, **103**, 11195–200.

Mayhew, P. J. and Glaizot, O. (2001). Integrating theory of clutch size and body size evolution for parasitoids. *Oikos*, **92**, 372–6.

Maynard Smith, J. (1966). Sympatric speciation. *American Naturalist*, **100**, 637–50.

Maynard Smith, J. (1971). The origin and maintenance of sex. In *Group Selection*, ed. G. C. Williams. Chicago, IL: Aldine-Atherton, pp. 163–75.

Maynard Smith, J. (1978). *The Evolution of Sex*. Cambridge: Cambridge University Press.

Maynard Smith, J. (1982). *Evolution and the Theory of Games*. Cambridge: Cambridge University Press.

Maynard Smith, J. (1988). Evolutionary progress and levels of selection. In *Evolutionary Progress*, ed. M. H. Nitecki. Chicago, IL: University of Chicago Press, pp. 219–30.

Maynard Smith, J. and Harper, D. (2003). *Animal Signals*. Oxford: Oxford University Press.

Maynard Smith, J. and Szathmáry, E. (1995). *The Major Transitions in Evolution*. Oxford: Oxford University Press.

Maynard Smith, J. and Szathmáry, E. (1999). *The Origins of Life*. Oxford: Oxford University Press.

Maynard Smith, J., Burian, R., Kauffman, S., *et al.* (1985). Developmental constraints and evolution. *Quarterly Review of Biology*, **60**, 265–87.

Mayr, E., (1942). *Systematics and the Origin of Species*. New York: Columbia University Press.

Mayr, E. (1963). *Animal Species and Evolution*. Cambridge, MA: Harvard University Press.

Mayr, E. (1974). Behavior programs and evolutionary strategies. *American Scientist*, **62**, 650–9.

Mayr, E. (1980). Some thoughts on the history of the evolutionary synthesis. In *The Evolutionary Synthesis*, ed. E. Mayr and W. B. Provine. Cambridge, MA: Harvard University Press, pp. 1–48.

Mayr, E. (1982). *The Growth of Biological Thought: Diversity, Evolution and Inheritance*. Cambridge, MA: Harvard University Press.

Mayr, E. (1988). *Toward a New Philosophy of Biology*. Cambridge, MA: Harvard University Press.

Mayr, E. and Provine, W. B. (1980). *The Evolutionary Synthesis*. Cambridge, MA: Harvard University Press.

McFadden, B. J. (2005). Fossil horses: evidence for evolution. *Science*, **307**, 1728–30.

McGinnis, W. (1994). A century of homeosis, a decade of homeoboxes. *Genetics*, **137**, 607–11.

McGinnis, W., Levine, M. S., Hafen, E., Kuroiwa, A. and Gehring, W. J. (1984). A conserved DNA-sequence in homoeotic genes of the Drosophila antennapedia and bithorax complexes. *Nature*, **308**, 428–33.

McGrew, W. C., Marchant, L. F., Scott, S. E. and Tutin, C. E. G. (2001). Intergroup differences in a social custom of wild chimpanzees: the grooming hand-clasp of the Mahale mountains. *Current Anthropology*, **42**, 148–53.

McShea, D. W. (1996). Metazoan complexity and evolution: is there a trend? *Evolution*, **50**, 477–92.

Medawar, P. B. (1952). *The Uniqueness of the Individual*. London: Methuen.

Menand, L. (2002). *The Metaphysical Club*. London: Flamingo.

Mesoudi, A., Whiten, A. and Laland, K. N. (2004). Perspective: is human cultural evolution Darwinian? Evidence reviewed from the perspective of The Origin of Species. *Evolution*, **58**, 1–11.

Michiels, N. K. and Newman, L. J. (1998). Sex and violence in hermaphrodites. *Nature*, **391**, 647.

Migliano, A. B., Vinicius, L. and Lahr, M. M. (2007). Life history trade-offs explain the evolution of human pygmies. *Proceedings of the National Academy of Sciences of the USA*, **104**, 20216–19.

Mikkelsen, T. S., Hillier, L. W., Eichler, E. E., *et al.* (2005). Initial sequence of the chimpanzee genome and comparison with the human genome. *Nature*, **437**, 69–87.

Miller, G. F. (2000). *The Mating Mind: How Sexual Choice Shaped the Evolution of Human Nature*. New York: Doubleday.

Miranda, J. J. L. (2006). Conservation and diversity of ancient hemoglobins in bacteria. *Biochemical and Biophysical Research Communications*, **343**, 924–7.

Mithen, S. (1996). *The Prehistory of the Mind*. London: Thames & Hudson.

Mithen, S. (2007). *The Singing Neanderthals: The Origins of Music, Language, Mind, and Body*. Cambridge, MA: Harvard University Press.

Miura, T., Kamikouchi, A., Sawata, M., *et al.* (1999). Soldier caste-specific gene expression in the mandibular glands of Hodotermopsis japonica (Isoptera: Termopsidae). *Proceedings of the National Academy of Sciences of the USA*, **96**, 13874–9.

Møller, A. P. (1990). Parasites and sexual selection: current status of the Hamilton and Zuk hypothesis. *Journal of Evolutionary Biology*, **3**, 319–28.

Moore, B. R. (2004). The evolution of learning. *Biological Reviews*, **79**, 301–35.

Morgan, T. H. (1932). *The Scientific Basis of Evolution*. London: W. W. Norton.

Morgan, T. H., Bridges, C. B. and Sturtevant, A. H. (1925). The genetics of Drosophila. *Bibliographica Genetica*, **2**, 1–262.

Mosseau, T. A. and Fox, C. W., eds. (1998). *Maternal Effects as Adaptations*. Oxford: Oxford University Press.

Muller, H. J. (1932). Some genetic aspects of sex. *American Naturalist*, **66**, 118–38.

Muller, H. J. (1939). Reversibility in evolution considered from the standpoint of genetics. *Biological Reviews of the Cambridge Philosophical Society*, **14**, 261–80.

Muller, H. J. (1964). The relation of recombination to mutational advance. *Mutation Research*, **1**, 2–9.

Muller, M. N. and Wrangham, R. (2002). Sexual mimicry in hyenas. *Quarterly Review of Biology*, **77**, 3–16.

Nagel, T. (1998). Reductionism and antireductionism. In *The Limits of Reductionism in Biology*, ed. L. Wolpert. Chichester, UK: Wiley & Sons, pp. 3–14.

Narita, Y. and Kuratani, S. (2005). Evolution of the vertebral formulae in mammals: a perspective on developmental constraints. *Journal of Experimental Zoology Part B*, **304**, 91–106.

Nicolis, G. and Nicolis, C. (2007). *Foundations of Complex Systems*. Singapore: World Scientific.

Nicolis, G. and Prigogine, I. (1977). *Self-Organization in Nonequilibrium Systems: From Dissipative Structures to Order through Fluctuation*. New York: John Wiley.

Noad, M. J., Cato, D. H., Bryden, M. M., Jenner, M. N. and Jenner, K. C. S. (2000). Cultural revolution in whale songs. *Nature*, **408**, 537.

Noë, R. and Bshary, R. (1997). The formation of red colobus: diana monkey associations under predation pressure from chimpanzees. *Proceedings of the Royal Society Series B*, **264**, 253–9.

Nowak, M. A. (2006). Five rules for the evolution of cooperation. *Science*, **314**, 1560–3.

Nowak, M. and Sigmund, K. (1993). A strategy of win stay, lose shift that outperforms tit-for-tat in the prisoners-dilemma game. *Nature*, **364**, 56–8.

Nowak, M. A. and Sigmund, K. (2005). Evolution of indirect reciprocity. *Nature*, **437**, 1291–8.

Nowak, M. A., Plotkin, J. B. and Jansen, V. A. A. (2000). The evolution of syntactic communication. *Nature*, **404**, 495–8.

Odling-Smee, F. J., Laland, K. N. and Feldman, M. W. (2003). *Niche Construction: The Neglected Process in Evolution*. Princeton, NJ: Princeton University Press.

Ohno, S. (1972). An argument for the genetic simplicity of man and other mammals. *Journal of Human Evolution*, **1**, 651–62.

Olendorf, R., Getty, T. and Scribner, K. (2004). Cooperative nest defense in red-winged blackbirds: reciprocal altruism, kinship or by-product mutualism? *Proceedings of the Royal Society Series B*, **271**, 177–82.

Orgel, L. E. and Crick, F. H. C. (1980). Selfish DNA: the ultimate parasite. *Nature*, **284**, 604–7.

O'Riain, M. J., Jarvis, J. U. M. and Faulkes, C. G. (1996). A dispersive morph in the naked mole-rat. *Nature*, **380**, 619–21.

O'Riain, M. J., Jarvis, J. U. M., Alexander, R., Buffenstein, R. and Peeters, C. (2000). Morphological castes in a vertebrate. *Proceedings of the National Academy of Sciences of the USA*, **97**, 13194–7.

Orr, H. A. (1998). The population genetics of adaptation: the distribution of factors fixed during adaptive evolution. *Evolution*, **52**, 935–49.

Orr, H. A. (2000). Adaptation and the cost of complexity. *Evolution*, **54**, 13–20.

Orr, H. A. (2001). The "sizes" of mutations fixed in phenotypic evolution: a response to Clarke and Arthur. *Evolution and Development*, **3**, 121–3.

Orr, H. A. (2005). The genetic theory of adaptation: a brief history. *Nature Reviews Genetics*, **6**, 119–27.

Osborn, H. F. (1926). The problem of the origin of species as it appeared to Darwin in 1859 and as it appears to us to-day. *Science*, **64**, 337–41.

Ospovat, D. (1980). *The Development of Darwin's Theory*. Cambridge: Cambridge University Press.

Otto, S. P. and Gerstein, A. C. (2008). The evolution of haploidy and diploidy. *Current Biology*, **18**, R1121–4.

Otto, S. P. and Lenormand, T. (2002). Resolving the paradox of sex and recombination. *Nature Reviews Genetics*, **3**, 252–61.

Packer, C., Tatar, M. and Collins, A. (1998). Reproductive cessation in female mammals. *Nature*, **392**, 807–11.

Padian, K. (2001). Owen's Parthian shot – Charles Darwin may have had the science, but Richard Owen could write a lethal letter. *Nature*, **412**, 123–4.

Pagel, M. and Mace, R. (2004). The cultural wealth of nations. *Nature*, **428**, 275–8.

Palacios, M. G., Cunnick, J. E., Winkler, D. W. and Vleck, C. M. (2007). Immunosenescence in some but not all immune components in a free-living vertebrate, the tree swallow. *Proceedings of the Royal Society Series B*, **274**, 951–7.

Paland, S. and Lynch, M. (2006). Transitions to asexuality result in excess amino acid substitutions. *Science*, **311**, 990–2.

Panhuis, T. M., Butlin, R., Zuk, M. and Tregenza, T. (2001). Sexual selection and speciation. *Trends in Ecology and Evolution*, **16**, 364–71.

Panksepp, J. and Panksepp, J. B. (2000). The seven sins of evolutionary psychology. *Evolution and Cognition*, **6**, 108–31.

Parker, G. A. (1970). Sperm competition and its evolutionary consequences in insects. *Biological Reviews*, **45**, 525–67.

Payne, R. J. H. and Krakauer, D. C. (1997). Sexual selection, space, and speciation. *Evolution*, **51**, 1–9.

Peabody, R. B. and Brodie, E. D. (1975). Effect of temperature, salinity and photoperiod on number of trunk vertebrae in *Ambystoma maculatum*. *Copeia*, 741–6.

Pennisi, E. (2004). Searching for the genome's second code. *Science*, **306**, 632–5.

Penrose, R. (1989). *The Emperor's New Mind: Concerning Computers, Minds and The Laws of Physics*. Oxford: Oxford University Press.

Perry, S., Baker, M., Fedigan, L., *et al.* (2003). Social conventions in wild white-faced capuchin monkeys: evidence for traditions in a neotropical primate. *Current Anthropology*, **44**, 241–68.

Peterson, K. J., Arenas-Mena, C. and Davidson, E. H. (2000). The A/P axis in echinoderm ontogeny and evolution: evidence from fossils and molecules, *Evolution and Development*, **2**, 93–101.

Peterson, K. J. and Davidson, E. H. (2000). Regulatory evolution and the origin of the bilaterians. *Proceedings of the National Academy of Sciences of the USA*, **97**, 4430–3.

Pettay, J. E., Kruuk, L. E. B., Jokela, J. and Lummaa, V. (2005). Heritability and genetic constraints of life-history trait evolution in pre-industrial humans. *Proceedings of the National Academy of Sciences of the USA*, **102**, 2838–43.

Pineda, D., Gonzalez, J., Callaerts, P., *et al.* (2000). Searching for the prototypic eye genetic network: sine oculis is essential for eye regeneration in planarians. *Proceedings of the National Academy of Sciences of the USA*, **97**, 4525–9.

Pollard, K. S., Salama, S. R., Lambert, N., *et al.* (2006). An RNA gene expressed during cortical development evolved rapidly in humans. *Nature*, **443**, 167–72.

Power, C. (1998). Old wives' tales: the gossip hypothesis and the reliability of cheap signals. In *Approaches to the Evolution of Language: Social and Cognitive Bases*, ed. J. R. Hurford, M. Studdert-Kennedy and C. Knight. Cambridge: Cambridge University Press, pp. 111–29.

Prabhakar, S., Noonan, J. P., Paabo, S. and Rubin, E. M. (2006). Accelerated evolution of conserved noncoding sequences in humans. *Science*, **314**, 786.

Prenter, J., MacNeil, C. and Elwood, R. W. (2006). Sexual cannibalism and mate choice. *Animal Behaviour*, **71**, 481–90.

Presgraves, D. C., Balagopalan, L., Abmayr, S. M. and Orr, H. A. (2003). Adaptive evolution drives divergence of a hybrid inviability gene between two species of Drosophila. *Nature*, **423**, 715–19.

Putters, F. A. and van den Assem, J. (1985). Precise sex ratio in a parasitic wasp: the result of counting eggs. *Behavioral Ecology and Sociobiology*, **17**, 219–24.

Queller, D. C. (1997). Why do females care more than males? *Proceedings of the Royal Society Series B,* **264**, 1555–7.

Queller, D. C. (2008). Behavioural ecology: the social side of wild yeast. *Nature*, **456**, 589–90.

Queller, D. C., Zacchi, F., Cervo, R., *et al.* (2000). Unrelated helpers in a social insect. *Nature*, **405**, 784–7.

Quiring, R., Walldorf, U., Kloter, U. and Gehring, W. J. (1994). Homology of the *eyeless* gene of *Drosophila* to the *Small eye* gene in mice and *Aniridia* in humans. *Science*, **265**, 785–9.

Rachlin, H. and Green, L. (1972). Commitment, choice and self-control. *Journal of Experimental Analysis of Behavior*, **17**, 15–22.

Raff, R. A. (1996). *The Shape of Life*. Chicago, IL: University of Chicago Press.

Rankin, D. J., Bargum, K. and Kokko, H. (2007). The tragedy of the commons in evolutionary biology. *Trends in Ecology and Evolution*, **22**, 643–51.

Rao, A. L. N., Dreher, T. W., Marsh L. E. and Hall, T. C. (1989). Telomeric function of the tRNA-like structure of brome mosaic virus RNA. *Proceedings of the National Academy of Sciences of the USA*, **86**, 5335–9.

Raoult, D. and Forterre, P. (2008). Redefining viruses: lessons from Mimivirus. *Nature Reviews Microbiology*, **6**, 315–16.

Ratnieks, F. L. W. and Wenseleers, T. (2005). Policing insect societies. *Science*, **307**, 54–6.

Read, F. (1988). Sexual selection and the role of parasites. *Trends in Ecology and Evolution*, **3**, 97–101.

Reader, S. M. (2006). Evo-devo, modularity, and evolvability: insights for cultural evolution. *Behavioral and Brain Sciences*, **29**, 361–2.

Reader, S. M. and Laland, K. N. (1999). Do animals have memes? *Journal of Memetics*, **3**,100–8.

Reeve, H. K. and Keller, L. (1999). Levels of selection: burying the units-of-selection debate and unearthing the crucial new issues. In *Levels of Selection in Evolution*, ed. L. Keller. Princeton, NJ: Princeton University Press, pp. 3–14.

Reeve, H. K., Westneat, D. F., Noon, W. A., Sherman, P. W. and Aquadro, C. F. (1990). DNA 'fingerprinting' reveals high levels of inbreeding in colonies of the eusocial naked mole-rat. *Proceedings of the National Academy of Sciences of the USA*, **87**, 2496–500.

Reik, W. and Walter, J. (2001). Genomic imprinting: parental influence on the genome. *Nature Reviews Genetics*, **2**, 21–32.

Rendell, L. and Whitehead, H. (2001). Culture in whales and dolphins. *Behavioral and Brain Sciences*, **24**, 309–24.

Reno, P. L., Meindl, R. S., McCollum, M. A. and Lovejoy, C. O. (2003). Sexual dimorphism in Australopithecus afarensis was similar to that of modern humans. *Proceedings of the National Academy of Sciences of the USA*, **100**, 9404–9.

Rensch, B. (1960). *Evolution Above the Species Level*. New York: Columbia University Press.

Reynolds, W. W. and Reynolds, L. J. (1977). Zoogeography and the predator-prey 'arms race': a comparison of Eriphia and Nerita species from three faunal regions, *Hydrobiologia*, **56**, 63–7.

Rice, S. H. (2002a). The role of heterochrony in primate brain evolution. In *Human Evolution through Developmental Change*, ed. N. Minugh-Purvis and K. J. McNamara. Baltimore, MD: Johns Hopkins University Press, pp. 154–70.

Rice, W. R. (2002b). Experimental tests of the adaptive significance of sexual recombination. *Nature Reviews Genetics*, **3**, 241–51.

Richerson, P. J. and Boyd, R. (2001). The evolution of subjective commitment to groups: a tribal instincts hypothesis. In *Evolution and the Capacity for Commitment*, ed. R. M. Nesse. New York: Russell Sage, pp. 186–220.

Richerson, P. J., Boyd, R. and Henrich, J. (2003). The cultural evolution of human cooperation. In *The Genetic and Cultural Evolution of Cooperation*, ed. P. Hammerstein. Cambridge, MA: MIT Press, pp. 357–88.

Ritchie, M. G. (1996). The shape of female mating preferences. *Proceedings of the National Academy of Sciences of the USA*, **93**, 14628–31.

Ritchie, M. G. (2007). Sexual selection and speciation. *Annual Review of Ecology Evolution and Systematics*, **38**, 79–102.

Rivera-Pomar, R. and Jackle, H. (1996). From gradients to stripes in *Drosophila* embryogenesis: filling in the gaps. *Trends in Genetics*, **12**, 478–83.

Roberts, C. J. and Lowe, C. R. (1975). Where have all conceptions gone? *Lancet*, **1**, 498–9.

Robertson, A. V., Ramsden, C., Niedzwiecki, J., Fu, J. Z. and Bogart, J. P. (2006). An unexpected recent ancestor of unisexual *Ambystoma*. *Molecular Ecology*, **15**, 3339–51.

Robson, S. L. and Wood, B. (2008). Hominin life history: reconstruction and evolution. *Journal of Anatomy*, **212**, 394–425.

Rose, M. R. (1991). *Evolutionary Biology of Aging*. New York: Oxford University Press.

Rose, M. R., Rauser, C. L. and Mueller, L. D. (2005). Late life: a new frontier for physiology. *Physiological and Biochemical Zoology*, **78**, 869–78.

Rosenberg, K. and Trevathan, W. R. (1996). Bipedalism and human birth: the obstetrical dilemma revisited. *Evolutionary Anthropology*, **4**, 161–8.

Rosenberg, M. S. (2001). The systematics and taxonomy of fiddler crabs: a phylogeny of the genus *Uca*. *Journal of Crustacean Biology*, **21**, 839–69.

Royle, N. J., Hartley, I. R. and Parker, G. A., (2002). Sexual conflict reduces offspring fitness in zebra finches. *Nature*, **416**, 733–6.

Ruppert, E. E. and Barnes, R. D. (1994). *Invertebrate Zoology*, 6th edn. London: Thomson Learning.

Ruse, M. (1996). *From Monad to Man*. Cambridge, MA: Harvard University Press.

Salvini-Plawen, L. V. and Mayr, E. (1977). On the evolution of photoreceptors and eyes. *Evolutionary Biology*, **10**, 207–63.

Sanchez-Elsner, T., Gou, D. W., Kremmer, E. and Sauer, F. (2006). Noncoding RNAs of Trithorax response elements recruit Drosophila Ash1 to *Ultrabithorax*. *Science*, **311**, 1118–23.

Sanfey, A. G., Rilling, J. K., Aronson, J. A., Nystrom, L. E. and Cohen, J. D. (2003). The neural basis of economic decision-making in the ultimatum game. *Science*, **300**, 1755–8.

Sawamura, K. and Yamamoto, M. T. (1997). Characterization of a reproductive isolation gene, zygotic hybrid rescue, of *Drosophila melanogaster* by using minichromosomes. *Heredity*, **79**, 97–103.

Schärer, L. (2009). Tests of sex allocation theory in simultaneously hermaphroditic animals. *Evolution*, **63**, 1377–405.

Schilthuizen, M. (2000). Dualism and conflicts in understanding speciation. *BioEssays*, **22**, 1134–41.

Schneider, E. D. and Sagan, D. (2005). *Into the Cool: Energy Flow, Thermodynamics, and Life*. Chicago, IL: Chicago University Press.

Schrödinger, E. (1944). *What is Life? With Mind and Matter and Autobiographical Sketches*. Cambridge: Cambridge University Press.

Schwab, I. R. (2001). A roving eye. *British Journal of Ophthalmology*, **85**, 1276.

Scott, E. C. (2005). *Evolution vs. Creationism: An Introduction*. Berkeley, CA: University of California Press.

Scott, M. P. and Weiner, A. J. (1984). Structural relationships among genes that control development: sequence homology between the Antennapedia, Ultrabithorax, and fushi tarazu loci of Drosophila. *Proceedings of the National Academy of Sciences of the USA*, **81**, 4115–19.

Sebens, K. P. (1987). The ecology of indeterminate growth in animals. *Annual Review of Ecology and Systematics*, **18**, 371–407.

Seehausen, O, Terai, Y., Magalhaes, I. S., *et al.* (2008). Speciation through sensory drive in cichlid fish. *Nature*, **455**, 620–6.

Seyfarth, R. M. and Cheney, D. L. (1992). Meaning and mind in monkeys. *Scientific American*, **267**, 122–8.

Shackleton, L. A. and Holmes, E. C. (2008). The role of alternative genetic codes in viral evolution and emergence. *Journal of Theoretical Biology*, **254**, 128–34.

Shanley, D. P., Sear, R., Mace, R. and Kirkwood, T. B. L. (2007). Testing evolutionary theories of menopause. *Proceedings of the Royal Society Series B*, **274**, 2943–9.

Shannon, C. E. (1948). A mathematical theory of communication. *Bell System Technical Journal*, **27**, 379–423.

Shea, B. T. (1983). Pedomorphosis and neoteny in the pygmy chimpanzee. *Science*, **222**, 521–2.

Sherman, P. W. (1977). Nepotism and evolution of alarm calls. *Science*, **197**, 1246–53.

Shull, A. F. (1935). Weismann and Haeckel: one hundred years. *Science*, **81**, 443–52.

Shuster, S. M. and Wade, M. J. (2003). *Mating Systems and Mating Strategies*. Princeton, NJ: Princeton University Press.

Silk, J. B., Brosnan, S. F., Vonk, J., *et al.* (2005). Chimpanzees are indifferent to the welfare of unrelated group members. *Nature*, **437**, 1357–9.

Simon, J. C., Rispe, C. and Sunnucks, P. (2002). Ecology and evolution of sex in aphids. *Trends in Ecology and Evolution*, **17**, 34–9.

Simmons, P. and Young, D. (1999). *Nerve Cells and Animal Behaviour*, 2nd edn. Cambridge: Cambridge University Press.

Simpson, G. G. (1944). *Tempo and Mode in Evolution*. New York: Columbia University Press.

Simpson, G. G. (1949). *The Meaning of Evolution*. New Haven, CT: Yale University Press.

Simpson, G. G. (1953). *The Major Features of Evolution*. New York: Columbia University Press.

Simpson, G. G. (1964). The nonprevalence of humanoids. *Science*, **143**, 769–75.

Siomi, H. and Siomi, M. C. (2009). On the road to reading the RNA-interference code. *Nature*, **457**, 396–404.

Small, S., Blair, A. and Levine, M. (1992). Regulation of even-skipped stripe-2 in the Drosophila embryo. *Embo Journal*, **11**, 4047–57.

Smolin L. (1997). *The Life of the Cosmos*. London: Phoenix.

Smukalla, S., Caldara, M., Pochet, N., *et al.* (2008). Flo1 is a variable green beard gene that drives biofilm-like cooperation in budding yeast. *Cell*, **135**, 726–37.

Sole, R. V., Fernandez, P. and Kauffman, S. A. (2003). Adaptive walks in a gene network model of morphogenesis: insights into the Cambrian explosion. *International Journal of Developmental Biology*, **47**, 685–93.

Solis, E., Aviles, J. M., de la Cruz, C., Valencia, J. and Sorci, G. (2008). Winter male plumage coloration correlates with breeding status in a cooperative breeding species. *Behavioral Ecology*, **19**, 391–7.

Sommerfeld, R. D., Krambeck, H. J. and Milinski, M. (2008). Multiple gossip statements and their effect on reputation and trustworthiness. *Proceedings of the Royal Society Series B*, **275**, 2529–36.

Squire, L. R. (1987). *Memory and Brain*. New York: Oxford University Press.

Stach, T., Winter, J., Bouquet, J. M., Chourrout, D. and Schnabel, R. (2008). Embryology of a planktonic tunicate reveals traces of sessility. *Proceedings of the National Academy of Sciences of the USA*, **105**, 7229–34.

Stearns, S. C., ed. (1987). *The Evolution of Sex and its Consequences*. Basel, Switzerland: Birkhauser.

Stearns, S. C. (1992). *The Evolution of Life Histories*. Oxford: Oxford University Press.

Stedman, H. H., Kozyak, B. W., Nelson, A., *et al.* (2004). Myosin gene mutation correlates with anatomical changes in the human lineage. *Nature*, **428**, 415–18.

Stephens, C. (2005). Senescence: even bacteria get old. *Current Biology*, **15**, R308–10.

Stephens, D. W., McLinn, C. M. and Stevens, J. R. (2002). Discounting and reciprocity in an iterated prisoner's dilemma. *Science*, **298**, 2216–18.

Stern, D. L. (2000). Perspective: evolutionary developmental biology and the problem of variation. *Evolution*, **54**, 1079–91.

Stevens, J. R. and Hauser, M. D. (2004). Why be nice? Psychological constraints on the evolution of cooperation. *Trends in Cognitive Sciences*, **8**, 60–5.

Strassmann, J. E. and Queller, D. C. (2007). Insect societies as divided organisms: the complexities of purpose and cross-purpose. *Proceedings of the National Academy of Sciences of the USA*, **104**, (Supplement 1), 8619–26.

Strassmann, J. E., Zhu, Y. and Queller, D. C. (2000). Altruism and social cheating in the social amoeba Dictyostelium discoideum. *Nature*, **408**, 965–7.

Stratikopoulos, E., Szabolcs, M., Dragatsis, I., Klinakis, A. and Efstratiadis, A. (2008). The hormonal action of Igf1 in postnatal mouse growth. *Proceedings of the National Academy of Sciences of the USA*, **105**, 19378–83.

Stratton, M. R., Campbell, P. J. and Futreal, P. A. (2009). The cancer genome. *Nature*, **458**, 719–24.

Striedter, G. F. (2005). *Principles of Brain Evolution*. Sunderland, MA: Sinauer Associates.

Sturtevant, A. H. (1920). Genetic studies on Drosophila simulans. I. Introduction: hybrids with Drosophila melanogaster. *Genetics*, **5**, 488–500.

Sumner, S., Pereboom, J. J. M. and Jordan, W. C. (2006). Differential gene expression and phenotypic plasticity in behavioural castes of the primitively eusocial wasp, Polistes canadensis. *Proceedings of the Royal Society Series B,* **273**, 19–26.

Sundström, L., Chapuisat, M. and Keller, L. (1996). Conditional manipulation of sex ratios by ant workers: a test of kin selection theory. *Science,* **274**, 993–5.

Surani, A. A. (2007). Germ cells: the eternal link between generations. *Comptes Rendus Biologies,* **330**, 474–8.

Suzuki, S. and Akiyama, E. (2005). Reputation and the evolution of cooperation in sizable groups. *Proceedings of the Royal Society Series B,* **272**, 1373–7.

Swalla, B., Just, M., Pederson, E. and Jeffery, W. (1999). A multigene locus containing the Manx and bobcat genes is required for development of chordate features in the ascidian tadpole larva. *Development,* **126**, 1643–53.

Szathmáry, E. and Maynard Smith, J. M. (1997). From replicators to reproducers: the first major transitions leading to life. *Journal of Theoretical Biology,* **187**, 555–71.

Taupin, P. (2006). Adult neurogenesis in mammals. *Current Opinion in Molecular Therapeutics,* **8**, 345–51.

Thornton, A. and McAuliffe, K. (2006). Teaching in wild meerkats. *Science,* **313**, 227–9.

Thurston, H. (1994). *Early Astronomy.* New York: Springer.

Tibbetts, E. A. and Dale, J. (2007). Individual recognition: it is good to be different. *Trends in Ecology and Evolution,* **22**, 529–37.

Tishkoff, S. A., Reed, F. A., Ranciaro, A., *et al.* (2007). Convergent adaptation of human lactase persistence in Africa and Europe. *Nature Genetics,* **39**, 31–40.

Trivers, R. L. (1971). Evolution of reciprocal altruism. *Quarterly Review of Biology,* **46**, 35–57.

Trivers, R. L. (1972). Parental investment and sexual selection. In *Sexual Selection and the Descent of Man, 1871–1971,* ed. B. Campbell. Chicago, IL: Aldine-Atherton, pp. 136–79.

Trivers, R. L. and Hare, H. (1976). Haplo diploidy and the evolution of the social insects. *Science,* **191**, 249–63.

Tuljapurkar, S. D., Puleston, C. O. and Gurven, M. D. (2007). Why men matter: mating patterns drive evolution of human lifespan. *PLoS One,* **2**, e785.

Turner, G. F. and Burrows, M. T. (1995). A model of sympatric speciation by sexual selection. *Proceedings of the Royal Society Series B,* **260**, 287–92.

Vachon, G., Cohen, B., Pfeifle, C., *et al.* (1992). Homeotic genes of the Bithorax complex repress limb development in the abdomen of the Drosophila embryo through the target gene distal-less. *Cell,* **71**, 437–50.

van Doorn, G. S., Noest, A. J. and Hogeweg, P. (1998). Sympatric speciation and extinction driven by environment dependent sexual selection. *Proceedings of the Royal Society Series B,* **265**, 1915–19.

van Schaik, C. P., Ancrenaz, M., Borgen, G., *et al.* (2003). Orangutan cultures and the evolution of material culture. *Science,* **299**, 102–5.

Vermeij, G. J. (1994). The evolutionary interaction among species: selection, escalation, and coevolution. *Annual Review of Ecology and Systematics,* **25**, 219–36.

Vermeij, G. J. (2006). Historical contingency and the purported uniqueness of evolutionary innovations. *Proceedings of the National Academy of Sciences of the USA,* **103**, 1804–9.

Vickaryous, M. K. and Hall, B. K. (2006). Human cell type diversity, evolution, development, and classification with special reference to cells derived from the neural crest. *Biological Reviews*, **81**, 425–55.

Vinicius, L. (2005). Human encephalization and developmental timing. *Journal of Human Evolution*, **49**, 762–76.

Vonk, F. J. and Richardson, M. K. (2008). Developmental biology – serpent clocks tick faster. *Nature*, **454**, 282–3.

Vrba, E. S. (1998). Multiphasic growth models and the evolution of prolonged growth exemplified by human brain evolution. *Journal of Theoretical Biology*, **190**, 227–39.

Wade, M. J. (2002). A gene's eye view of epistasis, selection and speciation. *Journal of Evolutionary Biology*, **15**, 337–46.

Wagner, G. P. and Altenberg, L. (1996). Perspective: complex adaptations and the evolution of evolvability. *Evolution*, **50**, 967–76.

Wagner, G. P., Pavlicev, M. and Cheverud, J. M. (2007). The road to modularity. *Nature Reviews Genetics*, **8**, 921–31.

Wagner, G. P., Kenney-Hunt, J. P., Pavlicev, M., *et al.* (2008). Pleiotropic scaling of gene effects and the 'cost of complexity'. *Nature*, **452**, 470–2.

Wagner, W. and Wagner, G. P. (2003). Examining the modularity concept in evolutionary psychology: the level of genes, mind, and culture. *Journal of Cultural and Evolutionary Psychology*, **1**, 135–66.

Walker, F. O. (2007). Huntington's disease. *Lancet*, **369**, 218–28.

Walker, M. L. (1995). Menopause in female Rhesus monkeys. *American Journal of Primatology*, **35**, 59–71.

Warren, R. W., Nagy, L., Selegue, J., Gates, J. and Carroll, S. (1994). Evolution of homeotic gene-regulation and function in flies and butterflies. *Nature*, **372**, 458–61.

Watanabe, T. K. (1979). A gene that rescues the lethal hybrids between D. melanogaster and D. simulans. *Japanese Journal of Genetics*, **54**, 325–31.

Watson, D. M. S. (1929). Adaptation. *Nature*, **124**, 231–4.

Weil, T., Korb, J. and Rehli, M. (2009). Comparison of queen-specific gene expression in related lower termite species. *Molecular Biology and Evolution*, **26**, 1841–50.

Weiner, A. M. and Maizels, N. (1987). 3 terminal tRNA-like structures tag genomic RNA molecules for replication: implications for the origin of protein synthesis. *Proceedings of the National Academy of Sciences of the USA*, **84**, 7383–7.

Weismann, A. (1889). *Essay upon Heredity and Kindred Biological Problems*. Oxford: Clarendon Press.

Weiss, K. M. (1973). Demographic models for anthropology. Society for American Archaeology, Memoir No. 27. *American Antiquity*, **38**, 1–186.

Weitzman, M. L. (2001). Gamma discounting. *American Economic Review*, **91**, 260–71.

Werren, J. H. (1980). Sex-ratio adaptations to local mate competition in a parasitic wasp. *Science*, **208**, 1157–9.

West, G. B., Brown, J. H. and Enquist, B. J. (2001). A general model for ontogenetic growth. *Nature*, **413**, 628–31.

West, K., Cohen, A. and Baron, M. (1991). Morphology and behavior of crabs and gastropods from Lake Tanganyika, Africa: implications for lacustrine predator-prey coevolution. *Evolution*, **45**, 589–607.

West-Eberhard, M. J. (1983). Sexual selection, social competition, and speciation. *Quarterly Review of Biology*, **58**, 155–83.

Western, D. and Ssemakula, J. (1982). Life history patterns in birds and mammals and their evolutionary interpretation. *Oecologia*, **54**, 281–90.

Westneat, D. F. and Birkhead, T. R. (1998). Alternative hypotheses linking the immune system and mate choice for good genes. *Proceedings of the Royal Society Series B*, **265**, 1065–73.

Weston, E. M. and Lister, A. M. (2009). Insular dwarfism in hippos and a model for brain size reduction in *Homo floresiensis*. *Nature*, **459**, 85–8.

Wheeler, J. A. and Ford, K. (1998). *Geons, Black Holes and Quantum Foam*. New York: W. W. Norton.

White, M. J. D. (1978). *Modes of Speciation*. San Francisco, CA: W. H. Freeman.

Whiten, A., Goodall, J., McGrew, W. C., *et al.* (1999). Cultures in chimpanzees. *Nature*, **399**, 682–5.

Whitfield, J. (2004). Everything you always wanted to know about sexes. *PLoS Biology*, **2**, e183.

Whitlock, M. C. and Phillips, P. C. (2000). The exquisite corpse: a shifting view of the shifting balance. *Trends in Ecology and Evolution*, **15**, 347–8.

Wicken, J. S. (1987). *Evolution, Thermodynamics and Information: Extending the Darwinian Program*. Oxford: Oxford University Press.

Williams, G. C. (1957). Pleiotropy, natural-selection, and the evolution of senescence. *Evolution*, **11**, 398–411.

Williams, G. C. (1966). *Adaptation and Natural Selection*. Princeton, NJ: Princeton University Press.

Williams, G. C. (1975). *Sex and Evolution*. Princeton, NJ: Princeton University Press.

Williams, G. C. (1996). *Plan and Purpose in Nature*. London: Weidenfeld & Nicolson.

Wilson, D. S. and Sober, E. (1994). Reintroducing group selection to the human behavioral sciences. *Behavioral and Brain Sciences*, **17**, 585–608.

Wilson, E. O. (1975). *Sociobiology: The New Synthesis*. Cambridge, MA: Harvard University Press.

Wilson, E. O. and Hölldobler, B. (2005). Eusociality: origin and consequences. *Proceedings of the National Academy of Sciences of the USA*, **102**, 13367–71.

Woese, C. R. (2002). On the evolution of cells. *Proceedings of the National Academy of Sciences of the USA*, **99**, 8742–7.

Wolpert, L. (1969). Positional information and spatial pattern of cellular differentiation. *Journal of Theoretical Biology*, **25**, 1–47.

Wong, B. B. M. and Candolin, U. (2005). How is female mate choice affected by male competition? *Biological Reviews*, **80**, 559–71.

Wong, J. T. (1991). Origin of genetically encoded protein synthesis: a model based on selection for RNA peptidation. *Origins of Life and Evolution of the Biosphere*, **21**, 165–76.

Wrangham, R. W., de Waal, F. B. M. and McGrew, W. C. (1994). The challenge of behavioral diversity. In *Chimpanzee Cultures*, ed. R. Wrangham, W. C. McGrew, F. B. M. de Waal and P. G. Heltne. Harvard, MA: Harvard University Press, pp. 1–18.

Wray, G. A. (2007). The evolutionary significance of cis-regulatory mutations. *Nature Reviews Genetics*, **8**, 206–16.

Wright, S. (1931). Evolution in Mendelian populations. *Genetics*, **16**, 97–159.

Wright, S. (1932). The roles of mutation, inbreeding, crossbreeding and selection in evolution. *Proceedings of the Sixth International Congress of Genetics*, **1**, 356–66.

Wright, S. (1977). *Evolution and the Genetics of Populations. Volume 3: Experimental Results and Evolutionary Deductions*. Chicago, IL: University of Chicago Press.

Wynne-Edwards, V. C. (1962). *Animal Dispersion in Relation to Social Behavior*. London: Oliver & Boyd.

Zahavi, A. and Zahavi, A. (1997). *The Handicap Principle: A Missing Piece of Darwin's Puzzle*. Oxford: Oxford University Press.

Zak, P. J., Stanton, A. A. and Ahmadi, S. (2007). Oxytocin increases generosity in humans. *PLoS One*, **2**, e1128.

Zeggini, E., Scott, L. J., Saxena, R., *et al.* (2008). Meta-analysis of genome-wide association data and large-scale replication identifies additional susceptibility loci for type 2 diabetes. *Nature Genetics*, **40**, 638–45.

Zera, A. J. and Harshman, L. G. (2001). The physiology of life history trade-offs in animals. *Annual Review of Ecology and Systematics*, **32**, 95–126.

Index

African naked mole rats, 165
aggregation, 27, 30, 31, 155, 186, 197
altruism, 163, 167
  and kin selection, 160
altruistic punishment, 176, 180
animal societies, 154, 160, 183, 200
Anisogamy, 137
Avery, J., 187

Barbieri, M., 33, 35, 189
behavioural code, 33, 34, 153, 201, 203
biological complexity, 22, 25, 27, 36, 157, 184, 186, 204
  cost of, 51
  increase in, 197, 202, 206
biological information, 25, 30, 152, 153, 186, 188, 201
  and thermodynamics, 187
  carriers of, 189
brain, 200
  as information carrier, 184, 189, 193
Buss, L., 28, 189
by-product mutualism, 172

centipedes, 16
Charnov, E., 119, 121, 139
cis-regulatory region, 74, 85, 89, 191
  evolution, 91
computers
  as non-biological information carriers, 204
contingency, 4, 15, 201
Convergence, 18
Conway Morris, S., 19
co-operation, 157, 168, 173
  and brain size, 171
  in small-scale societies, 182
co-operative breeding, 164
Crick, F., 24, 104, 188
cultural group selection, 177
culture, 35, 195
  material culture, 196, 203

Darwin, C., 1, 46, 102, 129, 202
  and biological complexity, 206
  and sexual selection, 143
  evolution of human morality, 177
  on baboon 'hero', 158
  on complexity, 7
  on evolutionary progress, 12
  on speciation, 62
  on species selection, 10
Darwinism, 1, 12
Dawkins, R., 69, 196
de Beer, G., 191
developmental code, 32, 72, 75, 99, 191, 201
developmental complexity, 26
Dictator game, 176, 180
DNA
  as information carrier, 189
Dobzhansky, T., 12
dolphins
  super-alliances, 172
Doyne Farmer, J., 188
Drosophila
  axis specification, 82
  body plan evolution, 96

electron, 7
entropy, 187
epistasis, 55, 68, 153
Euler-Lotka equation, 143
eusocial insects, 161, 163, 174, 176
  conflict over sex ratio, 164
evolution
  of animal societies, 155
  of body size, 121
  of galaxies, 8
  of sex, 134
Evolutionary constraints, 15
evolutionary progress, 21
extended phenotype, 196

Fehr, E., 175
Feynman, R., 7
Fishbacher, U., 175